BRUCE
SPRINGSTEEN
AND THE
E STREET BAND—
THE ILLUSTRATED
HISTORY

BOSS

GILLIAN G. GAAR

Voyageur
Press

Quarto is the authority on a wide range of topics.

Quarto educates, entertains and enriches the lives of our readers—enthusiasts and lovers of hands-on living.

www.quartoknows.com

First published in 2016 by Voyageur Press, an imprint of
Quarto Publishing Group USA Inc., 400 First Avenue North, Suite 400,
Minneapolis, MN 55401 USA. Telephone: (612) 344-8100 Fax: (612) 344-8692

quartoknows.com
Visit our blogs at quartoknows.com

Voyageur Press titles are also available at discounts in bulk quantity for industrial or sales-promotional use. For details contact the Special Sales Manager at
Quarto Publishing Group USA Inc., 400 First Avenue North, Suite 400,
Minneapolis, MN 55401 USA.

10 9 8 7 6 5 4 3 2 1

ISBN: 978-0-7603-4972-4

Library of Congress Cataloging-in-Publication Data
Names: Gaar, Gillian G., 1959-
Title: Boss : Bruce Springsteen and the E Street Band : the illustrated
  history / by Gillian G. Gaar.
Description: Minneapolis, MN : Voyageur Press, 2016. | Includes index.
Identifiers: LCCN 2016002289 | ISBN 9780760349724 (plc)
Subjects: LCSH: Springsteen, Bruce. | E Street Band. | Rock musicians—United
  States. | Springsteen, Bruce—Portraits. | E Street Band—Portraits. |
  Rock musicians—United States—Portraits.
Classification: LCC ML420.S77 G25 2016 | DDC 782.42166092—dc23
LC record available at http://lccn.loc.gov/2016002289

Acquiring Editor: Todd R. Berger
Project Manager: Caitlin Fultz
Art Director: Cindy Samargia Laun
Book Design and Layout: Brad Norr Design

On the front cover: *Richard E. Aaron/Redferns*
On the back cover: *Paul Bergen/Redferns*
On the frontis: © *Claudia Candido / Alamy Stock Photo*
On the title page: © *epa european pressphoto agency b.v. / Alamy Stock Photo*
On the endpapers: *Kevin Winter/DMI/The LIFE Picture Collection/Getty Images,*
  THOMAS LOHNES/AFP/Getty Images, Paul Bergen/Redferns,
  L. Busacca/Larry Busacca/Wireimage
On the title page: *Rich Lipski/The Washington Post/Getty Images*

Printed in China

CONTENTS

INTRODUCTION
ELVIS, BRUCE, AND ROCK 'N' ROLL DREAMS

They were the television shows that transfixed the nation. Elvis Presley, after making his national TV debut on *Stage Show*, then outraging the country with his swiveling hips on *The Milton Berle Show*, then being stuffed into a tux in a vain attempt to neuter him on *The Steve Allen Show*, was finally going to appear on the most popular variety program in the United States. The King of Rock 'n' Roll made three landmark appearances on *The Ed Sullivan Show*: September 9, 1956; October 28, 1956; and January 6, 1957. He would not be seen on television again for another three years.

Bruce Springsteen, who was just about to turn seven when that first appearance aired, was watching. Elvis sounded different, looked different, and moved differently from every other male singer he had ever seen. Certainly there would be other musical influences in Bruce's life. But the original inspiration to make music—and, more specifically, to make rock 'n' roll music—goes back to Elvis.

The kid who watched Elvis bop his way through "Don't Be Cruel" and "Hound Dog" would have been flabbergasted to hear that one day he'd be a rock star too—called "the future of rock 'n' roll," no less—the inheritor of Elvis's crown. Young Bruce grew up believing in the redemptive power of rock 'n' roll. But by the time he ascended to star status, he could also see his childhood hero's story as a cautionary tale.

Both men grew up in families of little means (though at least Springsteen always had electricity and running water at home). Both loved music of every genre, absorbing it wherever it could be found. And in the early years of their careers, they evinced a similar determination. Prior to recording for Sun Records, Elvis dropped by the studio on several occasions, making demos, asking if studio owner Sam Phillips might be looking for a singer, ingratiating himself with the office manager, Marion Keisker, who finally persuaded her boss to give the kid a break. Springsteen was so keen on making music his career that he never even sought a day job: he allowed nothing to distract him from his goal. He turned down a contract with music impresario Bill Graham because he didn't think his band was ready, and he kept forming groups and

(opposite)
Springsteen at the Oakland-Alameda County Coliseum in October 1980, during *The River* tour; the record was his first double album. *Ed Perlstein/Redferns*

Elvis Presley rehearsing for his *Ed Sullivan Show* appearance in January 1957. Springsteen adored the King of Rock 'n' Roll and frequently performed Presley's songs in concert. *Michael Ochs Archives/Getty Images*

breaking them up, tinkering with the lineup until he was truly satisfied with his players.

When Springsteen speaks of Elvis in concert it is always with reverence: "It was like he came along and whispered some dream in everybody's ear and somehow we all dreamed it," he said, introducing Elvis's "Follow That Dream" during a concert. In April 1976, he famously jumped over the gates of Graceland, in an attempt to meet the King (who wasn't home).

In May 1977, he saw Elvis in concert but was dismayed to see his hero's obvious deterioration. Just three months later, Elvis was dead. "I remember I was sitting at home when a friend of mine called and told me that he'd died," Springsteen said during a 1981 concert, "and it wasn't that big a surprise at the time, 'cause I'd seen him a few months earlier in Philadelphia. I thought a lot about it, how somebody who'd had so much could in the end lose so bad, and how dreams don't mean nothing unless you're strong enough to fight for 'em and make 'em come true."

The high price of fame weighed heavily on Springsteen. His first big influx of attention, in the 1970s, left him feeling uneasy. "I used to feel I always was in control," he told the *New Musical Express* in 1975. "But now I'm not so sure." Asked about his own image at a press conference in 1972, Elvis had answered, "Well, the image is one thing, and a human being is another. It's very hard to live up to an image." Springsteen would certainly have agreed.

Elvis was very much on Springsteen's mind while Springsteen recorded his most well-known album, *Born in the U.S.A.* During the sessions he recorded a version (as yet unreleased) of "Follow That Dream." In stark contrast to Elvis's upbeat original, Springsteen slows down the tempo and recasts the song as mournful, as if the singer is chasing a dream that may never come true. He also recorded "Johnny Bye Bye," a tribute depicting the sad loss of his one-time idol, found dead with "a whole lot of trouble running through his veins." As he later told *Rolling Stone,* "The type of fame Elvis had…the pressure of it, the isolation that it seems to require, has gotta be really painful." His own blistering rise to stardom, following the release of *Born in the U.S.A.,* would soon leave him feeling "Bruced out."

Elvis was the biggest solo male rock star of the 1950s; Springsteen was the biggest solo male rock star of the 1980s. When Springsteen sings in "Johnny Bye Bye" that Johnny didn't have to die, he speaks from his own experience. He saw the traps that ensnared Elvis and became determined to avoid them in his own career. He was far more involved in producing his work than Elvis ever was. He refused to be isolated; instead of locking himself away in a mansion, Springsteen thought nothing of dropping into local clubs to sit in with whoever was playing that night. And while his own manager was as tough a negotiator as Elvis's, Springsteen never let himself be controlled; in the end, the final decisions were always his own.

Springsteen is one of rock's most compelling live performers. *Ed Perlstein/Redferns/Getty Images*

Elvis's rock 'n' roll dreams inspired Springsteen to make his dreams a reality—and they would take him to places he never imagined. Over time, his musical interests broadened beyond rock 'n' roll, and he recorded country, blues, folk, and gospel music (just like Elvis). Over time, his political views grew from a general support of the average person to increasingly explicit activism. But at the root of everything is his love of rock 'n' roll. "I had serious ideas about rock music," he told the *New Musical Express* in 1996. "I believed it should be fun—dancing, screwing, having a good time. But I also believed it was capable of conveying serious ideas." It's serious fun: Springsteen has mastered the tricky balancing act of taking his music seriously and wearing his fame lightly. Which is why, for Bruce Springsteen, rock 'n' roll dreams will never die.

—Gillian G. Gaar
Seattle, Washington, December 2015

GREETINGS FROM
ASBURY PARK

Working-class hero. There couldn't be a better name for Bruce Frederick Springsteen.

Springsteen mythologized the lives of ordinary people in his songs and made them seem extraordinary. The rebels. The drifters. The lost souls who yearned to escape their impoverished surroundings. But the myths were all grounded in reality, a reality drawn from the fabric of Springsteen's youth.

His father, Doug Springsteen, was born and raised in the small township of Freehold, New Jersey, a half hour's drive inland from the Jersey Shore, almost fifty miles south of New York City. He dropped out of high school to take a job as a laborer, then joined the army in 1943, when he turned eighteen, at the height of World War II. Perhaps his years in the service dulled his sense of ambition; perhaps he had little to begin with. But after his hitch, he couldn't summon up the energy to do much more than live off his veteran's benefits—until one night in 1946 when he went on a double date with a friend and met Adele Zerilli.

Zerilli's parents emigrated from Italy, and she and her two sisters were born and raised in Brooklyn. Her father became a lawyer, but he was later sent to prison for embezzlement. Before his incarceration, he managed to purchase a farmhouse just outside Freehold for his three daughters to live in, his wife having divorced him in the wake of the scandal. Zerilli was working as a secretary when she met Doug Springsteen and was underwhelmed by his immediate offer of marriage, telling him he would have to get a job before she'd even consider his proposal. Doug promptly went out and secured a job at a Ford auto plant in Edison, New Jersey, and the two married on February 22, 1947. Bruce arrived on September 23, 1949, born in Monmouth Memorial Hospital in Long Branch, New Jersey. In 1951, Virginia (whom everyone called Ginny), was born, followed by a second daughter, Pamela, in 1962.

After Virginia's birth, the family moved in with Bruce's paternal grandparents. Bruce's father had had an older sister (also named Virginia) who died at age five when she was hit by a truck, and her parents, Fred and Alice Springsteen, had been devastated by the loss. The two doted on their first grandchild, to the point that Bruce's sister—the second Virginia—felt neglected. Springsteen admitted in biographer Peter Carlin's 2012 biography *Bruce* that his role was "to replace the lost child . . . which is an enormous burden." The family regularly went out to Saint Rose of Lima cemetery, where Virginia Springsteen had been buried in 1927, to tend her gravesite.

Doug Springsteen tended to drift from job to job, working in various factories, as a security guard or as a truck driver. It was up to Adele Springsteen, the one with a steady job, to provide some measure of security. Bruce was especially close to his grandfather; the two spent a lot of time together, fixing the broken radios that they found thrown away in the

(previous spread)
Springsteen and Clemons at RAI Congress Hall in Amsterdam, Holland, on November 23, 1975. It was the band's first time overseas, and Springsteen was nervous about how he would be received. *Gijsbert Hanekroot/Redferns*

neighborhood. But discipline was lax when his mother wasn't home, and Bruce often stayed up late at night, sneaking out to watch television when everyone else was asleep.

When Bruce was old enough for school, his mom decided it was time the family had a home of their own, and they moved to a house a few blocks away. (They would move again after Pamela was born.) He was sent to Saint Rose of Lima School, a Catholic institution, but it was an uncomfortable fit. Bruce rebelled against the school's many rules and spent a lot of time in the principal's office. (He later claimed a nun once forced him to sit in the trash can next to her desk because he'd been misbehaving.) He was rarely in trouble for fighting with other boys, though; it was the system he rebelled against.

He played Little League baseball, but by 1957 his primary interest became music. It helped him break out of his self-imposed shell. "I tend to be an isolationist by nature," he told *Rolling Stone* in 1992. "Then music came along, and I latched onto it as a way to combat that part of myself." And the reason behind his new passion could be summed up in a single name: Elvis.

There had always been music in the Springsteen household. The radio was usually on, his mother and her sisters enjoyed dancing to music, and Bruce occasionally fiddled with the spinet in his aunt Dora's living room. But no one galvanized him like Elvis Presley, who gave three incendiary performances on *The Ed Sullivan Show* on September 9 and October 28, 1956, and January 6, 1957. The last appearance was likely the one Bruce saw; the previous gyrations of the King of Rock 'n' Roll on *Ed Sullivan* had so scandalized audiences that the television cameras were kept fixed firmly above his waist for the January appearance.

To Bruce, it looked like Elvis was having a ball, and he couldn't wait to join in. "It looked like he was playing, like a child is drawn to play," he told Carlin. "It looked like so much fun. Imagine throwing out all the self-consciousness that's sort of like a blanket over you. What would happen if you threw all that off for two and a half minutes, three minutes, as a performer!" Unlike other parents of the era, Bruce's mother shared his interest in Elvis, and she agreed to get him a guitar when he asked for one. But his first round with the instrument ended in a stalemate. His mother rented an acoustic guitar from a music store, where Bruce went to take lessons, but, typically, he resisted formal training. He quickly lost interest in learning how to play the instrument.

But music nonetheless became an all-consuming passion. He kept his ear glued to the radio, picking up New York City stations such as WINS and WMCA, absorbing the likes of Chuck Berry, Buddy Holly, Sam Cooke, Roy Orbison, Ray Charles—the cream of popular radio. (He was tickled that Philadelphia vocal group the Orlons did a song with the same name as the road he lived on: "South Street.") On June 29, 1962, his mother took him and his sister to their first concert, a Dick Clark package show in Atlantic City, New

In 1972, the year Springsteen signed with his first manager, Mike Appel. *Michael Ochs Archives/Getty Images*

Jersey, featuring the Shirelles, Freddy Cannon, and Bobby Rydell, headlined by the King of Twist himself, Chubby Checker.

By the following year, Bruce had developed a feeling for the power of rock 'n' roll. It would now be the Beatles who would firmly propel him back to the guitar. When he first heard the Beatles' breakthrough hit in America, "I Want to Hold Your Hand," while riding in the car with his mother, he was so excited he jumped out and ran to the nearest phone to call his girlfriend and tell her about it. He watched the Beatles when they appeared on *Ed Sullivan* in February 1964, and the band's subsequent flurry of hits, the high-spirited antics in their first feature film, *A Hard Day's Night*, and the influx of other British Invasion acts that followed (the Rolling Stones, the Kinks, the Animals), made Bruce determined to pick up the guitar again—and stick with it this time.

He spent $18 of his hard-earned money on an acoustic guitar and, armed with a copy of the songbook *100 Greatest American Folk Songs*, from his older cousin Frank, set about learning his craft. The first song he learned was "Greensleeves." The song was in E minor, which, he noted to his biographer and friend Dave Marsh in spring 2006, had a major impact on his later work: "I started off in a minor key, and that led me down that road ever since."

By the end of the year he was accomplished enough that he knew he needed a better instrument, and his mother took out a loan in order to buy her son his first electric guitar, a black-and-gold Kent model (made in Japan), for Christmas 1964. The first rock song he learned to play on it was "Twist and Shout," originally by the Isley Brothers and widely popularized by the Beatles.

The guitar became his obsession. His days at Freehold Regional High School were just something to get through until he could return to playing, up in his room, ignoring his father's shouts from downstairs about the noise. Despite Doug Springsteen's protests, Bruce continued to practice, even when his father pounded the ceiling with a broom handle in a vain attempt to get his son to quiet down. It was just one of many disagreements that would arise between father and son during Bruce's teenage years. His music was too loud. His hair was too long. When Bruce tried racing through the family kitchen, only to be stopped by his father's request to sit down and talk with him as he worked his way through endless cigarettes and a six-pack of beer, Bruce would sigh, knowing that the best intentions would invariably lead to yet another argument. Springsteen later worked his father's admonitions into his stage raps. "We'd start talking about nothing much," he said during one show in 1976. "How I was doing. Pretty soon he'd ask me what I thought I was doing with myself, and we'd always end up screaming at each other."

But music was always there. By the spring of 1965, he'd landed a spot in a local band, the Rogues, as a rhythm guitarist, and he played a handful of shows with the band. But he was subsequently kicked out of the group, ostensibly over the poor quality of his guitar. Dragging himself back home, he learned how to play the Rolling Stones' "It's All Over Now" to console himself.

His sister Ginny was dating a fellow Freehold student named George Theiss, lead singer and guitarist in a band made up of high school friends who started out under the name the Sierras. The band even had a manager, Gordon "Tex" Vinyard, who lived next door to the band's drummer, Bart Haynes. He had gotten to know the group after complaining about their noisy rehearsals. After meeting the boys, he took a liking to them and agreed to help them out, even finding them a bass player, twenty-eight-year-old Frank Marziotti, who owned the local Chevron station; despite the age difference, he fit in well. Vinyard also offered his own living room for rehearsals. The Sierras soon took on the name Castiles, after a popular shampoo.

When Bruce learned the Castiles were looking for a lead guitarist, he offered his services and came by Vinyard's house one night to audition, with Theiss in attendance. Bruce was then invited back to play with the full band, which also included vocalist Danny Hyland (later replaced by Richie Goldstein and then by Paul Popkin). Bruce made sure he had a couple other songs under his belt before he returned and won over the group with his skill. He was in. "I guarantee you that once I had the job, I went home and started to woodshed like a mad dog," he told Carlin.

The Castiles played the teen dance circuit in the area: school dances (including some held at Saint Rose of Lima), pizza parlors, the Freehold Elks Club, and battle-of-the-bands contests. "So many styles were overlapping at that point in time that you would have a doo-wop singing group with full pompadours and matching suits set up next to our band playing a garage version of Them's 'Mystic Eyes,' set up next to a full thirteen-piece soul show band," Springsteen recalled of the latter events. One especially memorable date was at the Marlboro State Psychiatric Hospital. "This guy in a suit got up and introduced us for twenty minutes, saying we were greater than the Beatles," Springsteen later cracked, "then the doctors came up and took him away."

The Castiles avoided covering the Beatles—too many other groups were doing that—but didn't hesitate to play songs by other British Invasion acts. One black-and-white promo shot shows the group in matching outfits: white ruffled shirts and dark vests, with everyone's hair (except for Marziotti's) falling into their eyes. They stand with their arms folded, staring down at the camera, trying to look tough. The matching outfits wouldn't last long; later promo photos show them in jeans, slouching, though even with their long hair they're more clean cut than scruffy.

In 1966 Marziotti moved on, and he was replaced by another high school student, Curt Fluhr. Haynes also planned to take his leave. Having finished high school, he joined the US Marines and was sent to Vietnam (where he would be killed in action in October 1967). He was replaced in the band by Vinny Maniello. The two new Castiles joined just in time for the band's sole recording session on May 18, 1966, at Mr. Music Inc. studio in Bricktown, New Jersey. The band recorded a single, "Baby I"/"That's What You Get," cowritten by Springsteen and Theiss. The former was a kiss-off to an ex-girlfriend, set to a garage rock beat with a touch of surf guitar. The latter was more mournful, a dip into teenage melodrama as Theiss bemoaned the love he had lost—because she died. The single wasn't properly released: "It was released to the extent that for $100 you get a hundred of them," Springsteen later said in a radio interview.

By late 1966, the Castiles had managed to break out of New Jersey and landed a regular gig at a very prestigious venue, Cafe Wha? in New York City. Bob Dylan had played the legendary Greenwich Village club, as had the Velvet Underground; Jimi Hendrix, playing under the name Jimmy James and the Blue Flames, had appeared there just a few months before, prior to leaving for London and international stardom. The Castiles generally played on the weekends, daytime shows that were set up for teenage audiences, with no alcohol served. By this time the group had added an organist, Bob Alfano, to the lineup. It was exciting to be in the Big Apple; Springsteen loved checking out the scene in the other Village clubs. But when the gigs were over, the band headed back to Freehold.

Springsteen graduated from high school in June 1967 but was turned away from the graduation ceremony on June 19 because his hair was too long. That fall he entered Ocean County Community College (now Ocean

County College), more to avoid the draft than to fulfill any desire to further his education. Though he later dropped out and was called up in 1969, he was determined not to go, having already lost one friend to the war. "People were frightened and everybody was trying to figure out how to get out of the draft," he told *Mojo* in 1999. He played up a motorcycle accident he had had at age seventeen that had given him a serious concussion; that, and what he described as his "crazy" behavior when he went in for his physical convinced the authorities he was not military material.

By this time, he was writing songs for himself, not for the band, to perform, appearing at local coffeehouses to share his efforts. Perhaps he sensed the Castiles were coming to an end. In August 1968, a citywide drugs raid in Freehold landed Fluhr, Maniello, and Popkin in jail. That ended the group.

But Springsteen wasn't at loose ends for long. Within days he joined John Graham and Mike Burke—bassist and drummer, respectively, for a local band called Something Blue—in forming a new group, the Earth Band (later shortened to Earth); Alfano, from the Castiles, sat in occasionally on the organ. On August 16 the group played what is believed to be their first show at the Off Broad Street Coffee House in Red Bank, New Jersey. An ad for the engagement shows that Springsteen was already being singled out for special attention; the group was billed as "Earth with Bruce Springsteen (formerly with the Castiles)."

Earth's repertoire included some Castiles songs, along with covers of Jimi Hendrix, Cream, and Steppenwolf. The group had a short lifespan, fizzling out by February 1969. Their most notable performances were in New York City in December 1968. The first was particularly unusual: Earth was hired to portray a band in a softcore porn film entitled *N.Y.P.D.: Now You're Practically Dead*, in a scene shot at the rock venue Fillmore East. Earth didn't play; they mimed to the music of another band, Rhinoceros, while naked people cavorted on the stage and the catwalk above the band, as if at a Greenwich Village "happening" (at one point, a pair of women's underwear fell through the air to land on Springsteen's guitar neck). The band received a generous $350 for their work. But the film was never released, and no footage has surfaced to date.

A second NYC date was more conventional: the band played a show at the Hotel Diplomat's Crystal Ballroom on December 28, sharing the bill with

Springsteen in performance in 1973, a year that saw the release of his first two albums. *Michael Ochs Archives/Getty Images*

another local act, Baker Street Division. The show was a benefit to raise funds for a medical clinic, and to help spur ticket sales the promoters arranged for buses to take Earth's New Jersey fans to the Big Apple. The show eventually drew a crowd of around 1,800 people—the largest audience Springsteen had played for. And it almost led to a bigger payoff, for representatives from both Columbia Records and Elektra Records approached Earth's managers, Fran Duffy and Rick Spachner, after the show, each wanting to work with the group. But parental consent was needed in order for a deal to be signed, as the band members were still underage, and Graham's and Burke's parents preferred that

An outtake from the photo session for the *Darkness on the Edge of Town* album. *Michael Ochs Archives/ Getty Images*

their sons not continue to pursue a career in rock 'n' roll and refused to sign the offered contract. So the band decided it was time to break up.

Earth played their last show at a special "Saint Valentine's Day Massacre" gig at the IAMA (Italian American Men's Association) Clubhouse in Long Branch, New Jersey. Watching from the audience was Vini "Mad Dog" Lopez, a drummer who had been in a variety of local bands. He knew Springsteen from the music scene; one of his previous bands, Sonny and the Starfighters, had even competed against the Castiles in a battle-of-the-bands show at the Matawan-Keyport Roller Drome in Matawan, New Jersey.

Now Lopez was looking to put together a new band. He had met a man named Carl "Tinker" West who had a strong interest in music. West had abandoned a promising career as an aerospace engineer in favor of founding Challenger Surfboards in Mission Beach, California, selling boards he designed and crafted himself. He also enjoyed playing guitar and designing and building amplifiers. By the time he met Lopez, he had relocated his company, now named Challenger Eastern Surfboards, to Wanamassa, New Jersey (just outside Asbury Park). And he was thinking about getting more involved in music, having become acquainted with the area's musicians.

West had met Lopez when Mad Dog was in a band called Moment of Truth. "Tinker told us he thought we were good and suggested that we play original music instead of cover tunes," Lopez told the website Castiles.net. "He said we wouldn't go anywhere doing covers and that if we wrote our own songs we could have something unique." Tinker told Lopez to give him a call if he ever started doing original music.

So, ever since Moment of Truth had broken up, Lopez had been on a mission. He'd been hearing stories about how good Springsteen had become and, after seeing him play with Earth, invited him to come over to the Upstage for a jam. The Upstage was a popular Asbury Park hangout for musicians, owned by Margaret and Tom Potter, who also owned the Green Mermaid coffeehouse one floor below the Upstage (the building's ground floor space was given over to a Thom McAn shoe store). It was an all-ages club until midnight; then the minors were sent home, and the venue reopened as an after-hours club at 1:00 a.m. The club's wide array of instruments, available for anyone to pick up and use, enhanced its jam sessions.

Springsteen knew the Upstage well but had never played there himself. Now, as February 22 became February 23, 1969, he arrived at the club, went upstairs, and asked to borrow Margaret Potter's Stratocaster. He then began playing what she later recalled as "some blues thing." She was so excited by what she heard that she went downstairs to the Green Mermaid to spread the news: "Hey guys, there's some kid up there who can really play!"

Lopez was also at the club, hanging out with keyboard player Danny Federici. "When I got to the top of the staircase, there was Bruce with the way he looked in those days, with the hair and suspenders with no shirt, playing away," he told the *New York Times*. "I said: 'Look at that guy play. He's got charisma.'" Springsteen had been jamming with Vinnie Roslin (previously a member of the Sierras, before the band had become the Castiles) on bass and "Big Bad" Bobby Williams on drums. When the jam came to an end, Lopez recalled, "Danny and I went up to him and said, 'Next set, let's us guys play.' And we did, and we made the band."

Tinker saw the musicians play at another late-night jam at the Upstage and agreed to take them on. He also made Challenger Eastern available as a rehearsal space—and even as a temporary residence, when the musicians needed somewhere to stay. Since everyone was a veteran of the Jersey Shore scene, they had no trouble lining up gigs. The band started out under the name Child; when they learned there was another band with the same name, they changed it to Steel Mill at the end of 1969.

"Steel Mill was a lot of different music combined together," Lopez remembered in January 2007. "It was hard rock. It was country. It was jazz. . . . We were free to experiment and express ourselves, unlike the cover bands. It was riding on the wave of the heavier metal sounds of Hendrix and Led Zeppelin and the jam sounds of 10 Years After and Canned Heat. It was a hard rocking band." In January 1999, Springsteen described Steel Mill as "basically a riff-oriented hard-rock thing."

By summer 1969 the band had played their first out-of-state show in Virginia, and they returned to the state frequently to play college gigs. Doug Albitz, a friend of West's from California, even offered them a slot at the Woodstock Music and Art Fair, billed as "three days of peace and music" and held over the weekend of August 15–18 in Bethel, New York. But Child (as they were still known) was playing the Student Prince in Asbury Park that weekend and turned it down. West went up to the festival on his own and was instantly filled with regret about the decision. "I was walking around thinking, 'Fuck! I'm an idiot! Why'd I leave the band in New Jersey?'" he told Carlin. "But the band was booked, we needed the money, and that was that."

The band worked steadily throughout the rest of the year, playing shows with Iron Butterfly and Chicago, then known as the Chicago Transit Authority. Then Albitz came through with another offer, one that the band took: playing a New Year's Eve show at the Esalen Institute, a picturesque retreat in Big Sur, California, that offered seminars in meditation, yoga, and other alternative disciplines. Steel Mill played a farewell show at Challenger Eastern to raise funds for the trip. They wanted to explore other opportunities in the Bay Area as well and weren't sure when they'd return to the East Coast.

They arrived on December 30, 1969, weary from hours on the road, and helped themselves to the freshly baked bread they were offered, not realizing it was laced with marijuana. It was a shock for Springsteen, as the most clean-living member of the group. As Randall Whited, one of West's employees, recalled, Springsteen "did not party like the rest of us. . . . He did not drink or smoke as I recall. Quite the healthy one—which was not the norm in those wild '60s."

After the New Year's Eve show and a second performance at Esalen on January 2, 1970, they headed for San Francisco. An audition at the Avalon Ballroom didn't lead to any work at the club, but then they got a lucky break. Steel Mill was booked as the opener for a Boz Scaggs show at the Matrix on January 13. When Scaggs fell ill, Steel Mill stepped up to play the entire show. Philip Elwood, music critic for the *San Francisco Examiner*, was in the audience, having planned to review Scaggs. Instead, his write-up, which

Springsteen was always proud of his New Jersey roots. *Michael Ochs Archives/Getty Images*

appeared in the next day's edition, was a rave about the New Jersey imports. "I have never been so overwhelmed by an unknown band," he wrote, calling the show "one of the most memorable evenings of rock in a long time." The band was quickly booked for another date at the Matrix on January 22, opening for the Elvin Bishop Band.

The Matrix shows brought Steel Mill to the attention of promoter Bill Graham, who booked them for two dates at his club, the Fillmore West, on February 9 and 18. Also performing at the latter show was the band Grin, led by a nineteen-year-old guitarist named Nils Lofgren who had made his name playing on Neil Young's album *After the Gold Rush*. Although Springsteen was initially intimidated by Lofgren's skill on the instrument, he soon warmed up to the guitarist.

Graham also arranged for the group to audition for his Fillmore Records label, setting up a demo session on February 22 at Pacific Recording Studio in San Mateo—the same city that Springsteen's parents and younger sister Pamela had moved to the previous summer, Doug Springsteen feeling that life might be better in California. The band recorded three songs: the sprawling rocker "Guilty (Send That Boy to Jail)" (a song that had a lot of resonance in this era of student protest), "Goin' Back to Georgia," a slice of country-rock, and a straightforward country ballad, "The Train Song." Graham liked their work and offered them a contract. But the advance was small—just $1,000—and Graham wanted all the publishing rights to Springsteen's songs as well. No dice. Springsteen later explained that he wasn't convinced the group was good enough yet: "I didn't have the confidence in the band that other people seemed to have."

Roslin had been the only member of the band strongly in favor of the deal. Now that they'd turned it down, Springsteen decided to fire him, though he left it to Lopez to deliver the bad news. Roslin didn't fit in, Springsteen felt, and he'd become increasingly distracted during Steel Mill's sojourn in California, missing rehearsals and turning up late for shows.

The rest of Steel Mill felt there was nothing more they could accomplish, so they headed home, driving back across the country after a show at the College of Marin in Kentfield, California, on February 24, straight through to Richmond, Virginia, where they had a show booked at the Free University on February 27. Soon after, their new bassist, Steve Van Zandt, joined.

Springsteen had known Van Zandt—also nicknamed "Miami Steve" and "Little Steven"—for some time, having met the guitarist in the mid-1960s. He was like a long-lost brother to Springsteen; each had the same passionate interest in music, and the two spent hours talking about their favorite songs, instruments, and musicians. Springsteen's suggestion that Van Zandt join the group was as much about spending more time with him as his musicianship. Nor did Miami Steve have any qualms about switching from guitar to bass.

Springsteen returned to the Bottom Line in New York in August 1975 in triumph with his breakthrough album, *Born to Run*. Steve Morley/Redferns

Steel Mill was soon back in the swing of things. The band drew good crowds, and it wasn't unusual for each band member to earn $500 a gig, a substantial amount in those days. There were fun times: on May 2, 1970, the band tried to crash a music festival held at the University of North Carolina in Chapel Hill (headlined by James Taylor and Joe Cocker), setting up their gear as if they were scheduled to play, but getting kicked out when organizers realized they weren't on the bill. There were frustrating times, as when Lopez let his "Mad Dog" persona off the leash during a show at Virginia Commonwealth University in Richmond on May 23; the plug was pulled at 11:00 p.m., but Mad Dog kept pounding away at his drums and ended up getting arrested.

They continued opening for name acts as well, such as a June 13 show at the Ocean Ice Palace in Bricktown, New Jersey, opening for Grand Funk Railroad. And their reputation led to an invitation to perform at the Third

Annual Nashville Music Festival on August 29 as one of the few acts on the bill without a record contract. Springsteen was thrilled at the chance to share the same stage with Roy Orbison, one of his teenage idols.

It was around this time that Springsteen first struck up an acquaintance with Patti Scialfa, then an aspiring singer and songwriter. She had called Springsteen when he was living at West's surfboard factory and asked about joining the band. On learning she was still in high school, Springsteen demurred, telling her, "Well, we have to travel, so you should stay in school." But their paths were destined to cross again.

The turning point for Steel Mill came at a September 11 show at the Clearwater Swim Club in Atlantic Highlands, New Jersey. Lopez had been busted again, this time when the police raided the house where he was spending the night; when the cops found six pounds of marijuana, they arrested everyone staying there. Steel Mill was playing the show to raise funds for Lopez's legal defense. Dave Hazlett, drummer with another local

★ ★

Steve Van Zandt

Springsteen met Steve Van Zandt when they were both teenagers, playing the Jersey Shore circuit in their respective bands. They've been close friends and colleagues ever since.

Steven Lento was born November 22, 1950, in Boston, Massachusetts, later moving with his family to New Jersey. His parents divorced, and when his mother remarried he took on the last name of his new stepfather, Van Zandt. "Little Steven" is one of his nicknames, and Springsteen christened him "Miami Steve" due to his love of Florida.

After seeing the Beatles on *Ed Sullivan*, Steve formed his first band, the Whirlwinds. He later played with oldies act the Dovells, whose "Bristol Stomp" had been a hit in 1961, playing rock 'n' roll revival shows with the likes of Dion and Little Richard. Prior to signing on with Springsteen, he cofounded the band Southside Johnny & the Asbury Jukes.

Steve launched a solo career in 1982 with the album *Men without Women*, and his involvement with Artists United

Bruce Springsteen with Steven Van Zandt in 2009. The two musicians have a firm friendship that's lasted over four decades. *CLAUS FISKER/AFP/Getty Images*

Against Apartheid helped inspire Springsteen to become more politically involved. In 1999 he joined the cast of the hit TV series *The Sopranos*, and in 2012 took the starring role in the English/Norwegian series *Lilyhammer*. He also hosts the radio show *Little Steven's Underground Garage* and runs a label, Wicked Cool Records.

Van Zandt is always ready for another tour with the E Street band, telling *The Globe and Mail*, "I'm not sure how often we'll do it, but I expect to keep going out on tour with the E Street Band as far as the eye can see."

Springsteen was an energetic live performer, here surprising keyboardist Danny Federici by climbing up on his piano during a show at the Electric Ballroom in Atlanta, Georgia, on August 21, 1975. *Tom Hill/WireImage/ Getty Images*

Springsteen on stage in 1975, the year he attained his first big commercial success with *Born to Run. Michael Ochs Archives/Getty Images*

band, Mercy Flight, took Lopez's place at the gig; Mercy Flight's former lead singer, Robbin Thompson, was another new member in the group.

The outdoor show started smoothly enough at 5:00 p.m. Three bands played before Steel Mill, who were headlining. The trouble began when the police in attendance, already fitted with riot gear, decided to strictly observe the 10:00 p.m. curfew. The band was playing "He's Guilty"—a song whose sentiments would only further provoke the law—when the police descended, battling their way to the stage and arresting audience members for illicit drug use along the way. Springsteen recalled that when a cop was thrown into the swimming pool, everything exploded.

When the police finally made it to the stage, they cut the power. But someone in the crew managed to restore it, leading the police to arrest every crew member they could get their hands on. One of the crew was seriously injured when he was whacked over the head with a police officer's heavy flashlight. The cops again managed to turn off the sound, but Bruce wouldn't quit, continuing to sing "Guilty" a cappella as chaos erupted around him. But eventually, fearing that their gear would be confiscated, the band packed up quickly and roared off in West's truck. Federici had engineered his own escape; after pushing over a speaker stack on some encroaching cops, he took off running, making such a quick getaway he was nicknamed "The Phantom." A warrant was issued for his arrest, and after dodging the authorities for a while he finally turned himself in to clear the matter up. The police made more than twenty arrests that night, with reports of ten police officers injured.

The band performed seven more shows over the rest of the year, opening for Ike and Tina Turner in Richmond, Virginia, on October 10; returning to Nashville, Tennessee, for a show on October 24; and opening for Black Sabbath on November 27 at Asbury Park's Sunshine In. Springsteen then headed to San Mateo, California, for the Christmas holidays to see his family. Taking a break from the band helped him think about the direction he wanted

A leather-jacketed Springsteen, circa 1975. *Monty Fresco/Evening Standard/Getty Images*

to take his music. Inspired by the work of Van Morrison and Joe Cocker, he wanted to create something bigger and bolder than Steel Mill; less a rock band and more a musical troupe with an R & B feel. He didn't want to rejigger Steel Mill; it was simpler to break it up and start over again.

The rest of the band was disappointed, but not terribly surprised; they had a sense that Springsteen was destined for bigger things. When Steel Mill had played Nashville in August, Thompson noticed that the record company people who dropped by backstage spent their time talking to Springsteen and not the rest of the band. Although Van Zandt and Lopez would continue to play with Springsteen, the band put Steel Mill to rest after three final shows in January 1971. Steel Mill's last two gigs were sold-out shows at the Upstage on January 22 and 23. Springsteen fixed his eyes on his next musical adventure.

FROM
JERSEY
TO
JUNGLELAND

Steel Mill might have ended, but Springsteen wasn't at loose ends for long. A week after the band's final appearance at the Upstage, he was back at the same venue on January 29, 1971, sitting in with Steve Van Zandt & the Big Bad Bobby Williams Band. That outfit featured not only Van Zandt on vocals and guitar and Williams on drums and vocals, but also Garry Tallent on bass, David Sancious on organ, and Southside Johnny Lyon on harmonica and vocals. Springsteen would work with these same musicians many times over the coming years.

The Upstage remained a major Springsteen hangout; he dropped by to join in the jam sessions and also played acoustic sets downstairs at the Green Mermaid. On March 18, 1971, he tapped his pool of fellow musicians to form a band to play a dance in Deal, New Jersey, organized by the Young Hebrew Association. Backing Springsteen that night were Van Zandt, Tallent, Sancious, and Lopez.

The same crew was on hand for a more high-profile date later that month, opening for the Allman Brothers on March 27 at Asbury Park's Sunshine In. West had been asked if Steel Mill was available to open, and while the band was no more, Springsteen wasn't going to let a chance like this go by. He embellished the lineup by adding John "Hotkeys" Waasdorp on electric piano, Albany "Al" Tellone on sax and vocals, Bobby Feigenbaum on tenor sax, and Williams as a second drummer; West was even invited to play the congas. Springsteen added a performance-art touch to the group by arranging for a baton twirler and for some friends to play Monopoly onstage during the show. The collective took the jokey name Bruce Springsteen & Friendly Enemies, and their performance drew a thumbs-up from the Allmans.

Springsteen and most of the Friendly Enemies played similarly styled shows as Dr. Zoom & the Sonic Boom (with backing vocals provided by a group of singers dubbed "Zoomettes"). The sets included Steel Mill material such as "Goin' Back to Georgia," rock 'n' roll classics including "Roll Over Beethoven," Carole King's "Will You Love Me Tomorrow," Bob Dylan's "It Takes a Lot to Laugh, It Takes a Train to Cry," and the group's own "Zoom Theme." "Dr. Zoom was just a fun band that had all of our friends in it," Lopez told Castiles.net in 2007. "We put it together quickly to keep working and make an income."

During this period, Springsteen also played some shows under the name Bruce Springsteen and the Red Hot Mammas. In May he briefly joined the Sundance Blues Band as a guitarist, alongside Van Zandt, Lyon, Tallent, and Lopez. But he was itching to step out under his own name and that summer formed the Bruce Springsteen Band, leaving no doubt as to the main attraction.

It was around this time that Springsteen acquired the nickname of "the Boss." Nicknames were popular in his crowd, and over the years various explanations have been offered for his nickname's origin, including his skill in

(previous spread)
The '70s-era Springsteen was most often seen playing a Fender Telecaster. *Michael Ochs Archives/ Getty Images*

(opposite)
Though an unabashed rock 'n' roller, Springsteen also performed more acoustically based material. *Michael Ochs Archives/Getty Images*

playing Monopoly and the fact that he passed out money to the rest of the band after shows. It was an inside joke among friends that later embarrassed him: he called the nickname "idiotic." "It's the bane of my entire career," he told Gavin Martin of the *New Musical Express* in 1996. "I've learned to live with it but I've hated it, y'know. Basically it was a casual thing. Somebody said it when the paychecks came out at the end of the month and then it ended up being this stupid thing—in my mind anyway. But, hey, so it goes."

The Bruce Springsteen Band made their first-known performance on July 10, 1971, at an outdoor event called the 2nd Annual Nothings Festival at Brookdale Community College in Lincroft, New Jersey. The lineup featured Springsteen, Van Zandt, Tallent, Sancious, Lopez, a horn section with Feigenbaum on sax and Harvey Cherlin on trumpet, and Delores Holmes and Barbara Dinkins on backing vocals. West filled in occasionally on congas. "The Bruce Springsteen Band moved on to rhythm and blues," Lopez explained in 2007, "more towards the sound that we think of Bruce today."

The band captured attention right away. The following night, when they opened for Humble Pie at the Sunshine In, the band's guitarist, Peter Frampton, was impressed enough to offer Springsteen the opening slot for the rest of their tour. He also offered to give them a plug at Humble Pie's label, A&M Records. But West wasn't interested. The band kept busy, venturing up to New York on July 23 to play the Guggenheim Bandshell in Lincoln Center's Damrosch Park. But for the most part, they stuck to the familiar turf of New Jersey and Virginia.

It was during the band's fall residency at the Student Prince in Asbury Park, New Jersey, that Springsteen encountered another musician who would play an important role in his career. In September, Karen Cassidy, a former girlfriend of Springsteen's, advised him to go down the street to the Wonder Bar and check out a band called Norman Seldin & the Joyful Noyze, featuring a great sax player, one Clarence Clemons, whose towering stature gave him the obvious nickname "the Big Man." Springsteen did so and was suitably impressed. Cassidy then suggested Clemons stop by the Student Prince sometime to check out Springsteen's band, which he did—and quickly found himself jamming with the group. Springsteen and Clemons later recounted a mythologized version of this encounter, saying that when Clemons entered the club, he brought with him a force so strong that the door blew right off its hinges ("It was raining and thundering like a motherfucker," Clemons gleefully wrote in his 2009 memoir, *Big Man: Real Life & Tall Tales*). Springsteen loved playing with Clemons, and the feeling was mutual. "I will never, ever forget the feeling I got when we hit that first note," the Big Man later told biographer Carlin. "It was like I'd been searching for so long, and now, thank God, I am finally, finally, where I'm supposed to be." Nonetheless, he wouldn't join Springsteen's band for another year.

More changes were in the air. In October it was announced that the Upstage would be closing. Springsteen performed at the club for the last time on October 29; the club's final night was October 30, when the Bruce Springsteen Band played Virginia Commonwealth University in Richmond. In November, Springsteen told West he no longer wanted to be managed by him. West was agreeable, although he continued to run sound for the Bruce Springsteen Band.

West was also destined to be instrumental in hooking Springsteen up with the man who would change everything for him: Mike Appel. West mixed sound for the band Montana Flintlock (which also worked under the name Tumbleweed), and Appel and his partner Jim Cretecos had worked briefly with the band in Nashville. Appel had started his career in music in a high school band called the Humbugs. He later joined the Balloon Farm (cowriting their sole hit, "A Question of Temperature") and went on to work as a producer and songwriter. He was currently working for the Wes Farrell Organization and enjoying some success writing songs for the TV show *The Partridge Family*, about a family who becomes a rock band, based loosely on a real-life rock band family, the Cowsills.

West arranged an audition for Springsteen at Appel's office in New York City and drove Springsteen to the Big Apple in his car. After introductions, Springsteen explained what he wanted: "I'm tired of being a big fish in a little pond."

"Fine," Appel responded, "Let's hear what you've got."

Springsteen performed two songs for Appel, on acoustic guitar and piano, including the number "Baby Doll." Appel was underwhelmed. He didn't hear anything distinctive or interesting in Springsteen's work, telling him, "There's just nothing here that anyone is going to get excited about." But he wasn't totally dismissive; he told Springsteen to come back when he'd written some better songs.

That gave Springsteen something to think about. He had been playing the club circuit for six years now, and while there was no shortage of work, he seemed destined to remain in bar bands. But how to get out? After a final show at the Student Prince on December 19, Springsteen traveled back to California to see his family during the holidays and pondered his options. "I did some auditioning, but I realized really quickly that I wasn't gonna be able to live out there," he told Bob Costas in a 1995 radio interview. "There were just a lot of musicians, and while it was a much bigger music scene, I was a nobody."

So January 1972 found Springsteen back in New Jersey. He sat in with the Sundance Blues Band and got the Bruce Springsteen Band going again. Then he took a deep breath, picked up the phone, and called Appel, reminding him of their previous meeting and saying that he'd written some new songs. Did Appel want to hear them? He did. And so on Valentine's Day, Springsteen

October 2, 1985, the final night of the *Born in the U.S.A.* tour, at the Los Angeles Memorial Coliseum. *Bob Riha Jr/WireImage*

headed back to New York, where Appel, Cretecos, and Bob Spitz (a song plugger, publishing administrator, and future rock biographer), waited to hear what he could do. Spitz brought along a tape recorder.

Springsteen played eight songs for the group: "No Need," "Cowboys of the Sea," "If I Was the Priest," "It's Hard to Be a Saint in the City," "The Angel," "Hollywood Kids," "Arabian Nights," and "For You." In stark contrast to their first meeting, Appel loved Springsteen's work—he was so taken with "It's Hard to Be a Saint in the City" he asked Springsteen to play it a second time—and said he was interested in signing Springsteen there and then. Appel and Cretecos had previously worked together with an act called Sir Lord Baltimore, and the two decided to form a new partnership to work with Springsteen. But first, they had to clear it with their boss, Wes Farrell. After hearing the tape of Springsteen's audition, Farrell passed on signing him. Appel and Cretecos promptly quit their jobs and set up Laurel Canyon Productions, moving into the same office building where Bob Dylan's manager, Albert Grossman, had an office.

Springsteen signed exclusive recording, publishing, and management contracts with Laurel Canyon at this time—contracts that would come back to haunt him. "My attitude when I was started was I would sign anything to make a record," he said in 2010 for an interview for the Australian TV program *Sunday Night.* "And of course it comes back and gets you later."

After signing, Springsteen recorded demos over the next few months for Appel and Cretecos, in the hopes of generating interest in his songwriting. But Springsteen and his new managers were primarily interested in securing a record contract. Appel headed straight for the top: Columbia Records, a subsidiary label of CBS Records. When he called the company, Appel first tried to arrange a meeting with the company's president, Clive Davis, but he was out of town, so Appel asked to speak to John Hammond instead. Hammond was legendary in the recording industry for signing Billie Holiday, Aretha Franklin, and Bob Dylan, among many others. Springsteen knew of Hammond's storied history and was excited and nervous when he arrived with Appel at Hammond's office on May 2, 1972, for his 10:30 a.m. audition.

He was soon cringing in embarrassment over Appel's brusque manner with Hammond. "So you're the man who is supposed to have discovered Bob Dylan," Appel announced. "Now, I want to see if you've got any ear, 'cause I've got somebody *better* than Dylan."

"I don't know what you're trying to prove," Hammond responded, "but you're succeeding in making me dislike you." Fortunately, he didn't throw the brash upstarts out, and Springsteen hastily went into his performance, playing—as recalled by those who were there—"Growin' Up," "It's Hard to Be a Saint in the City," "Mary Queen of Arkansas," and "If I Was the Priest."

Hammond loved the songs and was eager to sign Springsteen, instantly recognizing the kind of artist who would "last a generation." But he wanted to see Springsteen perform in front of an audience; after a few phone calls, Gaslight Au Go Go, a Greenwich Village club, agreed to let Springsteen play a few songs that night. Before the evening's scheduled performers, headliner Charlie Musselwhite and support act Garland Jeffreys, took the stage, Springsteen held forth with his acoustic guitar for half an hour, playing a handful of songs including "Growin' Up" and "It's Hard to Be a Saint in the City."

There weren't many people in the audience, but the only one of any consequence was Hammond, and Springsteen's performance only confirmed Hammond's initial response to his music. Now he only had to convince Columbia's president, Clive Davis. On May 3, Springsteen was once again in New York, recording a twelve-song demo at CBS Studios (four of those songs would appear on the 1998 rarities set *Tracks*). Davis heard the demo and asked to meet Springsteen, and a meeting was duly arranged. After hearing a few more songs in his office, Davis agreed to sign Springsteen, although the deal wasn't finalized until June 9. Springsteen wasn't signed to Columbia directly; he was signed to Laurel Canyon Productions, which signed the deal with the record company.

The contractual setup left Hammond uneasy, and he recommended that Appel show his contract with Springsteen to a lawyer he knew, William

Krasilovsky. According to one account, Krasilovsky told Appel, "Mike, this is a slave contract. If you're smart, you won't go through with it, because your artist—if he makes it—is going to hate you." In his own book, *Down Thunder Road*, Appel denied that Krasilovsky used the term "slave contract," recalling that the lawyer had merely suggested some revisions, which Appel agreed to make.

Sessions for Springsteen's debut album began in late June at 914 Sound Studio in Blauvelt, a small town forty-five minutes northwest of New York, chosen by Appel because it was inexpensive and he knew the owner, Brooks Arthur. Hammond had regarded Springsteen as a solo acoustic artist, but Springsteen insisted on recording with a band; the final album had both solo and band numbers. Springsteen enlisted Sancious, Tallent, and Lopez as his core band. Van Zandt was also asked to join the sessions, but he was touring with the Dovells, a Philadelphia vocal group known for their hit "Bristol Stomp." He did turn up to add a "sound effect"—hitting his amp so it boomed like thunder—for "Lost in the Flood."

Sessions ran until late October and were coproduced by Appel and Cretecos. They recorded songs featuring the band during the first two weeks, after which Springsteen concentrated on his solo material. By August, the album was complete. Its lineup was evenly divided between band recordings ("Does This Bus Stop at 82nd Street?," "Growin' Up," "It's Hard to Be a Saint in the City", "For You," and "Lost in the Flood") and Springsteen's solo numbers ("The Angel," "Mary Queen of Arkansas," "Arabian Nights," "Jazz Musician," and "Visitation at Fort Horn"). But when Davis listened to the album, he told Springsteen he didn't hear a hit single among any of the tracks. "To his credit, Bruce took that advice with the best possible attitude," Davis later wrote in his 2012 autobiography. The songs he wrote next, "Blinded by the Light" and "Spirit in the Night," turned out to be the album's strongest tracks. He brought in someone new to play on the tracks too: sax man Clemons. Springsteen had recently jammed with Clemons's band, Norman Seldin & the Joyful Noyze, at the Shipbottom Lounge in Point Pleasant Beach, New Jersey, on July 1. The two tracks were added to the album, and "Visitation," "Arabian Nights," and "Jazz Musician" were removed. Most of the eight outtakes from the sessions are available unofficially on the collector's circuit, along with outtakes from other albums; demo versions of "Mary Queen of Arkansas," "Growin'," "Growin' Up," "Does This Bus Stop at 82nd Street?," and "It's Hard to Be a Saint in the City" were officially released on the 1998 rarities collection *Tracks*.

Springsteen named his debut album after a touristy picture postcard he found that read "Greetings from Asbury Park, N.J."; the same postcard appeared on the cover. Davis was so impressed with Springsteen's work that he taped himself talking about Springsteen's importance and unique talents and played the recording over the company's closed-circuit television

GREETINGS FROM ASBURY PARK, N.J.

Released: January 1973
Chart Position: No. 60

Springsteen was twenty-three years old when he recorded *Greetings from Asbury Park, N.J.*, and he was already a veteran musician, having played in bands since he was fifteen. Now he finally had an outlet for all of his ideas. "I had all that stuff stored up for years," he later recalled. "The first album was a big outlet."

It was also something of a mix, given that Springsteen's manager and some of the people at his new label regarded him as an acoustic troubadour, while Springsteen emphasized he needed to rock out with a band. So *Greetings* became a compromise, a mix of rock 'n' roll and folk that, if nothing else, demonstrated the rising talent's versatility.

The album opens with the rollicking wordplay of "Blinded by the Light," its stream-of-consciousness-driven lyrics a key reason why Springsteen was so plagued by Bob Dylan comparisons in his early years. "Does This Bus Stop at 82nd Street?" is in a similar vein, a wide-eyed look at the cast of characters roaming the streets of Manhattan. "Growin' Up" is a slice of surreal autobiography. "Spirit in the Night" strides middle territory, a beguiling remembrance of a night on the town with a new love, a live favorite to this day. There's a warmth and a friendliness throughout the album that draws you in from the beginning.

"Mary Queen of Arkansas" presents the other side of Springsteen. The sole instrumentation is guitar and harmonica, and while the mournful tale seems to be about a broken relationship, there are lyrical hints of something more going on beneath the surface (such as Mary being neither "man enough for me to hate" or "woman enough for kissing"). "The Angel" is another contemplative number that highlights just how expressive Springsteen's voice can be.

There are clear signs of how Springsteen's career would progress on this first album. Most obviously, he would indulge his penchant for stripped-bare acoustic numbers on an entire album in the future. "For You" has the same kind of get-out-of-town urgency that would be the stepping off point for a number of songs. "Lost in the Flood" addresses the plight of veterans, a recurring theme in Springsteen's work. The album ends with "It's Hard to Be a Saint in the City," the track that so impressed Mike Appel when Springsteen auditioned for him, and the first of many road trips on which Springsteen would take his listeners.

When Springsteen played the album set live in its entirety for the first time on November 22, 2009, he joked, "This was the record that took us from way below zero to—one." But while it may have been a slower start than Springsteen wished, as the saying goes, a journey of a thousand miles begins with a single step.

network. It was decided to delay the release of the album until January 1973 so it wouldn't get lost in the holiday rush.

Springsteen had done few live performances while the album was being recorded. He made an early foray into politics when the Bruce Springsteen Band played a benefit for Senator George McGovern's Democratic presidential campaign at the Grant's Cinema III Theater in Red Bank, New Jersey, on July 5, an event that also included admission to that evening's film attraction, the cult favorite *Frogs* (Ray Milland's last film). But Springsteen made no speech in support of the candidate; he wasn't interested in being a spokesman for a cause—yet.

He also played a number of solo sets at Max's Kansas City in New York, opening for Dave Van Ronk. Later in the summer he played early evening shows at the club, and he often stuck around to watch protopunk act the New York Dolls take the stage after midnight. On September 9, he turned up as a surprise special guest at a Jackson Browne gig at the Bitter End in New York, after the opening act, David Blue, persuaded Browne to let Springsteen play. Springsteen played for an hour between Browne's and Blue's sets, and the two later became his good friends. During the same month, he also performed a song during Bonnie Raitt's show at Gaslight Au Go Go.

But Springsteen was itching to get back onstage, and he began putting his live band together. Tallent and Lopez were ready, but Sancious turned the offer down, so Springsteen sought out former Steel Mill keyboardist Federici and asked if he'd like to join. Springsteen also extended an invitation to Clemons, who played a final show with Norman Seldin on October 21 before signing on with Springsteen. The tour kicked off on October 28 at West Chester College in West Chester, Pennsylvania. A report in the college newspaper said Springsteen was "heckled off the stage," and there would be plenty of ups and downs as Springsteen began touring more extensively.

Next up were shows in New Jersey and Pennsylvania, a quick dash to Michigan, and a six-night residency at Kenny's Castaways in New York City. During the run, Springsteen and the band went up to Ossining Correctional Facility—Sing Sing Prison—for a daytime show on December 7 and then headed back to New York City for the shows that night at Kenny's. "It was good that they liked us," Bruce cracked about the prison appearance. The year ended with shows in Ohio.

Greetings was released on January 5, 1973. It got off to a slow start, rising only to No. 60 in the *Billboard* charts, and neither of the accompanying singles, "Blinded by the Light" (released in February) and "Spirit in the Night" (released in May), reached the charts at all. (Ironically, when Manfred Mann's Earth Band released their 1977 cover of "Blinded by the Light," it topped the charts). A promotional postcard had been sent out to hype the album, featuring the cover art on one side and the hopeful inscription "The most important new voice of Asbury Park, New Jersey. And perhaps the '70s as well" on the back.

The label also talked him up as "the next Bob Dylan," a comparison Springsteen always hated. "I don't know why people thought they needed a new Dylan," he said in 2009. "But it was just, I think he invented a language that didn't exist in popular song before, so when you came along and you built on that language, you were just immediately connected to it." And there were some positive reviews. "Bruce has a knack for bringing things to light in vivid images," Barbara Schoenweis wrote in the *Asbury Park Evening Press*. *Stereo Review* magazine named it Record of the Year. But sales were lagging.

So, the band stayed on the road, the only way they could make money. The new year opened with a four-night stand at the Main Point in Bryn Mawr, Pennsylvania, beginning January 3, 1974, followed by a two-week residency at Paul's Mall in Boston, opening for David Bromberg. During their time in Boston, the band made their first live radio performance, on WBCN, playing a six-song set (later released officially in the UK on the album *Bound for Glory*). At the end of the month, Springsteen was back at Max's Kansas City for six nights, opening for Biff Ross. One song from the first night, "Bishop Danced," later aired on the *King Biscuit Flower Hour* syndicated radio show, netting Springsteen more national exposure. (It later appeared on *Tracks*.) The Max's show also generated an item in *Rolling Stone*, but not because of the music; Hammond suffered a heart attack while at one of the shows, and his doctor charitably attributed it to "Hammond's enthusiasm" for Springsteen's onstage antics.

February saw Springsteen venturing beyond home territory, performing his first Los Angeles–area show at the Troubadour in West Hollywood on February 26. The press was invited for the occasion (though Springsteen wasn't the headliner), and while the show was hampered when Springsteen's amp blew after a few songs, forcing him to move to the piano, he received good notices in *Billboard* and the *Los Angeles Free Press*, where Peter Jay Philbin wrote, "Never have I been more impressed with a debuting singer than I was with Bruce Springsteen on Monday night."

After three more dates in California, Springsteen headed back east, and as winter became spring, most of the shows he played were on the East Coast: Massachusetts, Rhode Island, Connecticut, New York, Pennsylvania, Virginia, and only two shows in New Jersey. The April 24 show, the first of two gigs in Bryn Mawr, was broadcast live over Philadelphia station WMMR (later appearing on the *Bound for Glory* release). April 28 was an especially exciting night for Springsteen, as he opened for two rock 'n' roll icons, Jerry Lee Lewis and Chuck Berry. On hearing that Berry used pick-up bands for his dates, Springsteen was quick to volunteer the services of his band and got

Springsteen's homecoming show during the *Born to Run* tour, October 11, 1975, at the Monmouth Arts Center in Red Bank, in his home state of New Jersey. *Fin Costello/Redferns*

to close out the show, backing rock 'n' roll's poet laureate on classics such as "Maybelline," "Roll Over Beethoven," and "Johnny B. Goode."

On May 1, Springsteen was back in L.A., performing a show that was one of a special series of gigs CBS Records had organized, seven days of shows with bands on their roster, billed as "A Week to Remember." Davis, noting that Springsteen seemed intimidated by the size of the stage gave him a preshow pep talk: "Look, you know I love your music, but you have to take advantage of a stage this size. You can't let yourself be overwhelmed by it. Don't be daunted by it—use it!" The shows, at the Ahmanson Theatre, were all filmed so the footage could be shown at CBS Records' upcoming sales convention in July, where Springsteen would also perform. One song, "Wild Billy's Circus Story," was later released on a promotional EP.

Sessions for Springsteen's next album, *The Wild, the Innocent & the E Street Shuffle*, also began in May and ran through mid-September, at the same studio where *Greetings* had been recorded. Sancious was again brought in to play on the record, and he ended up joining the band as well. After playing a few shows in May, his first official gig with the band was a June 22 date in Seaside Heights, New Jersey. He was also destined to leave a more permanent mark on the band. At the time, he was living in his mother's home at 1105 E Street in Belmar, New Jersey. Looking at the street sign one day, Springsteen decided that should be the name of his backing group: the E Street Band.

Springsteen delighted the crowd at this December 21, 1975, date at Seneca College in Toronto, Ontario, by leaping into the audience. *Dick Darrell/Toronto Star via Getty Images*

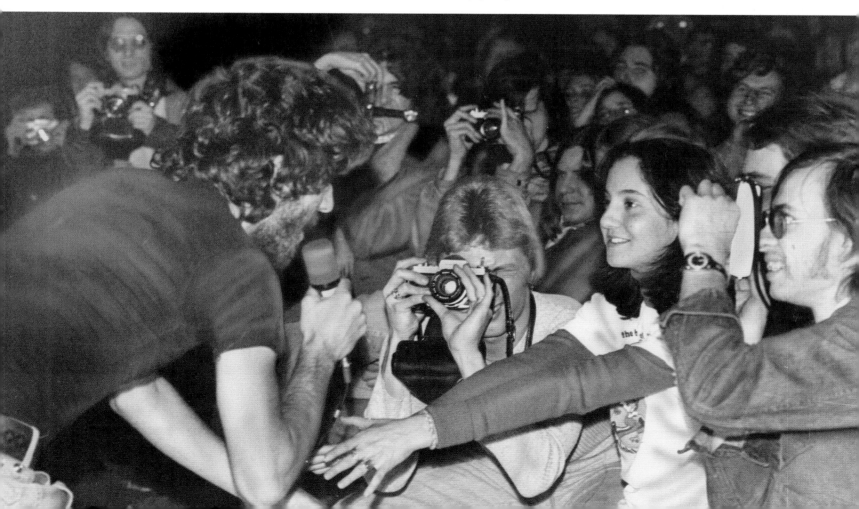

Opening Acts

Springsteen at the Palladium in New York City in October 1976. Gary "U.S." Bonds and Patti Smith guested during his three-night stand at the venue.
Allan Tannenbaum/Getty Images

Before becoming a headline act, Springsteen started out like any other performer, opening for a variety of artists. It resulted in some unexpected pairings. In 1972, Springsteen opened for stoner comedy act Cheech and Chong. The following year, he opened for a number of well-known acts, including Lou Reed, Stevie Wonder, and the Beach Boys.

But by 1974, Springsteen's acclaim as a live act had grown, even if commercial success hadn't quite caught up yet. And it was the latter that concerned Anne Murray's managers when Springsteen was picked to replace Boz Scaggs at the Schaefer Music Festival in New York on August 3, 1974. Murray was previously set to open for Scaggs. But if he was no longer on the bill, her managers argued, she should become the headliner, with Springsteen relegated to opening for her, given that she was the one with the hit records. Springsteen's booking agent, Barry Bell, told them they didn't realize what Springsteen's live show was like, telling them "You're not going to want to follow Bruce Springsteen in New York City." But Murray's managers stood firm.

And, to their dismay, they watched as a quarter of the audience left after Springsteen's set. Murray might've been the headliner, "But it was Springsteen's night, probably the biggest of his life," Robert Christgau wrote in the *Village Voice*, adding that by the time the show ended, three-quarters of the audience had left. Springsteen's time as an opening act was coming to an end.

As staying on the road was the only way to keep the money coming in ("If we don't play every week, we don't have money—it's as easy as that," Springsteen said in 1974), sessions were scheduled between live dates. Promotional appearances were shoehorned in as well: Springsteen performed before an invited audience on May 31 at the Alpha Sound Studios in Richmond, Virginia, which was broadcast live on local station WGOE. The night before, in Fayetteville, North Carolina, the band had started a thirteen-date tour opening for Chicago. It was to be an unhappy pairing for Springsteen, and the radio performance was one of few bright spots in the next two weeks.

Springsteen and Chicago were both on Columbia but had little else in common. He had always loved using horns to embellish his bands, but he preferred a looser, rawer sound in comparison to Chicago's radio-friendly jazz fusion style. As an opening act, Springsteen was limited to short sets, barely enough time to get started, he felt. He'd never played arenas before, and he didn't like them; too big, too cold, too impersonal. And he couldn't have been cheered by reviews such as Barbara Green's in the *Richmond New Leader*, which said he "looks like a parody of the early Bob Dylan," with an "undistinguished" voice (though she grudgingly conceded, "he has enough stage presence to catch one's eye").

The tour's nadir came on June 6, when the band played the Spectrum in Philadelphia. The crowd booed Springsteen. He responded with an obscene gesture and defiantly continued to play.

"The Chicago tour was a waste," said Barry Bell, who booked Springsteen's tours. "And it was just sad, almost, after seeing him in the clubs, doing two hours of energy and stories and charisma. Now here he was just another opening act on stage." The tour came to an end on June 15 at Madison Square Garden, Springsteen's debut at the venue where he had seen Elvis Presley perform the previous June. But Springsteen couldn't wait to get off the stage. After the show, he told Appel he didn't want to play another arena. Ever again.

He was soon back at the smaller venues where he felt more comfortable: three nights at Fat City in Seaside Heights, New Jersey, from June 22 to 24; five nights at the Main Point from July 5 to 9; and a six-night stand at Max's Kansas City from July 18 to 23, two shows a night, the opening act being a reggae band from Jamaica, the Wailers, whose lead singer was Bob Marley. The Max's engagement drew a rave from Michael Gross in the *Miscellany News*, who was mightily impressed by Bruce's live show: "I just can't explain Bruce Springsteen. All I know is that he must have loved the Ronettes as much as he loved Bob Dylan. Probably even more. He's so original that he gets the short end of any description. Just see him live and you'll know what I mean. He's one guy that vinyl hasn't done any justice to at all."

But the dynamic performer Gross had written about seemed MIA on July 27, when the band played at the CBS Records Sales Convention later in the month, part of a showcase at the Fairmont Hotel in San Francisco. Watching an exuberant set by Edgar Winter's White Trash, replete with fireworks and smoke bombs, Springsteen felt he had no way to compete with such razzle-dazzle and decided to open his own set with a new number, "4th of July, Asbury Park (Sandy)," accompanying himself on acoustic guitar while Federici played the accordion. Though he brought on the rest of the band for his four-song set, he didn't win many converts and later recalled, "All these ladies in gowns in the front rows had their fingers in their ears." It didn't help that while the acts were supposed to play fifteen-minute sets, Springsteen performed for over half an hour. As Hammond later put it, "Bruce came onstage with a chip on his shoulder and played way too long. People came to me and said, 'He really can't be that bad, can he, John?'"

It was a sign that Springsteen's label was starting to lose faith in him. He'd lost a big supporter earlier in the year when Davis resigned from the label amid allegations of financial misconduct. Now Charles Koppelman was the director of artists and repertoire (A&R), and he made his lack of interest in Springsteen clear. After coming up to 914 Studios to listen to an early version of the new album, he stunned everyone by stating, "Fellas, we may have run to the end of our days with Bruce Springsteen. This is not an album we are going to put out." Springsteen hastily remixed and resequenced the album, and it was deemed acceptable. But the reaction of his label left him shaken.

The Wild, the Innocent & the E Street Shuffle had finally been completed in September and released on November 5. There were eleven outtakes from the sessions; "Zero and Blind Terry," "Thundercrack," "Seaside Bar Song," and "Santa Ana" were later released on *Tracks*, and "The Fever" appeared as a bonus cut on the "best of" *Tracks* compilation *18 Tracks* (1999). To everyone's disappointment, it failed to chart. Appel was nonplussed: "How could anyone be this good, I wondered, and not be on the top of the charts?" But if sales were slow, they at least were steady; over the next year and a half the album would sell 175,000. And the critical reception was positive; Springsteen even tied with Elliott Murphy and Larry Norman in *Cashbox* as Best New Male Artist of the year.

Throughout the fall, Springsteen played up and down the East Coast. On an October 6 date at Villanova University in Villanova, Pennsylvania, he shared the bill with Jackson Browne, who had just released his second album, *For Everyman*. The up-and-coming duo Hall & Oates opened for them on another Max's Kansas City residency from November 6 to 10. Springsteen also opened for a few notable acts, including Brian Auger's Oblivion Express at Trenton State College in Ewing, New Jersey, on November 11; he was pleased to note that he was the big draw that night, as much of the audience left after his set. On November 25 he opened for blues legend John Mayall at the University of Massachusetts in Amherst. "What the people got to see last night was not Bob Dylan, not Van Morrison, but Bruce Springsteen, a polished, convincing performer in his own right," the *Massachusetts Daily Collegian* wrote of the show. "Bruce was energetic and overflowing with stage charisma." A week later, he opened again for Mayall on December 1 at Quinnipiac University in Hamden, Connecticut.

But money remained tight. In October, Appel decided that instead of Springsteen splitting the money with his bandmates, the band would have to go on salary. There was some grumbling, and Springsteen convinced his manager to guarantee the band members would get at least $35 a week. He was also forced to ask his mother for a loan; she agreed.

As 1974 began, some more administrative changes were in order; Appel became Springsteen's sole manager when Cretecos sold his interest to his partner for $1,500. Now Appel was running the entire show. He kept the band busy with gigs along the East Coast, in the Midwest, and in the South. There was

THE WILD, THE INNOCENT & THE E STREET SHUFFLE

BRUCE SPRINGSTEEN: THE WILD, THE INNOCENT & THE E STREET SHUFFLE

Released: September 1973
Chart Position: No. 59

Springsteen's second album gets off to a jaunty start with the sound of horns tuning up, before coming together for the band's homegrown dance, "The E Street Shuffle." It's an album brimming with confidence, yielding a few classics and much-loved live numbers.

For the latter, look no further than "Rosalita (Come Out Tonight)," a wonderfully exuberant song in which Springsteen pleads his case to the object of his desire with a delightful mix of freewheeling wordplay and tongue-in-cheek references to his own career as a musician. (He brags about the big advance he's received from his record company, at a time when the real Springsteen was barely earning enough to make ends meet.) In contrast, "4th of July, Asbury Park (Sandy)" is laid-back and dreamy, a night under the stars on the boardwalk at the Jersey Shore, though the lyrics indicate it won't be long before the singer chooses to move on from this seemingly idyllic scene.

Elsewhere, Springsteen spins stories about an eclectic cast of characters. "Kitty's Back" celebrates the title character's return with a stinging guitar opener and a great instrumental break with horns, guitars, and organ tumbling all over each other. "Wild Billy's Circus Story" looks behind the razzle-dazzle of carnival life and finds the poignancy that lies underneath, recasting "circus town" as a community of perennial outsiders, with the big boss man whispering words of temptation into the ears of a young innocent, hoping to lure him into the life under the big top. "Incident on 57th Street" recasts Romeo and Juliet as Spanish Johnny and Puerto Rican Jane. It's Springsteen in pure storytelling mode, unfurling the tale as if outlining a movie plot, creating an atmosphere so strong you can feel the sweatiness of the long, hot night.

The album closes with "New York City Serenade," opening with majestic piano playing by David Sancious (reminiscent of Gershwin's "Rhapsody in Blue"). It's the longest song on any of Springsteen's studio albums and quite different from everything else he'd done up to that point: not the acoustic singer-songwriter, not the no-holds-barred rock 'n' roller, but someone reaching beyond, pushing the boundaries to see where he might end up. The extended fadeout (two and half minutes—long enough for a pop song in itself) has Springsteen and the band simply reveling in the joy of making music—leaving no clear resolution for the song's protagonists, Billy and Diamond Jackie.

In contrast to his debut, it's an altogether superior album, so its initial failure to make an impression must surely have been frustrating for Springsteen. But though he didn't know it, that was about to change: *The Wild, the Innocent & the E Street Shuffle* would be the last of his studio albums to miss the Top 20.

a bump when Lopez's temper got the better of him before a February 12 show at the University of Kentucky in Lexington and he got into a fight with Steve Appel, his manager's brother, and the band's road manager. Lopez got fired, leading to the cancellation of the next few dates. "At that point, I didn't think the band was going to go too far and I didn't care either," Lopez later told the *New York Times*. "'I made a few mistakes, you know, everybody makes mistakes."

The band quickly found a replacement in Ernest "Boom" Carter. There was only time to arrange a single rehearsal before the band played a show at the Satellite Lounge in Cookstown, New Jersey, on February 23. Springsteen had tried to get the gig canceled, explaining they needed to break in a new member, but the club's owner, Carlo Rossi, refused and made threats against Springsteen and his manager. Rossi was known for his volcanic temper (when Foghat ignored Rossi's request to lower the volume, he had responded by shooting the band's amps), so the show went on. The band got through the engagement by playing lots of covers.

On March 3 the band played two shows at Georgetown University in Washington, DC, with the second show broadcast live on the radio. A March 7 show in Houston was also broadcast on the radio, and two days later the band recorded an eight-song session for Houston station KLOL-FM. The station also recorded the band's show that night at Liberty Hall.

But with support from his record label fading, Springsteen needed a whole lot more to get his career going. Little did he know that the career boost he needed was on the horizon.

Though Springsteen's run of shows at the Bottom Line in 1975 have been acclaimed as some of his best-ever gigs, none of the shows have been officially released. *Richard E. Aaron/Redferns*

"I SAW ROCK AND ROLL FUTURE AND ITS NAME IS BRUCE SPRINGSTEEN."

On April 9, 1974, Springsteen was in Cambridge, Massachusetts, to record another radio session for Boston station WBCN-FM and prepare for a four-night stand at Charlie's Place. The following night, between the first and the second shows, Springsteen stepped outside to check out a review of *The Wild, the Innocent & the E Street Shuffle* from the Boston weekly *Real Paper* that had been posted outside the club. As he was reading, a young man approached him and asked what he thought of the write-up. Springsteen said he liked it, and the man smiled and introduced himself as the writer of the piece—Jon Landau.

Landau was a serious music fan who had grown up listening to the Beatles and the Beach Boys, later moving on to Motown and soul artists such as Wilson Pickett and Otis Redding. He had played in a band called the Jellyroll, but after realizing his love of music didn't necessarily grant him musical skill, he decided to move into rock journalism, a budding field in the 1960s. He wrote for *Crawdaddy*, the first magazine that regarded rock 'n' roll as an art form, not just a teen phenomenon, and later became an editor at *Rolling Stone* while also writing for *Real Paper*. He had also worked as a producer on albums for Livingston Taylor, the J. Geils Band, and the MC5. Though Springsteen didn't know it at the time, his meeting with Landau would prove to be a life-changing encounter.

After the show, Landau and fellow rock scribe Dave Marsh hung out to talk with Springsteen and Appel. As coproducer of *The Wild, the Innocent & the E Street Shuffle*, Appel wasn't too pleased to hear that Landau hadn't thought much of the album's production, but both Landau and Marsh were enthusiastic about the live show, so his feelings were mollified—at least for the moment.

Landau was again in the audience when Springsteen returned to Cambridge on May 9, this time playing at the Harvard Square Theater. Springsteen was opening for Bonnie Raitt, and Landau planned to review the second show. Knowing that Landau was in the audience, Springsteen performed a new song he'd been working on, "Born to Run," and also played a longer set. The effort paid off. When Landau got home that night, he wrote a review that would tie him firmly to Springsteen's legend.

In a piece more an essay than review, Landau waxed lyrical about how much music had meant to him in his life, but admitted that after becoming a journalist, "I listen to music with a certain measure of detachment"—until witnessing Springsteen's performance at Charlie's Place, when his excitement reawakened.

"There is no one I would rather watch on a stage today," he wrote in the piece, entitled "Growing Young with Rock and Roll," which ran in the May 22, 1974, edition of *Real Paper*. "When his two-hour set ended I could only think, can anyone really be this good; can anyone say this much to me, can rock 'n' roll still speak with this kind of power and glory? And then I felt the sores on

Born to Run promotional pin, 1975

(previous spread)
Springsteen during the second night of a three-day residency at the Electric Ballroom in Atlanta, Georgia, in August 1975. *Tom Hill/WireImage/Getty Images*

my thighs where I had been pounding my hands in time for the entire concert and knew that the answer was yes." The piece ultimately became best known for this pronouncement: "I saw rock and roll future and its name is Bruce Springsteen. And on a night when I needed to feel young, he made me feel like I was hearing music for the very first time."

Columbia Records was thrilled; what a great tagline to use to promote their artist. "I saw rock and roll future and its name is Bruce Springsteen" was first used in an ad in *Rolling Stone*'s July 18, 1974, issue. (The somewhat awkward phrasing of the sentence meant it was also destined to be misquoted over the years, as "I saw rock and roll's future" or "I saw the future of rock and roll," among other variations.)

The hype embarrassed Springsteen. "I mean, who wants to come out onstage and be the future every night? Not me," he told British music weekly *Melody Maker*. But he was nonetheless gratified that Landau was such a strong supporter of his work, and he started calling him up to talk about music and dropping by to hang out when he was in Boston.

Springsteen returned to 914 Sound Studios in May to start work on his next record. It was Springsteen's last stand. His previous two albums had sold modestly, and he was in dire need of a hit to keep his record company happy and finally get his career off the ground. The first song he worked on was destined to be that hit, though took a while for the rest of the world to hear it. It was the song he had debuted for Landau's review: "Born to Run."

The song had an anthemic feeling from the beginning, with a bold melody that, in its final recorded version, had a full, lush density, a modern-day version of producer Phil Spector's "Wall of Sound" utilized on such hits as "Then He Kissed Me." It had all the hallmarks of a classic car song, celebrating the automobile as a means of escape from a dreary existence, with some playful innuendo thrown in. But there's also an underlying sadness; the longed-for escape is a dream that hasn't come true—and possibly never will. It would become Springsteen's signature song, and in 1980 a resolution introduced to the New Jersey state legislature attempted to make it the "Unofficial 'rock' theme of our state's youth" (the measure passed the House, but failed in the Senate).

Springsteen recorded the song at 914 Sound Studios with sessions spread out between May and October 1974 (he also recorded an early version of "Jungleland" at these sessions). Columbia liked the song but wouldn't release it; they wanted to wait until there was an album to promote. So in November, Appel sent copies of the track to select radio stations around the country; DJs were happy to air the exclusive song, and it generated a lot of interest. It also generated some frustration as well, as fans headed into the record stores to buy the single, only to find out it wasn't commercially available.

"Born to Run" single

In addition to serving as longtime drummer for the E Street Band, Max Weinberg was also Conan O'Brien's bandleader, on both *Late Night with Conan O'Brien* and *The Tonight Show with Conan O'Brien.* © John Ares / Alamy Stock Photo

The label was unhappy Appel had jumped the gun, but Springsteen was also unhappy with what he perceived as its lack of support. When Springsteen played Brown University on April 26, he did an interview with J. Garrett Andrews for *Fresh Fruit*, a supplement of the *Brown Daily Herald,* about the "different musical polices" that had come about as a result of Davis' departure. "Now I'm a pain in the ass to them is all and you know, they want to make somebody else famous," he groused. "Just let me make my music and leave me alone."

The article was published on May 1 and read by James Segelstein, the son of Irwin Segelstein, the new president of CBS Records. The younger Segelstein complained to his father, and the irritated elder Segelstein contacted Appel to complain about Springsteen badmouthing the company in the press. Appel suggested they get together to talk about it, and they arranged a lunch meeting. "And that became something of a turning point for Bruce, the precise moment when CBS began to change its attitude toward Springsteen," Appel later said. "They agreed to send Springsteen back into the studio to make a new album that day, to finance the rest of the album at the Record Plant, no hassles, whatever it takes to get the next record out."

There had been some lineup changes in the group. Sancious and Carter played their final show with Springsteen on August 14, 1974, the same date his backing band was billed as the "E Street Band" for the first time. The two musicians, who left to start their own band, Tone, were replaced by Roy Bittan on keyboards and Max Weinberg on drums. Violinist Suki Lahav, who had played on *The Wild, the Innocent & the E Street Shuffle,* made her first live

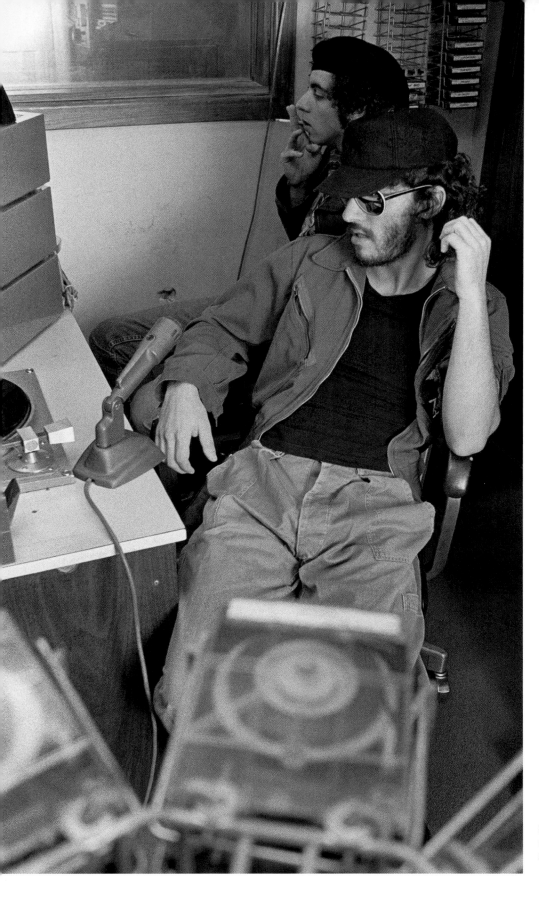

Springsteen and Van Zandt during an interview with radio station WQXI in Atlanta on March 27, 1976, a day after they'd played Atlanta's Fox Theatre. *Tom Hill/ WireImage/Getty Images*

appearance with the band at an October 4 show at Avery Fisher Hall, Lincoln Center, in New York City, and continued to make guest appearances with the group through March 1975. (Her husband, Louis Lahav, had also engineered Springsteen's first two albums.)

In March 1975 Springsteen also entered the studio to make his third album. He worked on it in a new, improved studio, the Record Plant in New York City, through July 1975, fitting in sessions alongside constant live dates. Springsteen liked to tinker with his songs, reworking them over and over until he was satisfied—no matter how long it took. He also brought in Landau to serve as coproducer, alongside Appel. It would not prove to be a happy union.

Landau brought a welcome dose of energy and drive to the sessions, and Appel viewed it as a threat to his authority. "I believe Landau had it in his mind all along, once he saw Springsteen and declared him rock and roll's future, to produce Springsteen and eventually take over his management," Appel later declared in his 1992 autobiography. At one point, toward the end of the sessions, Landau even called Appel to tell him that the tensions

Springsteen and Van Zandt harmonizing on stage during the *Born to Run* tour. *Fin Costello/Redferns*

between them were becoming too fraught, and he should stop coming to the studio. Appel grumbled about it, but complied—only to be visited by Springsteen a few days later, asking him to come back. Landau also apologized, and the situation calmed down. Discord also arose over a proposed live album that Appel and Columbia thought should be released in the interim before *Born to Run* was ready. Springsteen initially agreed, but changed his mind after Landau convinced him it wasn't a good idea. Appel was not pleased.

There were songs that didn't make the final cut. Known outtakes from the sessions include "Linda Let Me Be the One" and "So Young and in Love," both later released on *Tracks*; "Walking in the Street" and "Lonely Night in the Park," broadcast on E Street Radio in 2005; and "Janey Needs a Shooter," a song later recorded by Warren Zevon and released on his 1980 album *Bad Luck Streak in Dancing School*.

Born to Run also featured Springsteen's first iconic album cover. Photographer Eric Meola spent three hours taking pictures, and, when in studying the contact sheets later, was drawn to one particular image of Springsteen, wearing a leather jacket, casually holding his guitar (with an Elvis button pinned to the strap) while leaning against Clemons, who is playing his sax.

Columbia geared up to market the album, promising to put up a quarter of a million dollars for promotion. Bruce Springsteen and the E Street Band held a single rehearsal for the *Born to Run* tour, on July 19, 1975, at the Record Plant. The band hadn't played a show since a March 9 date in Washington, DC, but one rehearsal was all they'd get; the 116-show tour opened on July 20 at the Palace Concert Theatre in Providence, Rhode Island. Van Zandt was now officially part of the band, leaving the Asbury Jukes to take up Springsteen's offer to become a full-time E Streeter. Patti Scialfa had also auditioned for the band after Lahav left the group, but in the end Springsteen decided to not add another vocalist.

Four dates into the tour, the album's release was nearly called off. While in Kutztown, Pennsylvania, on July 25, Springsteen listened to an acetate of the album with the band, and he became so incensed at how bad the record sounded that he hurled it into the hotel's swimming pool. Appel kept his cool, telling Springsteen if he didn't like the album, they could scrap it and start over. "All you have to do is write eight or nine more songs as good as 'Jungleland' or 'Thunder Road.'" With that, Springsteen calmed down and soon agreed the album could come out as it was.

Two weeks before the album's release, Springsteen played a legendary run of shows from August 13 to 17 at the Bottom Line in New York City. Appel had wanted to bring Springsteen back to the Big Apple with a bang, at Madison Square Garden, but Springsteen refused, feeling he could better

Japanese promotional advertisement for *Born to Run* album

reach the audience in a smaller setting. The Bottom Line only held around four hundred people, versus the nearly twenty thousand that the Garden could host. Demand for tickets was fierce, especially because Columbia secured a quarter of all available tickets to distribute themselves.

Springsteen dazzled the audiences. The reaction of Dave Herman, a DJ at New York station WNEW, was typical: "I saw Springsteen for the first time last night. It's the most exciting rock 'n' roll show I've ever seen." The early show on the fifteenth was broadcast over WNEW, and an edited version of the broadcast was used to create the first Springsteen bootleg, *Bruce Springsteen*

Springsteen's five-night (ten-show) residency at New York's Bottom Line club in August 1975 was a career highlight. *Richard E. Aaron/Redferns*

The Bottom Line

Springsteen's ten shows at the Bottom Line in New York City, from August 13 to 17, 1975, are not just some of the finest performances of his career: they're also regarded as among the best concerts in rock history.

The *Born to Run* tour had begun the previous month, and the band was revved up and ready to go by the time they hit the Big Apple. Springsteen pulled out all the stops, leaping on tables, cracking corny jokes, proudly unveiling the new songs from *Born to Run* alongside rock classics like the Crystals' "Then He Kissed Me," Sam Cooke's "Having a Party" and the Drifters' "Up on the Roof." Critical response was strong, and Springsteen was also pleased with the shows. "There's nothin'—*nothin'*—in the world to get you playing better than a gig like that," he told *Rolling Stone*. "The band walked out of the Bottom Line twice as good as when they walked in."

But for all their acclaim, the shows have never been officially released. According to Bottom Line co-owner Allan Pepper, Springsteen had some of the shows videotaped; a brief excerpt of "Born to Run" can be seen in *Wings for Wheels*, a documentary about the making of *Born to Run*.

Numerous audio bootlegs have been released over the years, but fans still hold out hopes for an official release of the material one day.

Live, on Coral Records. At least some of the shows were filmed, though the footage has not been officially released.

Born to Run was finally released on September 1, 1975. It came almost two years after the release of *The Wild, the Innocent & the E Street Shuffle*, but it was worth the wait—it was the breakthrough album Springsteen had been longing for. There were good reviews: *Rolling Stone*'s Griel Marcus called it "a magnificent album that pays off on every bet ever placed on him—a '57 Chevy running on melted down Crystals records that shuts down every claim that has been made. And it should crack his future wide open."

"If I seem to OD on superlatives, it's only because *Born to Run* demands them," Lester Bangs wrote in *Creem*. There was much praise in other outlets as well, and the annual *Village Voice* Pazz & Jop critics' poll named it the third-best album of 1975.

This time, there was plenty of commercial success as well. After debuting in the lower reaches of the chart, the record climbed into the Top 10 in its second week of release, ultimately peaking at No. 3 in the *Billboard* charts. *Born to Run* became not only Springsteen's first gold record, with sales of half a million albums, but also the first album ever to get a platinum award from the Recording Industry Association of America for the sale of one million copies. Springsteen had made it. When he arrived in Red Bank, New Jersey, for an October 10 show at the Monmouth Arts Center, the marquee simply read "The Homecoming."

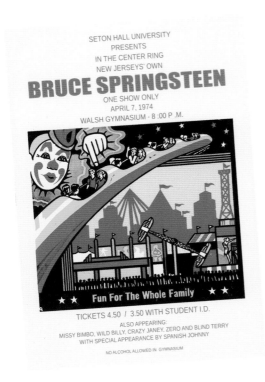

April 7, 1974, concert poster, New Jersey's Seton Hall University

Less than a week later, he was in Los Angeles for a residency at the Roxy on the Sunset Strip, with a single show on October 16, two shows each night on October 17 and 18, and a single show on October 19. A billboard advertising *Born to Run* went up on Sunset, another sign that Springsteen had arrived. His label made sure that the media and special guests were in attendance on opening night; when Springsteen spotted Carole King in the audience, he dedicated his cover of King's "Goin' Back" to her. The opening-night crowd was also dotted with celebrities such as Cher, Warren Beatty, Neil Diamond, and David Bowie. The next day, Springsteen and the band took a little time out to visit the "Happiest Place on Earth": Disneyland.

Springsteen then zipped back to New York to attend Mike Porco's sixty-first birthday party on October 23, 1975. Porco was the owner of New York City venue Gerde's Folk City, where Dylan had played his first New York dates in 1961. Springsteen and Dylan finally met at the party, and Dylan extended an offer for Springsteen to join his Rolling Thunder Revue tour (documented in the 1978 film *Renaldo & Clara*). Springsteen turned him down; he had plenty of touring commitments of his own, and he was on a roll.

At no time was that more evident than on October 27, 1975, when Springsteen graced the covers of both *Newsweek* and *Time*. It was quite a coup. When *Newsweek* had first requested an interview with Springsteen, Appel said they'd only agree if Springsteen was given the cover. To his surprise, *Newsweek* agreed. Appel then worked with Bob Altschuler, Columbia's vice president of publicity, to see if they could get Springsteen on the cover of *Time* as well. Appel used his usual brash touch, telling *Time* that they would eventually put Springsteen on their cover anyway, so why not do it now? *Time* agreed. Springsteen was amazed that they considered him worthy of a cover story at all: "I'm not the president," he said.

There were some unintended consequences from doing the stories. Maureen Orth interviewed Springsteen for *Newsweek*. During the interview she mentioned that Hammond was disappointed that Springsteen hadn't appeared in the TV special *The World of John Hammond*, honoring his career in music. Springsteen was surprised; he hadn't known about the show and later learned that Appel had turned down the request for his appearance. Springsteen also revealed to Orth that he was speaking to *Time* as well as *Newsweek*; she tried to persuade him not to speak to *Time* but did not succeed.

The *Newsweek* piece, "The Making of a Rock Star," focused on how Springsteen was being marketed. "Some people are asking whether Bruce Springsteen will be the biggest superstar or the biggest hype of the '70s," Orth observed. And while complimentary about Springsteen, the article also withheld a full endorsement, noting that Springsteen was still an artist of potential, or in the article's words, "a promising rookie." (For his part, Appel

BORN TO RUN

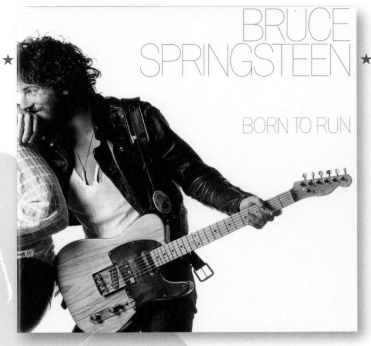

Released: August 1975
Chart Position: No. 3

Born to Run was the album that established Springsteen as a major star. It was his first record that stood as a complete work, a concept album of sorts, with a loose-knit narrative; as originally released on vinyl, side one and side two open with songs celebrating the thrill of escape ("Thunder Road" and "Born to Run," respectively), but the dreams of release are brought crashing down to earth in the closing songs on each side ("Backstreets" and "Jungleland").

"Thunder Road" starts out quietly, with only a piano and a wailing harmonica, then gradually rises in intensity as the ride takes off, the singer's determination to bust out of the "town full of losers" so fierce you can feel the wind blowing through your hair as you barrel down that mythic road with him. "Tenth Avenue Freeze-Out" is the band's origin story, with Springsteen in full-on blues shouter mode, introducing himself as "Bad Scooter" (one of his nicknames) and name-checking the Big Man as well. The glorious musical backing of "Night," lush and full in the best Phil Spector–girl group tradition, masks the underlying discontent of the lyrics, the song's protagonist stuck in a soul-destroying job, only coming alive when he's behind the wheel of his car. The mood is even more somber on "Backstreets," with the singer looking back in sadness at a relationship that failed despite repeated promises that "we'd live forever."

There are hints of discontent even amid the joyousness of "Born to Run." The music is exhilarating, generating the kind of excitement you want to last all night. But the last verse reveals that the dreams of escape are just that—dreams. The song's protagonist insists he and his girlfriend will get out "someday." But when and whether that day will actually come is a question left hanging.

"She's the One" depicts an alluring femme fatale, the kind of woman you yearn for, despite her deceitfulness. Yet the song isn't gloomy; there's an underlying Bo Diddley-esque beat that keeps it stepping lively and a great solo from the Big Man during the instrumental break. "Meeting Across the River" is another walk on the wild side, with a petty criminal seeking to meet his "connection" in what he hopes will be one last big score. It's a low-key number, with a haunting trumpet line helping to set the mood.

Then comes "Jungleland," a song that can only be described as epic, and not just due to its nine-and-a-half-minute length. It's a scenario straight out of a film, chronicling Magic Rat's last night on the town before his own dream "guns him down" and the world turns away in disinterest. The compelling narrative is matched by the skill of the musicians, each instrument a character in itself.

Born to Run fully deserves of all its accolades. It's Springsteen's first classic album.

was highly irritated to see that Landau was wrongly identified as Springsteen's manager in a photo caption.)

In contrast, Springsteen and his music were front and center in *Time*'s story, written by Jay Cocks, who had interviewed Springsteen on the flight to L.A. to do the Roxy shows. Though describing him as a "glorified gutter rat," Cocks was enthusiastic about Springsteen's music and live performing style. The Roxy shows, he wrote, "booted everyone back to the roots, shook 'em up good and got 'em all on their feet dancing. . . . Expecting a monochromatic street punk, the L.A. crowd got a dervish leaping on the tables, all arms and flailing dance steps, and a rock poet as well."

Springsteen was uneasy about the increasing attention, especially about suggestions that he might be all hype and no substance. "The hype just gets in the way," he told *Newsweek*'s Orth. He was uncertain how to react. "I was both elated and embarrassed by my good fortune," he later admitted in 2009. When he arrived for his first concert in London, England, on November 18, 1975, at the Hammersmith Odeon (now the Eventim Apollo), he was so irked by the posters proudly announcing, "Finally the world is ready for Bruce Springsteen," that he tore them down. He also asked that the custom-made buttons bearing the slogan "I have seen the future of rock 'n' roll at the Hammersmith Odeon" not be given out, and he walked around the auditorium taking promotional flyers off the seats.

Appel had wanted the show to be broadcast, but Springsteen was so nervous Appel decided not to, in case the performance wasn't strong enough. But he did arrange for it to be filmed. A few clips were released over the years, but the complete show wasn't officially available until 2005, when it was released on DVD as part of the *Born to Run 30th Anniversary Edition* package. Audio from the show was also released as a live CD in 2006. After shows in Sweden and the Netherlands, Springsteen returned to London for yet another show at the Hammersmith Odeon on November 24.

Back stateside, Springsteen's December schedule was full. His December 12 show in Greenvale, New York, was recorded, and one song from it, "Santa Claus Is Comin' to Town" was released as a radio promo single. (It later appeared on the 1981 children's charity album *In Harmony 2* and as the B-side of the "My Hometown" single in 1985.)

Even when he didn't have a show of his own, Springsteen just couldn't stay off the stage. On December 26, he was back at New York's Bottom Line for the opening night of Patti Smith's three-night residency at the club, joining in on the chorus of "Gloria." He closed out the year with a New Year's Eve show of his own at the Tower Theater in Philadelphia. Back in the city where

(top)
November 24, 1975, concert poster, London's Hammersmith Odeon

(above)
1975 promotional poster for *Born to Run* album

(opposite)
A moody shot of Springsteen in concert in 1976. *Fin Costello/Redferns*

(right)
October 27, 1975, cover of
Newsweek magazine

(far right)
October 27, 1975, cover of
Time magazine

he had once been booed offstage, he now cheekily changed the lyrics of "Rosalita (Come Out Tonight)" to reflect his newfound fame: "Tell your daddy I ain't no freak/ 'Cause I got my picture on the cover of *Time* and *Newsweek*." By this point, *Born to Run* had sold 1.2 million copies.

Springsteen evidently wasn't suffering from a hangover on New Year's Day. He dropped in at the Stone Pony in Asbury Park, New Jersey, to catch a show by Southside Johnny & the Asbury Jukes, accompanied by Van Zandt and Bittan, with all three musicians eventually joining the Jukes to play a number of songs. Van Zandt was involved in producing Southside Johnny's debut album, *I Don't Want to Go Home*, at the time, and Springsteen attended a number of sessions, earning credit as coarranger of the recordings of his own songs, "You Mean So Much to Me" and "The Fever" (the latter featuring a backing vocal from Clemons, credited as "Selmon T. Sachs" on the album's cover).

But in the new year, it didn't take long for the situation between Springsteen and Appel to come to a head. The two no longer seemed in sync over the direction of Springsteen's career. Appel thought it was the perfect time for a live album, to capitalize on the success of *Born to Run*, but Springsteen disagreed. Appel also had offers for radio and TV specials, but Springsteen wasn't interested. Springsteen turned down the chance to play at the closing ceremony of the 1976 Summer Olympics in Montreal, Quebec, Canada, as well as to headline a Fourth of July show at Philadelphia's John F. Kennedy Stadium, as he felt overwhelmed at the size of the venues; he wasn't yet comfortable playing in stadiums. And he considered Appel's suggestion of a summer tour to be performed in a tent to be grandiose and impractical.

More crucially, Springsteen's contract with Appel was set to expire in a year. Appel was eager to continue the arrangement and decided to use a half-million-dollar advance he'd received from Columbia as leverage, telling Springsteen that once they'd worked out a new contract, he would give him his share of the money under the new, more favorable terms.

But Springsteen, who was wondering why his bank account wasn't reflecting his apparent sales, was not in a mood to agree so readily. He talked over his frustrations with Landau, who advised him to hire an attorney and referred him to Myron "Mike" Mayer. Springsteen also had his accountant, Stephen Tenenbaum, do an audit of Laurel Canyon's accounts. Mayer was surprised at what Tenenbaum found. "Appel kept no books," Mayer told author Fred Goldman in his 1997 book *The Mansion on the Hill*.

★ ★

London Debut

When Springsteen arrived in London for his first shows outside of North America in November 1975, he was unaccountably nervous. His latest album, *Born to Run*, was the breakthrough hit he'd been waiting for, but the resulting flurry of attention had left him worried that his music was getting lost in the mix.

Springsteen's nerves were such that the first overseas date, November 18 at London's Hammersmith Odeon, wasn't broadcast live on the radio as planned, though the show was filmed. Springsteen was less talkative than usual during the sixteen-song set and later admitted he wasn't happy with the show, saying the second Hammersmith performance (on November 24) was much better.

The reviews were mixed. Philip Norman of *The Times* wrote that Springsteen was "wonderful. His is as devastating a talent as popular music has ever produced." However, Tony Tyler in the *New Musical Express* called the show a "middle-to-OK concert," and faulted Springsteen for his "basically weak voice" and "almost totally terrible" band. Springsteen himself had nothing good to say about the short tour. "We had four shows, got sandblasted, and scooted home," he

Springsteen's first concert at London's Hammersmith Odeon in November 1975 was his first-ever show overseas. *Tom Sheehan/Sony Music Archive/Getty Images*

told Peter Carlin in the biography *Bruce* (2012), jokingly adding another complaint about Europe: "We couldn't find any cheeseburgers! Europe in 1975 was very European."

It was not one of Springsteen's best nights by any account—until you actually watch the show, which was released on DVD as part of the *Born to Run* box set in 2005. Make no mistake: it's actually a strong performance by the Boss, and a key step on his way to international acclaim.

More hijinks with the Big Man during a December 11, 1975, date at Seton Hall University in South Orange, New Jersey. © *John Ares / Alamy Stock Photo*

"He had a good accountant, but the books consisted of two shopping bags full of paper, and he gave Bruce handouts." As Tenenbaum described it, "My audit reveals a classic case of the unconscionable exploitation of an unsophisticated and unrepresented performer by his manager for the manager's primary economic benefit."

Nonetheless, Springsteen didn't think it was necessary to cut ties with his manager completely, and he suggested that he and Appel simply start over again on new terms, a primary one being that he wanted the copyrights to his work back. Appel refused. In the meantime, Springsteen filed a claim with his record company for unpaid royalties. And he made it clear he wanted Landau to work with him on his next record. Appel naturally didn't want that to happen, and he resented Landau's increasing influence over Springsteen. "Jon was so enamored with Bruce he just couldn't live without him," he told author Clinton Heylin, "and whatever it took to get him 'married' to Bruce he would be willing to do." He informed Columbia that Laurel Canyon held the exclusive production rights to Springsteen's recordings and thus had a say in who could work with him. Meaning, no Landau.

It wasn't entirely a stalemate, for Bruce Springsteen and the E Street Band went back on the road in March 1976. On March 7, Springsteen dropped in at Carole King's show at the Beacon Theatre in New York and ended up joining her onstage to sing the hit she'd written with her then-husband, Gerry Goffin, for Little Eva, "The Loco-Motion." On the twenty-first of the month, everyone reconvened at the Stone Pony in Asbury Park, New Jersey, to warm up for the next leg of the *Born to Run* tour with a performance for a lucky few hundred invited guests.

The tour began on March 25 in Columbia, South Carolina. On April 28, Springsteen made his debut at the famed Grand Ole Opry House in Nashville, Tennessee. Four nights later the band was in Memphis, performing at the Ellis Auditorium; as a keen Elvis Presley fan, Springsteen may have appreciated that Elvis had performed at the same venue. Soul singer Eddie Floyd guested on a few songs during the show.

After the show, Springsteen, Van Zandt, and publicist Glen Brunman decided to find someplace to eat and caught a cab. When the cab driver said he knew of a restaurant near Graceland, Elvis's home, Springsteen excitedly asked him to stop by Graceland first. It was 3:00 a.m. when they pulled up at the famous gates, decorated with a musical staff and notes alongside silhouettes of Elvis. Springsteen could see lights on upstairs in the mansion, so he climbed the fence and headed for the front door. When he was stopped by a security guard, he pleaded his case, proudly announcing that he was an Elvis fan, and a musician too, a successful one; he'd been on the covers of *Time* and *Newsweek*, after all. But the disbelieving guard was unimpressed and escorted Springsteen off the grounds. "He thought I was just another crazy fan—which I was," Springsteen later told Dave Marsh in the 1979 biography *Born to Run*. He wouldn't have been able to meet his idol anyway; Elvis was performing in Lake Tahoe, California, that night.

There were some special appearances mixed in with regular gigs as well. When Southside Johnny & the Asbury Jukes took the stage at the Stone Pony on May 30 in celebration of the release of their album *I Don't Want to Go Home*, Springsteen and company were on hand, and Springsteen joined the band for their last number, "Having a Party." (Springsteen had first played the Stone Pony club on September 9, 1974, sitting in with Southside Johnny when the band was then known as the Blackberry Booze Band.) The show was broadcast live as well.

Springsteen then scored a half-hour set during *Crawdaddy* magazine's tenth birthday party, held at the Public Theater in New York on June 12. He also made a repeat appearance at the CBS Annual Sales Convention, held in L.A. on July 22, sitting in with Southside Johnny & the Asbury Jukes on two numbers. In August, when Southside Johnny's band was taking a break, Springsteen borrowed its horn section, dubbed the Miami Horns, for a few shows beginning August 1 in Red Bank, New Jersey.

But legal matters ramped up over the course of the summer. In May, Appel petitioned the court to put monies Springsteen earned from concerts in escrow, so he could draw his management commission; he was denied. Next, on July 27, Springsteen filed suit against Appel, Laurel Canyon Management Inc., Laurel Canyon Ltd., and Lauren Canyon Music Inc., for fraud, undue influence, breach of trust, and breach of contract. He asked for $1 million in damages. Appel's response was to countersue Springsteen, Landau, and CBS, Inc. He also filed a preliminary injunction to prevent Springsteen from recording his next album unless Laurel Canyon approved of the producer. On August 4, Springsteen fired Appel as his manager.

New York Supreme Court Judge Arnold L. Fein granted Appel's injunction, which was upheld twice on appeal; CBS Records President Walter Yetnikoff recalled in a 1977 *Rolling Stone* article Appel telling him he would "fight and possibly destroy" Springsteen's career. Springsteen's mother even wrote Appel, asking him to settle his differences with her son. Appel thought the gesture was sweet ("Can you imagine her innocence? It's just what a good mother would do to get her 'boys' back together again!"), but he remained unmoved.

As the case dragged on, the next leg of shows—nicknamed the "Lawsuit Tour"—opened in Phoenix, Arizona, on September 26. But when Springsteen was on tour, you never knew where he might turn up. On September 30, Springsteen and Van Zandt showed up to see the second show of Dion (of Dion and the Belmonts) at the Roxy in L.A.

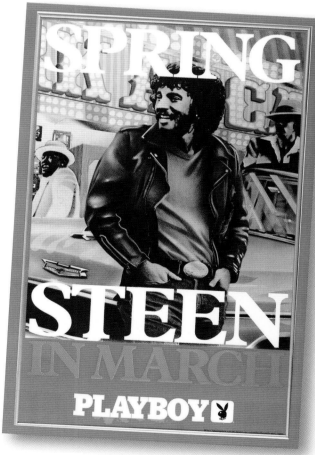

March 1976 Springsteen poster from *Playboy*

and wound up singing "A Teenager in Love" with him during the encore. Dion grandly introduced them as "honorary Belmonts." Of course, Van Zandt was already something of an honorary Belmont, having played as a backing musician for Dion during a New Year's show in Miami, Florida, in 1972; Springsteen had met Dion in 1975 at an L.A. recording session. On October 22, when he didn't have a show of his own scheduled, Springsteen went to a club in Hazlet, New Jersey, to see Gary U.S. Bonds. The club's owner spotted Springsteen in the audience and suggested that Bonds ask Springsteen to come up and join him. Bonds, having no idea who Springsteen was, responded, "Bruce who?" But his band members were excited and urged Bonds to get Springsteen onstage, where he was welcomed by exuberant applause. Springsteen played for about half the set and invited Bonds to catch one of his own shows in New York the next week at the Palladium.

The Palladium gigs, a six-show stand from October 28 to November 4, 1976 (with no show on Halloween), brought the first leg of the Lawsuit Tour to an end. Bonds took Springsteen up on his offer and attended the October 29 show, joining in onstage for "Twistin' the Night Away." The next night Patti Smith was in the audience, joining Springsteen on "Rosalita (Come Out

The Boss in a contemplative mood during a 1976 show.
Fin Costello/Redferns/Getty Images

Tonight)." On the final night, Ronnie Spector, of the Ronettes, appeared to sing some of the girl group's biggest hits: "Baby, I Love You," "Walking in the Rain," and their trademark song, "Be My Baby."

The rest of the year was relatively quiet. When Patti Smith was playing her own series of shows at the Bottom Line, Springsteen was on hand for both sets on November 26, playing guitar and occasional piano. In December he dropped in on sessions for Southside Johnny's second album, *This Time It's for Real*, released in May 1977, for which he cowrote two songs with Van Zandt, "Love on the Wrong Side of Town" and "Little Girl So Fine." On the first day of 1977, Springsteen, along with the E Street Band, backed Ronnie Spector during a recording session at CBS Studios in New York, with Van Zandt producing. They recorded a number of tracks, with the idea of releasing an album, but only "Say Goodbye to Hollywood" was officially released, as a single in April 1977. Springsteen wasn't credited on the record due to his ongoing legal tussle with Appel, which may be why the other tracks were not released. Later in the month, on January 22, he sat in with a local act, Pegasus, when they played a club called the Jail in Hillsdale, New Jersey; Springsteen's friend, Matty Delia, was the band's manager.

The next leg of the Lawsuit Tour began on February 7 in Albany, New York, and ran through March, closing with a March 25 date in Boston. Springsteen then had time to spare for a few Southside Johnny dates. On April 17 he sat in with the band when they played the Stone Pony, and he filled in on May 12 and 13 at the Monmouth Arts Center in Red Bank, New Jersey, after Southside Johnny became too ill to make the shows. Van Zandt drafted a cast of local talent he called the Asbury Park All-Star Revue, featuring members of the Asbury Jukes, the E Street Band, Ronnie Spector, and Springsteen. The scheduled four shows were scaled back to three and drew on each act's repertoire, meaning the sets veered joyously from "This Time It's for Real" to "Thunder Road" to "Be My Baby," and blues numbers such as "It Ain't the Meat (It's the Motion)." The next week Springsteen was back at the Stone Pony on May 19, sitting with the current house band, the Shakes, and ripping through the golden oldies "Jailhouse Rock" and "Sea Cruise."

Springsteen had always taken advantage of every opportunity to perform. But one reason for all this extracurricular activity was that he wasn't able to get back into the studio. He feared that the longer the legal battles continued, the more difficult it would be to revive his stalled career.

Springsteen in concert in 1975. His first gig of the year was at the Stone Pony in Asbury Park, New Jersey; he ended the year with a two-night stand at the Tower Theater in Philadelphia. © *Pictorial Press Ltd / Alamy Stock Photo*

PROVE IT
ALL NIGHT

4

Springsteen's legal woes cast a pall over his career well into 1977. So desperate was he to record that he filed an affidavit in December 1976 asking that he be allowed to record an album, with Landau producing, that would be held in the court's possession until the litigation was resolved; his request was denied. When he gave his deposition, he went "absolutely nuts," in Appel's words. "Every question I asked, instead of giving me a yes or a no answer, he would go on yelling and screaming and cursing and talking about what a bad person Appel was in the foulest, most gutterlike language," Appel's lawyer, Leonard Marks, recalled in Mike Appel's *Down Thunder Road*. Marks eventually stopped the deposition and asked that both parties meet with Judge Fein. Fein advised Springsteen privately that anything he said in his deposition could be used against him in a trial, and that he wasn't presenting himself in a very good light. Springsteen quickly toned down his behavior for the rest of his deposition.

But he'd also taken on a new attorney, Peter Parcher, and when he won a motion to submit an amended answer to Appel's complaint, the tide began to turn in his favor. It was clear that Appel had lost Springsteen as a client forever, and Appel's lawyer advised him to settle.

On May 28, 1977, everything was resolved. Appel would receive a payment of $800,000, as well as royalty rights on the first three albums and half the publishing on the first three albums. Springsteen got what he most wanted: control of his future songs. (In 1983, Appel sold his share of the publishing to Springsteen; the following year, he sold his share of the royalty rights to Springsteen as well.) He renegotiated a new, more favorable contract with Columbia as well. He was free.

The day the lawsuit was settled, Springsteen got a firsthand lesson on what could happen to an artist if he didn't keep a tight hold on his career. He and Van Zandt drove to Philadelphia to see Elvis, who was playing at the Spectrum. Shocked at Elvis's bloated appearance and lackluster performance, they drove home in silence. Looking back at the show later, Springsteen reflected, "It was not a good night." Later, he observed of the King of Rock 'n' Roll, "Here was a guy who had it all and he lost it, or maybe just let it slip through his fingers, 'cause somewhere, somehow, he just stopped caring. He let himself get fat and became a cartoon—a caricature."

But the evening did inspire Springsteen to write the rockabilly-flavored song "Fire," the kind of song he might have wanted to hear Elvis sing. (He noted that the songs Elvis had most seemed to enjoy performing at that disappointing show were the dramatic numbers "American Trilogy" and "How Great Thou Art.") Robert Gordon was the first to release a studio version of the song, with Springsteen playing piano, on his 1978 album *Fresh Fish Special*, and the Pointer Sisters had a No. 2 hit with their 1979 version. Springsteen's own studio version didn't appear until 2010, on *The*

(previous spread)
Springsteen always admired Clemons's sartorial flair; the Big Man was partial to flashy suits.
Michael Putland/Getty Images

Promise: The Darkness on the Edge of Town box set.

Four days later, on June 1, Springsteen entered Atlantic Studios in New York, with Landau by his side, to begin work on his next album. Songs poured out of him, and the version of "Something in the Night" that he recorded at that first session appeared on the final album. He didn't stay at Atlantic for long; unhappy with the sound, he began working at the Record Plant as well. Springsteen's energy and eagerness to get back to recording fueled hopes that an album would be ready for release before the end of the year—and it nearly was. By the fall, Springsteen had compiled the tracks for an album he planned to call *Badlands*; the website Brucebase lists a provisional running order of "Badlands," Streets of Fire," "The Promised Land," "Independence Day," "Prove It All Night," "Candy's Boy," "Racing in the Street," and "Don't Look Back." But Springsteen scrapped the idea and went back to the drawing board. According to engineer Jimmy Iovine, Springsteen recorded as many as seventy songs, in varying stages of completion, during the sessions.

Springsteen absorbed numerous new influences, from the *Saturday Night Fever* soundtrack to the music of Hank Williams to the writings of John Steinbeck and Flannery O'Connor and the films of John Ford (the latter three at Landau's suggestion). *The Grapes of Wrath* (both Steinbeck's book and Ford's 1940 film) had particular resonance for him. It all fueled the desire for authenticity in his own work, especially songs that spoke to the common man. "Badlands," "Streets of Fire," "The Promised Land,"

Springsteen and Van Zandt at a New Year's Eve show in 1977 at the Capitol Theatre in Passaic, New Jersey, a night that also saw the E Street Band playing with fellow Jersey Shore musician Southside Johnny on a number of songs. *Michael Putland/Getty Images*

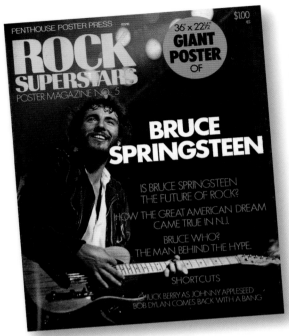

1975 *Rock Superstars* cover of *Born to Run* poster and program that ran in *Penthouse*

"Prove It All Night," "Candy's Boy" (retitled "Candy's Room"), and "Racing in the Street" appeared on the final album, which was named after its closing track, "Darkness on the Edge of Town," and featured striking new numbers such as "Adam Raised a Cain."

"I was interested now in writing music that felt not just New Jersey- or boardwalk-based," Springsteen said of the album in 2010. "I wanted to bring in the full landscape of the whole country." In an interview with NBC that same year, he called "Darkness" his "samurai song," explaining, "It was about stripping yourself down and finding what was essential, which is what I had to do at the time."

Springsteen had written so many songs that he was able to spread the wealth, giving Southside Johnny both "Hearts of Stone" and "Talk to Me" for his 1978 *Hearts of Stone* album, "The Rendezvous" to Greg Kihn, and "This Little Girl," to Gary U.S. Bonds. At Iovine's suggestion, he also gave an incomplete number, "Because the Night," to Patti Smith, as Iovine was producing Smith's *Easter* album at the same time. Smith wrote her own lyrics and released the track as a single in March 1978; it became her sole Top 40 single, peaking at No. 13. Springsteen's version, released on *The Promise* box set, used his original 1977 instrumental track with a newly recorded vocal. Nearly twenty outtakes from the *Darkness* sessions appeared on *The Promise*, including the title track, with bitter lyrics thought to refer to Springsteen's legal battles. He later said he'd left it off *Darkness* "because it felt to self-referential and I was uncomfortable with it. Maybe it was too close to the story I was actually living at the moment."

The album's cover shot was taken by a friend of Smith's, Frank Stefanko. Springsteen posed by the window in the bedroom of Stefanko's home in Haddonfield, New Jersey. "When I saw the picture I said, 'That's the guy in the songs,'" Springsteen said in an interview for Saint Louis radio station KSHE. "Frank stripped away all your celebrity and left you with your essence. That's what that record was about."

Born to Run had finally opened the doors for Springsteen. Now the upcoming release of *Darkness on the Edge of Town* had to show he could keep the momentum going. And he'd have a new partner to help him along the way. In July 1978, Landau officially became Springsteen's manager, a position he still holds along with Barbara Carr (Dave Marsh's wife).

Darkness on the Edge of Town, released on June 2, 1978, wasn't quite the smash that *Born to Run* had been, but it fared well enough on the charts, reaching No. 5 and selling more than three million copies. The album's singles were only modest hits ("Prove It All Night" reached the Top 40, peaking at No. 33, and "Badlands" climbed to No. 42). But for Springsteen, it was enough to just have an album out and a tour lined up to promote it. Until the tour began, his only noteworthy performance of the year was a guest appearance

DARKNESS ON THE EDGE OF TOWN

Released: June 1978
Chart Position: No. 5 (US), No. 16 (UK)

There was a gap of nearly three years between *Born to Run* and *Darkness on the Edge of Town*, and Springsteen surely wondered if he'd ever get his career revved up again. While *Darkness* might not have had the visceral excitement of its predecessor, the strength of its songwriting reveals Springsteen as an artist fully in command of his creative gifts.

"It ain't no sin to be glad you're alive," Springsteen declares in triumph on the opening song, "Badlands." But the celebratory mood doesn't last for long. The turbulence of Springsteen's fraught relationship with his father is the focus of "Adam Raised a Cain," a tough, uncompromising number with a searing guitar line. "Something in the Night" sets a somber tone, depicting the moment when dreams come to a crashing halt.

Springsteen's albums are filled with the stories of those who struggle to survive on the fringes of society, and "Candy's Room" describes one of those characters. The bracing, rapid-fire beat underscores the desperation of the scenario: the song's protagonist is in love with a prostitute, aching to take away her sadness, but failing to grasp that it runs deeper than he'll ever know. Side one of the original vinyl album ended with "Racing in the Street." It's a painful song of loss, made all the more powerful by its stripped-down piano backing. The couple it depicts has nothing to look back on but their

youthful glory days; there's little hope of redemption in the future. Side note: race car driver Richie Schultz later informed Springsteen of an error in his lyric: Fuelie heads wouldn't fit on a 1969 Chevy 396, as he sings in the opening line.

"The Promised Land" offers a far more optimistic outlook, with a moderate rock beat buoying up a singer who holds onto his faith no matter what dark clouds loom ahead. "Factory" is another song rooted in the Springsteen's father's experience as a working man, dutifully going through the factory gates every day, the years of never-ending toil transforming eager young men into leaden souls with "death in their eyes."

In "Streets of Fire" Springsteen dives into the blues; it's a terrific vocal workout, and the accompanying music is just as smoldering. (Check out the guitar work during the instrumental break.) "Prove It All Night" rightly became a live favorite, a powerful number about the determination to reach out in the face of adversity. And the title track brings it all to a close, the singer alone, having lost everything, but still trying to stand tall.

"By the end of *Darkness* I'd found my adult voice," Springsteen wrote in *Songs*, a collection of his lyrics. Springsteen's characters—and Springsteen himself—were learning that after partying all night, you still have to face the dawn.

Springsteen stays just out of reach of the fans at a December 16, 1978, show at Winterland in San Francisco. *Clayton Call/Redferns*

at Warren Zevon's March 17 show at hip New York club Trax; some accounts have him joining Zevon when he performed his signature hit, "Werewolves of London," while others disagree—but whether or not it happened, it wasn't much of a gig.

On May 19, Bruce Springsteen and the E Street Band warmed up with a lengthy rehearsal at the Paramount Theatre in Asbury Park, New Jersey. The *Darkness* tour began on May 23 in Buffalo, New York, and ended on January 1, 1979 in, Richfield, Ohio. At 111 shows, it was Springsteen's longest tour to date, and also the first on which he started to play larger venues—not just theaters, but also the occasional stadium. This was thanks to Landau, who had persuaded Springsteen that it would benefit his career.

Most dates on the tour sold out. A number of shows were broadcast live (and thus quickly made available as bootlegs). Two days after playing the Forum in Inglewood (a suburb of Los Angeles), Springsteen moved to a smaller venue with a July 7 show at the Roxy that was broadcast on KMET-FM (prompting Springsteen to joke, "All them bootleggers out there in radioland, roll your tapes!"). (Some of the songs from this date were later released as bonus tracks on singles and as part of the 1986 *Live: 1975–85* box set.) Footage shot at the July 8 performance at Arizona Veterans Memorial Coliseum in Phoenix was used in promotional videos for "Prove It All Night," "Badlands," "Rosalita (Come Out Tonight)," "The Promised Land," and "Born to Run" (later released as part of the 2010 *The Promise* box set). There were a number of other radio broadcasts as well: the August 9 performance in Cleveland, Ohio, was broadcast by WMMS and simulcast over a number of other stations, and a December 15 show at San Francisco's Winterland Ballroom was broadcast on KSAN.

At a few shows, Springsteen surprised the audience by returning to play a couple more songs once the house lights had come up and people were beginning to leave. As early as September he began playing "Santa Claus Is Comin' to Town"—just because he felt like it. But he was also happy to show he wore his fame lightly; while in L.A. over the Fourth of July holiday, he and some members of the band climbed up and defaced a billboard on the Sunset Strip promoting *Darkness*, spraying "Prove It All Night" (one of the songs on *Darkness*) in block letters along the bottom.

Springsteen then headlined for the first time at Madison Square Garden, playing a three-night stand from August 21 to 23—a mere five years after he'd seen Elvis play the same venue. Friends and family attended all three shows, and on the first night, he dedicated "Factory" to Tex Vinyard, the Castiles' manager, and "Sweet Little Sixteen" to his sister Pamela. Pam appeared onstage the next night for the last song, "Quarter to Three," and Springsteen's mother Adele came out on the third night, teasingly asking him to play "Quarter to Three" again: "Mom, I should have never flown you from California," he joked back.

And of course Springsteen found time to have a little fun outside of his own shows. On June 23, he caught Warren Zevon's show at the Paramount Theatre in Portland, Oregon, and joined Zevon on "I'll Sleep When I'm Dead" during the encore. One fan recalled to the website Brucebase that Zevon wasn't in top form that evening and hadn't been able to draw a standing ovation—until Springsteen came out, and the place exploded. (Springsteen himself played the same venue the following night.) Springsteen later gave his song "Janey Needs a Shooter" to Warren, who wrote new music and some new lyrics for it and recorded it for his 1980 album *Bad Luck Streak in Dancing School*.

On July 6, Springsteen and actor Gary Busey were hanging out together at the Sundance Saloon in Calabasas, California, to see Busey's brother's group, the Old Dog Band, and caught the band's performance of Chuck Berry's "Carol." On August 25, after a show in New Haven, Connecticut, Springsteen and his band headed for a club

September 19–21, 1978, concert poster, Capitol Theater, Passaic, New Jersey

called Toad's Place, where John Cafferty & the Beaver Brown Band were playing; Springsteen and Clemons joined in on a few numbers, including Springsteen's own "Rosalita (Come Out Tonight)." Back in L.A., on October 17, Springsteen joined New Wavers the Knack (still a year away from their breakthrough smash "My Sharona") onstage at the Troubadour, on "Mona" and "Not Fade Away."

After the tour's end, everyone reconvened on January 11, 1979, for Clemons's thirty-seventh birthday party at the Lock Stock and Barrel in Fair Haven, New Jersey. Touring was over for now, but Springsteen immediately started work on his next album, recording songs on a cassette tape recorder. By March he was recording at the Power Station, in New York City, coproducing alongside Landau and Van Zandt. Springsteen soon brought in the band, with rehearsals held at his home studio in Holmdel, New Jersey, nicknamed Telegraph Hill Studios after its address on Telegraph Hill Road. By August, enough songs had been recorded for an album, provisionally entitled *The Ties That Bind* (after a song first developed during the *Darkness* sessions). According to Brucebase, the running order would have been "The Ties That Bind," "The Price You Pay," "Be True," "Ricky Wants a Man of Her Own," "Stolen Car," "I Wanna Marry You," "Loose Ends," "Hungry Heart," "The Man Who Got Away," and "Ramrod."

Sometimes you just can't reach those high notes unless you're on your back; Springsteen in concert in the late '70s. *George Rose/Getty Images*

Everyone then took a break, to prepare for a pair of concerts concert benefiting MUSE—Musicians United for Safe Energy, an antinuclear group. It was the first show by the full band all year, aside from Clarence's birthday bash. Springsteen himself had guested at a few shows, sitting in with Robert Gordon on "Fire" and "Heartbreak Hotel" at the Fast Lane in Asbury Park on March 14, and giving drop-in performances at various Asbury Park clubs. On June 3, various members of the band, including Springsteen, wound up performing during a wedding reception for Mark Brickman (their lighting director) and June Rudley (their travel agent), held at the Whisky a Go Go in West Hollywood, California. (Rickie Lee Jones and Boz Scaggs were among the other well-known guests who performed.)

MUSE was founded by musicians Jackson Browne, John Hall, Graham Nash, and Bonnie Raitt in 1979, following that year's accident at Three Mile Island, in which a Pennsylvania-based nuclear power plant experienced a partial meltdown. The concerts were meant to raise awareness of the dangers of nuclear energy, though Springsteen, who hadn't appeared at a concert for any political cause since the McGovern rally in 1972, wouldn't discuss the reasons for his participation. "Bruce felt that a statement wasn't appropriate—the music was enough," Landau told *Rolling Stone*. As a political activist, Springsteen was still just getting his toes in the water (though the Three Mile Island incident had inspired him to write the song "Roulette," later recorded and released as the B-side of the 1988 single "One Step Up").

The concerts were held September 19 through 23, with Springsteen appearing on September 21 and 22. He received a thunderous ovation, and on the first day the crowd spontaneously sang "Happy Birthday" to him, even though his actual birthday was on September 23. The second day was marred by an unpleasant incident in which Springsteen, angry at seeing his former girlfriend, photographer Lynn Goldsmith, taking pictures from the photo pit when she'd been asked not to, dragged her onstage and had her forcibly ejected from the venue. (Even Marsh called it "the most stupid public act of Springsteen's career.")

The band's performance of "Stay" (featuring Jackson Browne and Rosemary Butler) and a medley that kicked off with "Devil with a Blue Dress On" from the September 21 gig were included on the triple album documenting the shows, *No Nukes: The MUSE Concerts for a Non-Nuclear Future,* released in November 1979, the first live album by Bruce Springsteen and the E Street Band to be released. Performances of "The River" (from September 21), and "Thunder Road" and "Quarter to Three" (from September 22) were used in the *No Nukes* film, released in 1980.

After the MUSE concerts, something shifted. "The River" (based around the experience of his sister Ginny, who'd had to marry her high school

Springsteen during the "No Nukes" benefit concert on September 22, 1979, at Madison Square Garden. The subsequent film and soundtrack marked the first official release of live material from Springsteen.
Richard E. Aaron/Redferns

THE
RIVER

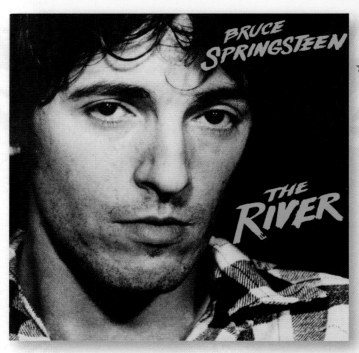

Released: October 1980
Chart Position: No. 1 (US), No. 2 (UK)

Springsteen has described *The River* as a continuation of the themes on *Darkness on the Edge of Town*. He wanted to delve even deeper into the lives of the characters, and one album wasn't enough this time. After working out provisional running orders for one disc, he realized that the statement he wanted to make could only be made on two discs.

The River represented a lot of firsts for Springsteen. It was not only his first double album, but also his first to top the charts. And it was the first album to spin off a hit single, "Hungry Heart," which he had planned to give to the Ramones until his manager talked him out of it. The Top 5 single matched a light pop melody with a bittersweet lyric about a man who left his family, following the pervasive pull of his "hungry heart."

The heartfelt title song is another key track. Springsteen acknowledged it was inspired by his sister's experience of marrying her high school sweetheart due to an unplanned pregnancy, on a day with "no wedding smiles," beginning a life together further stalled by a lack of available jobs. It's a harsh look at the daily struggle to survive, underscored by the wailing harmonica and Springsteen's world-weary vocal. Father and son struggle to come to terms on "Independence Day,"

as the son declares his freedom, his determination to escape the kind of life thrust upon his father. But there's a greater sense of understanding than in previous father-son numbers, an acceptance that people "see things in different ways."

There's a lot of defeat on the album. In the slow, mournful "Drive All Night," the singer hopes to find his way back into the arms of his loved one. "Point Blank" revisits the couple from "The River," now seemingly even more bereft of hope. The protagonist of "Stolen Car" is so invisible to the rest of world that even his crimes capture no attention.

All this melancholy is balanced by the album's upbeat numbers, and there are plenty of them. Songs like the jaunty opening track, which celebrates being alive even if it hurts. Songs like the rave-up "Sherry Darling" or "Two Hearts," the kind guaranteed to get you out on the dance floor. The punky "Crush on You" and the self-explanatory "You Can Look (But You Better Not Touch)" are just plain fun.

You can easily imagine the somber songs on one album and the rocking tracks on another. But the mixture of joy and pain throughout *The River* gives the album its richness and depth. It's the first Springsteen album to fully embrace the complexities of life, and how its sorrows are balanced by its joys.

boyfriend when she became pregnant) had debuted at the MUSE shows, and now Springsteen set out to write more material along the same lines: darker songs reflecting the hard times he saw around the country—and in his own family's history. Everyone went back into the studio, and by the time the sessions ended in May 1980, Springsteen had recorded around fifty songs. The tracks "Independence Day," "Point Blank," "The Ties That Bind," and "Sherry Darling" dated back to the *Darkness* era. "Be True," "Ricky Wants a Man of Her Own," "Loose Ends," and "The Man Who Got Away" were dropped from the provisional album's running order, but enough songs were added that *The River* became a double album.

"I handed it in with just one record and I took it back because I didn't feel it was big enough and I wanted to capture the themes that I'd been writing about *Darkness*," he later told *Rolling Stone* in 2015. "I wanted to keep those characters with me and at the same time added the music that made our live shows so much fun and enjoyable for our audience." Some of the thirty-odd tracks that didn't make the final cut later turned up as B-sides, on *Tracks*, and on the 2003 *The Essential Bruce Springsteen* compilation. Even more unreleased material from these sessions appeared on the 2015 box set, *The Ties That Bind: The River Collection*.

Springsteen and the E Street Band then spent some time recording with Gary U.S. Bonds, who was working on his album, 1981's *Dedication* (which featured three songs written during the *River* sessions, "This Little Girl," "Your Love," and the title track), biding their time until the release of *The River* on October 17. The double album became Springsteen's first No. 1 record, holding the top spot for four weeks; it eventually sold more than five million copies. The first single, "Hungry Heart" (which Springsteen had originally thought of giving to the Ramones, only to be talked out of it by Landau), also released in October, reached No. 5, Springsteen's highest position thus far in the singles chart; it also featured Flo & Eddie (formerly of the Turtles) on backing vocals. The next single, "Fade Away," released in January 1981, reached No. 20.

The band didn't perform at all in 1980, although Springsteen made a few appearances at the Fast Lane in Asbury Park, guesting with Atlantic City Expressway (featuring Jon Bon Jovi) in January and with the David Johansen Band in March. He also sang two songs, "Sweet Little Sixteen" and "Stay," with Jackson Browne during Browne's show at the Forum in Inglewood, California, in August. Springsteen's own *The River* tour kicked off on October 3 in Ann Arbor, Michigan, and ran for nearly a year, with 138 shows. There was an awkward start to the first show, when Springsteen forgot the words to the opening song, "Born to Run," but the audience surprised him by singing the words themselves. He played "Thunder Road" twice, once during the main set and again during the encore, when Bob Seger came out to provide guest vocals.

Springsteen had fun mixing it up during the shows, telling the band they wouldn't need a set list—he'd tell them what he wanted to play—and it was a credit to the musicians that they always pulled it off. It also encouraged the fans to see more than one concert; you'd never see the same show twice. One of Springsteen's more unusual side appearances on tour was in Seattle on October 23, the day before his concert at the Seattle Center Coliseum (now Key Arena). While walking around town he ran into Phil Hamilton, of the Lost Highway Band, who invited him to check out the group's show that evening. To Hamilton's surprise, Springsteen took him up on the offer, heading to the Old Timer's Café in Seattle's historic Pioneer Square district and sitting in for a few songs, including "Route 66," "Gloria," and "In the Midnight Hour." The following night, Springsteen dedicated "The River" to the Montana-based group.

The North American leg of the tour lasted until March 1981, with the occasional mishap. At a November 5 show in Tempe, Arizona, Springsteen misjudged a leap onto the speaker stack and fell off, sheepishly climbing back onstage afterward. The same show also saw him make what at the time was a rare political statement, in reference to Ronald Reagan's election as president the previous day. "I don't know what you guys think about what happened last night, but I think it's pretty frightening," he said prior to introducing "Badlands." The remark was met with approval by the critics, with Greil Marcus confidently predicting, "It is an almost certain bet that the songs Springsteen will now be writing will have something to do with the events of November 4."

Clemons, Springsteen, and Van Zandt in Rotterdam on April 29, 1981. The show opened with a cover of Creedence Clearwater Revival's "Run Through the Jungle." *Rob Verhorst/Redferns/Getty Images*

Another heartfelt moment came on December 9, when Springsteen performed the last of a three-night stand at the Spectrum in Philadelphia. Music fans were still reeling from the murder of John Lennon the night before in New York City, and Springsteen addressed the matter in his opening remarks. "I'd just like to say one thing," he began. "It's a hard night to come out and play tonight when so much has been lost. The first record that I ever learned was a record called 'Twist and Shout,' and if it wasn't for John Lennon, we'd all be in some place very different tonight. It's an unreasonable world and you have to live with a lot of things that are just unlivable; it's a hard thing to come out and play but there's just nothing else you can do." The concert fittingly ended with "Twist and Shout."

The Surprise Guest

While on break during *The River* tour in Saint Louis, Missouri, Springsteen decided to take in a movie and ended up seeing *Stardust Memories*, Woody Allen's caustic look at fame. A young man named Steve Satanovsky recognized him and asked if Springsteen would like to sit with him and his sister. Springsteen agreed. Afterward, Steve invited Springsteen to come home with him and meet his parents. As it was only eleven o'clock—not too late in Springsteen's mind—he decided to take Steve up on his offer.

But when they arrived, Steve's parents didn't believe it was Bruce Springsteen they'd welcomed into their home. Steve had to get one of his albums and hold it next to Springsteen's face before they realized it really was the Boss, causing Steve's mother, Sophie, to start screaming.

Once she calmed down, Sophie was quick to offer to make Springsteen a late-night snack. He spent the next few hours talking with the family and had Sophie call his mother to tell her he'd just eaten a home-cooked meal. Steve later drove Springsteen back to his hotel.

Springsteen mistakenly reported that the incident happened in Denver, but the Satanovskys live in Saint Louis. In a TV interview, Sophie Satanovsky said Springsteen's visit

Michael Marks/Michael Ochs Archives/Getty Images

happened in 1981, but the authoritative website Brucebase is more certain it happened in October 1980. When Bruce played Saint Louis on August 24, 2008, he dedicated "Twist and Shout" to Sophie.

Later that month, Springsteen played two of his longest-ever shows. On December 19, the second of two nights at Madison Square Garden, he treated the audience to thirty-four songs. He then bested that performance with thirty-eight songs at a New Year's Eve show at the Nassau Veterans Memorial Coliseum in Uniondale, New York. Both shows ran well over three hours. In addition to bootlegs, a number of songs from Uniondale later appeared on official releases: "4th of July, Asbury Park (Sandy)" on *Live/1975–85* (1986), "Merry Christmas Baby" on the *A Very Special Christmas* compilation (1987), "Rendezvous" on *Tracks* (1998), and "Held Up Without a Gun" on *The Essential Bruce Springsteen* (2003).

The tour included also included four shows in Canada, in Toronto, Ontario (January 20 and 21, 1981); Montreal, Quebec (January 23); and Ottawa, Ontario (January 24). "There is no doubt in my mind why this man is called 'The Boss,'" Lori Potrubacz wrote in *The Spirit* about the first Toronto show. "He sings with more power and emotion than any performer I've seen." John Griffin, in the *Montreal Gazette*, called the show "the single best rock concert I have ever seen since, well, since [Bruce] was last in town in 1978."

A European tour was set to begin after the end of the North American tour, but Springsteen begged off due to exhaustion and the dates were rescheduled to begin on April 7 in West Germany. It was Springsteen's first time in the country, on a tour that saw him making his live debut in numerous other European countries, including Switzerland, France, Spain, Belgium, Denmark, Norway, and Scotland. The tour also included six shows at London's Wembley Arena, during which he debuted a new song, the mournful "Johnny Bye Bye," about Elvis Presley's death; it was later recorded and released as the B-side of the 1985 single "I'm on Fire."

The band then took a few weeks off, aside from a "Survival Sunday" antinuke benefit on June 14 at the Hollywood Bowl, also featuring Jackson Browne, Graham Nash, and Bonnie Raitt. Springsteen dropped in to see Gary U.S. Bonds perform in San Francisco the next day and joined him onstage for a few numbers. And everyone was in attendance for drummer Max Weinberg's wedding on June 20 in East Orange, New Jersey, playing a set afterward at the reception.

It was back to work for the final leg of the tour on July 2, with another swing around the United States. On August 20 Springsteen played a benefit for the Vietnam Veterans of America Foundation at Los Angeles Memorial Coliseum. When he first came onstage, he told the crowd how nervous he'd been meeting members of the group the day before.

"It's like when you feel like you're walking down a dark street at night and out of the corner of your eye you see somebody getting hurt or somebody getting hit in the dark alley," he said, "but you keep walking on because you think it don't have nothing to do with you and you just want to get home. Well, Vietnam turned this whole country into that dark street and unless we're able to walk down those dark alleys and look into the eyes of the men and the women that are down there and the things that happened, we're never gonna be able to get home." He then opened the show with Creedence Clearwater Revival's protest song "Who'll Stop the Rain." Step by step, his involvement in politics was increasing.

The *River* tour finally came to an end on September 14 in Cincinnati, Ohio. There wouldn't be another major tour for two and a half years. But Bruce hardly dropped out of sight. Ten days after the tour ended, Springsteen and the band flew to Hawaii for Clemons's wedding in Honolulu and a performance

(opposite)
Springsteen at London's Wembley Arena on May 29, 1981, during *The River* tour. The show included the band's first ever performance of Jimmy Cliff's "Trapped." *David Corio/Redferns.*

at the reception. Back at home, if Springsteen happened to visit a New Jersey club, there was a good chance he'd get onstage at some point during the evening for a few songs with whoever was performing. He was especially fond of sitting in with Cats on a Smooth Surface, who had a Sunday-night residency at the Stone Pony in Asbury Park, as well as making regular appearances at Big Man's West, a club Clemons had opened in Red Bank, New Jersey. There was the occasional large-scale show, as when he appeared at the Rally for Disarmament on July 12, 1982, in New York's Central Park. He contributed to albums by his colleagues, such as Van Zandt's 1982 *Men Without Women* and Clemons's 1983 *Rescue.* He gave Donna Summer the song "Protection" for her 1982 self-titled album (and also performed on the track), and wrote, performed on, and coproduced Gary U.S. Bond's 1982 *On the Line* album.

Springsteen was also about to chart a new course on his next record. During breaks in the *River* tour he had recorded home demos, building up a lengthy backlog. On January 3, 1982, he recorded fourteen of these songs on a Teac Tascam four-track cassette recorder (according to Springsteen, at least; guitar tech Mike Batlan, who had bought the four-track deck for his boss, said recording actually began mid-December and ended on January 3). However it went down, Springsteen compiled the tape, added a live version of "Johnny Bye Bye," and sent it to his manager. He later wrote two additional songs, raising the final number of tracks to seventeen.

At this point the songs were still considered demos, prepared in the hope that it would make the recording process go faster. But when he recorded the songs with his band, he didn't like the results; the songs didn't benefit from additional instrumentation. Springsteen had a batch of more rock-oriented songs on hand as well, but decided to focus on the acoustic material first. He asked engineer Toby Scott, who had worked on *The River* and also mixed his live shows, if the entire album could be made from the original cassette. Scott agreed to give it a try and managed to overcome the limitations of the initial recording; at one point, doubtful the recording could ever be made to sound good enough, he floated the idea of making it a cassette-only release.

Springsteen thought of releasing a double-album set, with the rock songs on one record and the acoustic songs on the other. But in the end, he felt that having a single album would give the acoustic songs greater stature.

Of the seventeen songs, ten were chosen for the final album, *Nebraska,* named after its lead track. The album was released on September 30 and received good reviews, peaking at No. 3 on US charts, but the overall sales were minimal, especially in contrast to *The River* and *Born to Run.* Of the non-album tracks, "The Big Payback" turned up as the B-side of the European single "Open All Night," "Child Bride" and "Losin' Kind" were unreleased, and the rest would be rerecorded for Springsteen's next album.

Nonetheless, the album enhanced Springsteen's credibility. No one expected a spare, stripped-down album focusing on societal outcasts—Springsteen cited Howard Zinn's book *A People's History of the United States* as an inspiration for the album's songs— from a performer who had been positioning himself as a dynamic rock 'n' roller, and *Nebraska* was seen as a brave artistic statement. (In 2000, the compilation *Badlands: A Tribute to Bruce Springsteen's Nebraska* testified to how highly regarded the album came to be; the album was a straight recreation of *Nebraska*, with contributions from such artists as Chrissie Hynde, Los Lobos, Ani DiFranco, and Hank Williams III, among others.)

For the first time in Springsteen's career, the release of a new album wasn't accompanied by a tour. In late 1982, Springsteen moved to a house in the Hollywood Hills, Los Angeles, and contemplated his next move. As he recorded a new set of demos in L.A., he thought about releasing another solo album. He also thought of releasing some of the non-*Nebraska* songs he'd recorded with the band in the spring of 1982 as an album. But in the end he decided to go back east and start fresh.

Sessions began in May 1983 at the Hit Factory, and by July Springsteen had a provisional running order for his next album, with a working title of *Murder Incorporated*. But, dissatisfied once again, he decided to write more songs, returning to the studio

Springsteen and Clemons trade licks during an October 28, 1980, performance at the Oakland-Alameda County Coliseum. *Clayton Call/Redferns*

in September and working into February 1984, to Columbia's frustration, as the company had hoped to have a new album ready for the holiday season. And from their perspective, Springsteen's next album had to be a big one. His career had taken off with *Born to Run*, and *The River* had helped maintain the momentum, but for all its critical kudos, *Nebraska* hadn't generated similar sales.

There was certainly no shortage of material; by the end of the sessions, Springsteen had recorded around eighty songs. The title track was an older number, written back in the fall of 1981: "Born in the U.S.A." Springsteen had been asked to write a song for an upcoming film of the same name, directed by Paul Schrader. Springsteen had already been working on a song called "Vietnam" and adopted "Born in the U.S.A." as its new title, rewriting most of the lyrics. Written from the perspective of a Vietnam veteran, the song was a bitter critique of the life Springsteen might have experienced, had he not found success with rock 'n' roll. The song's working-class protagonist gets into trouble with the law and is sent off to fight in Vietnam as a result, returning home to no recognition, no glory, and no job—left with "nowhere to go" (Schrader's film was eventually released in 1985, retitled *Light of Day*, with Springsteen writing the title song).

Springsteen had recorded an acoustic demo of the song on the same day in January he'd recorded the songs for *Nebraska* (a version later released on *Tracks*), though he recognized it as a song that "should be done very hard rockin'," as he put it in a letter to Landau. The full band version easily came together at a session at the Power Station later that year, Springsteen in his finest blues shouter mode, transforming the song into what sounded like a celebratory anthem—if you hadn't read the lyrics. It was the musical arrangement, more than anything, that would lead to the song being so misinterpreted.

As usual, Springsteen continually tinkered with the rest of the album's running order. He thought of leaving "No Surrender" off the album, until Van Zandt argued against it. Then, when he finally thought he had the album completed, Landau told him something was missing—the kind of standout first single that would launch the album with a bang. Springsteen vehemently disagreed, but Jon wouldn't back down. More than a little irritated, Springsteen retired to try and come up with the right kind of song. He came up with a winner: "Dancing in the Dark," a song with the kind of pop lightness that one wouldn't expect from Springsteen, but which had an undeniable appeal.

Born in the U.S.A. had an iconic album cover as well, with Springsteen pictured facing a large American flag, hip cocked, a weatherworn baseball cap stuck in his rear jeans pocket. Noted rock photographer Annie Leibovitz took the photograph. Springsteen denied there was an hidden meaning in the photo; the Stars and Stripes were used simply because the first song on the album was "Born in the U.S.A."

The album thrilled the folks at Columbia, not only with "Dancing in the Dark," but also other potential hits they sensed on the album. They made plans for the album to be a major success; there would be singles, there would be dance remixes of the singles to broaden airplay both on the radio and in clubs, there would be videos, and, all being well, Springsteen would graduate to playing all stadium shows. "But you don't have to worry about this," Columbia Senior Vice President Al Teller assured Springsteen. "Go out and do what you do great." Springsteen was ready. But he probably wasn't expecting *Born in the U.S.A.* to change the trajectory of his entire career.

1980 ad for all Bruce Springsteeen and the E Street Band albums released by Columbia

BRUCE SPRINGSTEEN

NEBRASKA

NEBRASKA

Released: September 1982
Chart Position: No. 3 (US), No. 3 (UK)

With *Nebraska*, Springsteen made it plain that his career would not follow a conventional trajectory. His last three albums had been multi-platinum sellers, and most artists would have wanted to keep that momentum going. Instead, Springsteen released an album of songs originally meant to be demos, a largely acoustic collection that was completely unexpected from a rock performer in the pre-Unplugged era.

The album opens with the lonesome wail of a harmonica, well suited to the title track's bleak subject matter. The song was inspired by the real-life crimes of Charles Starkweather, who went on a shooting spree with his fourteen-year-old girlfriend in 1958, killing ten people. The chilling song is sung from the killer's perspective as he awaits his own death in the electric chair, attributing his motive for the senseless crimes to "a meanness in this world."

Springsteen had previously written about those scrabbling to survive on the fringes of society. But a number of Nebraska's characters are cut from different cloth, true outsiders who chose a criminal life because they had nothing left to lose. The protagonist in "Johnny 99" turns to murder after losing his job and his home. In "Highway Patrolman," a police officer is dispatched to pick up a suspect in a fight who turns out to be his own brother; he watches in despair as his brother flees to the Canadian border. The driver in the spooky "State Trooper" is a man on the edge, fearful of the violence that lurks within

him. The singer in "Atlantic City" becomes a hit man because it's the only work available in the would-be gambling mecca (Atlantic City's resurgence was some years away).

There's little in the way of light relief, but not everyone on the album is a killer. In the most upbeat number, "Open All Night" (the only song to feature an electric guitar), the singer is in a hurry only because he's anxious to get to his girlfriend. There are also numbers rooted in Springsteen's own experiences. "Used Car" is a poignant reminiscence about watching his father buy a used vehicle, vowing that he'll have the luck to be able to buy a new car someday. In a similar vein, "Mansion on the Hill" is not a cover of the Hank Williams song of the same name, but rather another portrait of outsiders looking in, the singer recalling the days when he and his sister peered through the gates at the richest house in town, contemplating the wonders within. In "My Father's House," the one-time rebel who longed to escape returns home in the hopes of finding the sanctuary he longs for.

The album ends with the bitter "Reason to Believe," a critique of the blind faith that Springsteen argues will only leave the believers disappointed. It's a sobering coda to an album that wearily concludes there isn't always a solution for every problem.

Columbia released *Born in the U.S.A.* on June 4, 1984. It was a smash, topping the *Billboard* charts in the United States and reaching No. 1 in ten other countries. (The album actually reached No. 1 *twice* in the United States; on August 2, Prince's *Purple Rain* knocked it down the chart, but on January 19, 1985, it captured the top spot again). It would be Springsteen's best-known and biggest-selling album, moving more than fifteen million copies in the U.S. and another thirty million worldwide. (It was also the first commercial CD manufactured in the United States.) By any standard, the album was a blockbuster.

The warm-up to the album's release, and the subsequent tour, began in early May 1985 with the release of "Dancing in the Dark." The single performed just as Landau had hoped, reaching No. 2 in the States and No. 1 on *Billboard*'s "Hot Mainstream Rock Tracks" chart. Columbia tapped film director Brian DePalma to direct the video, which was shot on June 28 and 29 at the Saint Paul Civic Center in Saint Paul, Minnesota. The first night was strictly a video shoot; the second night was the tour's opening date, and Bruce Springsteen and the E Street Band performed "Dancing in the Dark" twice during the show to allow De Palma to get all the footage he needed. It was a straight performance video, with Springsteen, given more freedom to move around stage by not playing a guitar, extending a hand to invite a young woman in the audience (future *Friends* star Courteney Cox) to dance along with him at the end, a bit of business he would carry over into his live shows, bringing some lucky young woman onstage to dance with him.

There were a few changes in the lineup for the tour. Regular E Streeters Tallent, Clemons, Federici, Bittan, and Weinberg were all present and accounted for. But Van Zandt had a flourishing solo career of his own and had told Springsteen he wouldn't be available for any touring. In February 1984, Springsteen invited guitarist Nils Lofgren to hang out with him for a weekend. Lofgren mentioned that if Springsteen was ever looking for a guitarist, he'd be interested, never imagining that Springsteen would take him up on the offer a few weeks later. There was also a female vocalist in the lineup: Patti Scialfa.

Since auditioning for Springsteen back in the 1970s, Patti had worked with Southside Johnny and David Johansen, in addition to writing and performing her own material solo and with a singing group called Trickster, which included Soozie Tyrell and Lisa Lowell. "We would only play on the streets," she later said of Trickster. "People would invite us to play clubs, but we thought playing clubs was selling out!"

Scialfa was offered the job just a few days before the tour began, and Springsteen frankly admitted he wasn't sure how it was going to work having

Born in the U.S.A. bumper sticker, circa 1984

(previous spread)
Springsteen giving his all at a show during the *Born in the U.S.A.* tour. *Ebet Roberts/Redferns*

a woman in the band. When she showed up wearing a frilly pastel top for opening night, he told her, "Maybe you should wear something not as pretty," and handed her one of his own T-shirts, emblazoned with the words "Broadway Motors."

"I tease him about it now," she told *Rolling Stone* in 2004. "I'm surprised he didn't ask me to get a haircut."

Springsteen was also reworking his own appearance. He'd embarked on a fitness program, and he was no longer a skinny, scruffy punk; now he sported sleeveless shirts to show off his newly developed muscles, was clean-shaven, and tied a bandana around his head to hold back his curly hair. This pumped-up, highly masculinized look would define Springsteen's image for some time to come. But it was never rigidly macho; Springsteen's sense of playfulness kept him from taking his image too seriously. And he joked that his nightly exertions on the stage caused him to lose three to five pounds a night.

The tour's first leg crisscrossed the United States and Canada. At the end of July, the second single from *Born in the U.S.A.* was released; "Cover Me" reached No. 7. A run of ten sold-out shows at Brendan Byrne Arena in East Rutherford, New Jersey, spread out between August 5 and August 20, was enlivened by a few special guests: John Entwistle turned up August 11 to play along on the closing number, "Twist and Shout," and Southside Johnny did the same the following night (and Springsteen's parents were on hand for the August 9 show). Van Zandt might not have been an official E Streeter on the tour but nonetheless made his presence felt, turning up at eight different shows, beginning with the August 20 show. Springsteen played to over two hundred thousand people at the East Rutherford shows; two days later he was back at the Stone Pony, sitting in with the band La Bamba and the Hubcaps.

Springsteen then played the Capital Centre in Largo, Maryland, on August 25, 26, and 28. There was an unexpected guest in the audience on August 25: conservative pundit George Will. Max Weinberg's wife, Rebecca, had enjoyed watching Will and fellow political commentator Sam Donaldson debate on the TV show *This Week with David Brinkley* and suggested they be invited to see Springsteen in performance. Will accepted, and he subsequently wrote a column about Springsteen that would have enormous ramifications for the musician.

In the syndicated piece, first published on September 13, 1985, Will admitted to feeling somewhat out of place at the concert, in his bowtie and double-breasted suit, stuffing his ears with the cotton that Rebecca Weinberg had thoughtfully given to him after a few songs because of the volume, and admitting, "I may be the only 43-year-old American so out of the swim that I do not even know what marijuana smoke smells like." But he was effusive in his praise of Springsteen, citing his work ethic: "In an age of lackadaisical

(*top*)
August 31, 1985, parking pass, *Born in the U.S.A.* tour, Giants Stadium, East Rutherford, New Jersey

(*above*)
August 31, 1985, ticket, *Born in the U.S.A.* tour, Giants Stadium, East Rutherford, New Jersey

BORN IN THE U.S.A.

Released: June 1984
Chart Position: No. 1 (US), No. 1 (UK)

Born to Run made Springsteen a star. Born in the U.S.A. made him a superstar.

It also had a quite a different sound from his previous albums, drenched in the echoing synthesizer typical of mid-1980s rock. It was the era of high-tech multi-platinum albums by the likes of Michael Jackson, David Bowie, and Madonna. Saleswise, Springsteen was right up there with them. But he never lost hold of his heart and soul.

It was Springsteen's most accessible album to date. The bright, poppy sound of album's first single, "Dancing in the Dark," is so engaging, it's easy to miss the bittersweet undercurrent of the lyric. That is also true of album's famous title track, its anthemic bombast masking bitter lyrical observations. Similarly, "No Surrender" has a joyously uptempo beat, but there's a sadness in the way the narrator looks back at his youth, a time before "hearts of fire grow cold."

Looking back at the past with a sense of regret is another recurring theme on the album. The farewell in "Bobby Jean" sounds like it's addressed to a friend, not a romantic partner; and it is thought to be about Springsteen's friendship with Van Zandt, who left the E Street Band prior to the Born in the U.S.A. tour. In "Glory Days," the narrator sings of watching his high school friends (the star athlete, the beauty queen), as well as his own father, falling from grace; he vows he won't end up the same way, but acknowledges he probably will.

There are a few songs of people struggling with hard times, as in the downbeat "Downbound Train." But a number of the album's songs are celebratory. The high-stepping "Cover Me" was originally intended for Donna Summer (and you can certainly imagine the Queen of Disco giving it a whirl), but Landau suggested Springsteen take it on himself; he does, with gusto (there's a nice guitar solo too). "Darlington County" is a fun tale of two would-be Lotharios on the prowl down South, the singer escaping just ahead of his buddy, last seen handcuffed to a police car. Even the singer in "I'm Goin' Down," about a difficult love affair, doesn't sound too distraught.

The rollicking "Working on the Highway" straddles both camps with a neat circular lyric; the highway worker in the first verse has become a prison laborer on the same highway in the last. And "I'm on Fire" is ostensibly an admission of lust, but Springsteen opts for a restrained delivery coupled with a tense, edgy beat.

The album ends on an elegiac note with "My Hometown," which features a musical backing that wouldn't have been out of place on Nebraska as the singer sadly takes his leave of a town in decline. Is this all that being "born in the U.S.A." will get you?

It's a pensive note to end on, making the point that Born in the U.S.A. is far more complex than it might appear at first glance.

effort and slipshod products, anyone who does anything—anything legal—conspicuously well and with zest is a national asset. Springsteen's tour is hard, honest work and evidence of the astonishing vitality of America's regions and generations." He also touted his presumed patriotism: "I have not got a clue about Springsteen's politics, if any, but flags get waved at his concerts while he sings songs about hard times. He is no whiner, and the recitation of closed factories and other problems always seems punctuated by a grand, cheerful affirmation: 'Born in the U.S.A.!'" Will concluded his piece by agreeing, "There still is nothing quite like being born in the U.S.A."

Six days after Will's column appeared, President Ronald Reagan, in the midst of running for reelection, jumped on the Springsteen bandwagon himself. During a speech in Hammonton, New Jersey on September 19, Reagan said, "America's future rests in a thousand dreams inside your hearts; it rests in the message of hope in the songs of a man so many young Americans admire: New Jersey's own Bruce Springsteen. And helping you make those dreams come true is what this job of mine is all about."

It wasn't the last time the lyrics to "Born in the U.S.A." would be misinterpreted by those who focused on the chorus and overlooked the lyrics, but it was certainly the time it attracted the most attention. It also demanded a response. Springsteen chose to issue his reply during a show in Pittsburgh on September 21, stating, "The President was mentioning my name the other day, and I kind of got to wondering what his favorite album must've been. I don't think it was the *Nebraska* album. I don't think he's been listening to this one," by way of introducing "Johnny 99," about a man who goes on a shooting spree after losing his job.

However much his songs addressed the concerns of the ordinary person, Springsteen had so far steered clear of making explicit political statements. But now the time had come to take a stand, if for no other reason than to differentiate himself from the forces seeking to misappropriate his message. His comments during shows became more pointed, as when he began introducing "Born to Run" by saying, "Let freedom ring—but it's no good if it's just for one. It's got to be for everyone." He began arranging for organizations such as local food banks and charity medical clinics to set up tables at his concerts and promoting the groups from the stage as well. Instead of just describing the problems of everyday life, Springsteen now began stressing the importance of taking action. And even as he became a bigger and bigger star, he worked to maintain a connection with his audience; at some shows, he would send a member of his entourage to bring people sitting in the back rows of the arena to prime seats upfront.

"Born in the U.S.A." was the next single, released in late October and reaching No. 9. The video, directed by acclaimed, socially conscious filmmaker John Sayles, took a restrained approach, showing Springsteen singing the

Promotional poster for *Born in the U.S.A.* Euro-Tour, 1985

song in concert, interspersed with footage of small-town America. The most sobering shot showed a military cemetery. January 1985 saw the release of a dramatic remix of the song by Arthur Baker on a twelve-inch single, which brought Springsteen's vocal up in the mix and heightened the song's bitter undercurrents.

The tour hit Los Angeles on October 25, 1984, with Springsteen playing seven shows at the Los Angeles Memorial Sports Arena. While Springsteen was in town Barry Bell, one of his booking agents, introduced him to Julianne Phillips, who worked as a model in New York and had moved to L.A. to further her acting career (she would become best known for a costarring role in the 1990s TV series *Sisters*). The two began dating, and during breaks on the tour, Springsteen returned to L.A. to be with her.

He had other reasons to be in Los Angeles as well. On January 28, 1985, he walked into A&M Studios in Hollywood to participate in the recording of the benefit single "We Are the World" (missing the American Music Awards held the same night, where "Dancing in the Dark" won Best Single). The song, written by Michael Jackson and Lionel Richie, was inspired by the UK charity single "Do They Know It's Christmas?," which raised money for African famine relief. Proceeds for "We Are the World" were earmarked for the same cause, disbursed through the organization United Support of Artists for Africa. At the session Springsteen found himself in the company not only of Jackson and Richie, but also Diana Ross, Billy Joel, Tina Turner, Stevie Wonder, and Paul Simon, among other luminaries. The distinguished artists were greeted by a sign that read, "Please check your egos at the door." The single was released in March and quickly topped the charts, and went on to win four Grammys; sales of the single, album, and accompanying merchandise raised more than $50 million by the end of 1986 ($108 million in 2016 dollars).

February 1985 saw the release of "I'm On Fire," which reached No. 6. The video, shot later that month and directed by Sayles, was Springsteen's first narrative video. He played an auto mechanic whose skills draw the attention of an attractive owner of a white Thunderbird. She flirtatiously gives him her car keys, but on dropping off her vehicle he decides that discretion is the better part of valor and, instead of ringing her doorbell, leaves the keys in her mailbox. On February 26, he attended the Grammy Awards with Julianne Phillips and his mother, winning his first Grammy for "Dancing in the Dark," which received the Best Male Rock Vocal.

The following month, the band hit the road again, playing their first dates in Australia (beginning March 21) and Japan (beginning April 10). On March 22 Springsteen found time to drop in on Neil Young's performance at the Sydney Entertainment Centre to trade licks on a rousing performance of "Down by the River."

(opposite)
Springsteen during the *Born in the U.S.A.* tour. The album spun off seven Top 10 singles in the United States. *L. Busacca/Larry Busacca/Wireimage/ Getty Images*

The final show on this leg of the tour was April 24 in Osaka, Japan, after which the band had a five-week break before the tour recommenced in Ireland. In between, Springsteen and Phillips decided to get married. In order to keep the media at bay, the two planned to hold the ceremony in Phillips's hometown of Lake Oswego, Oregon, near Portland. But word leaked out, and when the couple arrived, there were reporters crowded in front of the bride-to-be's family home. Springsteen still managed to hold a bachelor party of sorts—a small gathering as opposed to a drunken blowout—at a local bar, amusing his friends by singing along to the songs playing on the jukebox, including his own releases. The wedding was held just after midnight on May 13 at Our Lady of the Lake church, and the reception took place at the Oswego Lake Country Club on May 14. The couple then flew to Lake Como in Italy for their honeymoon.

★ ★

Julianne Phillips

Springsteen married Julianne Phillips seven months after meeting her, but it was a relationship not destined to last. *Ron Galella/WireImage*

Springsteen's relationship with Julianne Phillips started out as a white-hot romance. They married just over six months after they met. But by their third wedding anniversary the marriage had fallen apart.

Julianne was born on May 6, 1960, in Evanston, Illinois, and soon moved with her family to Lake Oswego, Oregon. She became interested in acting when she took an acting course at Brooks College in Long Beach, California. She later moved to New York City and signed with the Elite modeling agency. Prior to meeting Springsteen, she had appeared in the TV movies *Summer Fantasy* and *His Mistress*.

She took a few acting parts while married to Springsteen, but her acting career didn't really pick up until after the couple's divorce. Among other films, she appeared in *Skin Deep* with John Ritter and *Fletch Lives* with Chevy Chase. From 1991 to 1996 she had role on the TV series *Sisters*, playing the youngest sister, Frankie.

Julianne left acting in 1997 and has since maintained a low public profile. Her settlement in the divorce was said to have been between $16 and $20 million.

In late May the two returned to New Jersey. "Glory Days" was set as the next single release from *Born in the U.S.A.*, with the video once again directed by Sayles. After an opening sequence showing Springsteen first at work on a construction site and then practicing baseball pitches alone, thinking back to the "glory days" of his youth; the video switches to Maxwell's, a club in Hoboken, for a straight performance clip of Springsteen with the band (including both Van Zandt and Lofgren). At the video's end, Springsteen's character is seen pitching baseball again, this time to his son, until his wife arrives to pick them up (the wife played by Springsteen's real wife, Julianne). The single reached No. 5. Then the European leg of the tour began, with the band's first appearance in Ireland drawing a massive crowd of one hundred thousand fans at Slane Castle, northwest of Dublin. Dates in England, Sweden, Netherlands, West Germany, Italy, and France followed, culminating with three sold-out shows at Wembley Stadium in London and a final date in Leeds on July 7.

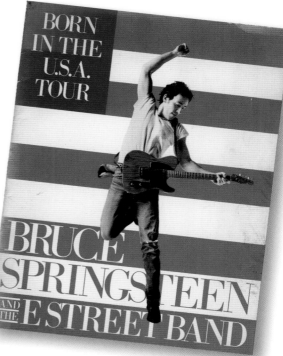

Program, *Born in the U.S.A.* tour, 1985

The bandana headband became a signature look for Springsteen during the *Born in the U.S.A.* tour. *Richard McCaffrey/Michael Ochs Archives/Getty Images*

A sellout crowd at London's Wembley Stadium anxiously awaits Springsteen to take the stage on July 3, 1985. *Dave Hogan/Hulton Archive/Getty Images*

Then came a month-long break before another US leg. In July, Springsteen furthered the awakening of his political voice by contributing to a song Van Zandt had put together to raise awareness about apartheid, "Sun City." The song's title referred to a casino in South Africa that had been declared an "independent state" by the government in order to allow such activities as gambling, which were banned in the rest of the country; it was strictly segregated. The United Nations had called for a "cultural boycott" of the country due to its repressive regime, but some big-name acts nonetheless performed at Sun City in the mistaken belief it was not really a part of South Africa.

Van Zandt wanted to draw attention to the issue. "I had been researching American foreign policy post–World War II just to educate myself," he told the website *Fast Company* in 2013. "I was quite shocked to find that we were not always the good guys. So I decided to write about that in my solo records . . . and also combine a bit of journalism with the rock art form." After meeting with anti-apartheid activists in the country and explaining, "We can win this thing on TV" (he recalled, "they looked at me like I had two heads"), he enlisted his friend Danny Schechter to help with the project. The two enlisted a wide variety of artists to contribute to the song, including Miles Davis, Bonnie Raitt, Joey Ramone, and George Clinton. Van Zandt had been hesitant to approach Springsteen, not wanting him to feel pressured to participate because of their friendship. But Springsteen was happy to do so. The single was released in October, credited to Artists United Against Apartheid, and reached No. 38 in the US charts (No. 21 in the United Kingdom). The single, and the album of the same name, helped raise more than a million dollars for anti-apartheid causes.

But the big charity news that month was the Live Aid concerts, which raised money for African famine relief, held on July 13 at London's Wembley

Stadium and JFK Stadium in Philadelphia. Surprisingly, Springsteen did not perform, though he had been asked. Springsteen later said he hadn't realized how big the shows would turn out to be and wished that he'd at least played a short set of acoustic songs.

The final leg of the tour began August 5 in Washington, DC. Yet another single from *Born in the U.S.A.*, "I'm Goin' Down," was released the same month, reaching No. 9. The tour closed with four shows at the Los Angeles Memorial Coliseum. On October 2, the final night, Landau made a surprise guest appearance on guitar on "Rockin' All Over the World" and "Glory Days," and Julianne was that evening's "Dancing in the Dark" choice.

It was a successful tour, and it made Springsteen a major rock star. But, typically, he remained as uneasy about his elevated status as a star as he had about the "future of rock 'n' roll" hype. "By the end of that whole thing, I just kind of felt 'Bruced' out," he told *Rolling Stone* in 1992 about the tour. "You can get enslaved by your own myth or your own image, for the lack of a better word." He wouldn't tour again for over two years.

In November, the final single from *Born in the U.S.A.*, "My Hometown," was released and reached No. 6. That made Springsteen one of the few artists to have seven Top 10 singles pulled from a single album (only Michael Jackson's *Thriller* and Janet Jackson's *Rhythm Nation 1814* achieved the same feat).

The single also inadvertently lead to Springsteen's next project. In search of a B-side, he initially thought of using a live version of Edwin Starr's protest song "War," which he had added to the set in L.A. Landau agreed it was a good choice, but argued that it shouldn't be relegated to a B-side. Instead, the live recording of "Santa Claus Is Comin' to Town" from the December 12, 1975, show in Long Island was used as the B-side, and after Landau listened to the recordings of Springsteen's stand at the Coliseum, he sent Springsteen a tape with four songs from the third show: "War," "Seeds," "The River," and "Born in the U.S.A." They were all great performances. Maybe it was time to put together the long-awaited live album?

Springsteen had always been resistant to doing a live album. But Landau pointed out he didn't have to do it the usual way: presenting a complete show from start to finish. He could do something different, something that would better represent his career as a live performer. Springsteen agreed to consider the idea and left it to Chuck Plotkin, who had mixed *The River*, to listen to all the live tapes while he waited in New Jersey.

While that project was in the works, Springsteen took time in January 1986 to support workers at the 3M plant in Freehold, New Jersey, the same factory where his father and grandfather had worked, and that Springsteen had referenced in the songs "Factory" and "My Hometown." Springsteen and most of the E Street Band (Lofgren and Bittan were unavailable) played the Jam '86 Hometown Benefit at the Stone Pony on January 19; he also donated

An airborne Springsteen during the *Born in the U.S.A.* tour. *The LIFE Picture Collection/Getty Images*

money to a production of *Lady Beth* that the unemployed workers staged in September at the Stone Pony and performed on the benefit single "We've Got to Love," credited to Jersey Artists for Mankind, released in May.

In February, Springsteen joined Plotkin in L.A. to go through the best of the live recordings. With input from Landau, they whittled the tracks down to forty songs and aimed for a fall release. Aside from the box, Springsteen lay low for most of the year, with only one confirmed performance at the Stone Pony on March 2. In October he was interviewed for the documentary *John Hammond: From Bessie Smith to Bruce Springsteen,* released in 1990. And on October 13 he performed at the first Bridge School Benefit Concert in Mountain View, California, an annual event organized by Neil Young and his then-wife Pegi, raising funds for the school for children with developmental disabilities. Springsteen performed a set with Lofgren and Federici, as well as a solo rendition of "You Can Look (But You Better Not Touch)" and joined Young in a performance of "Helpless"; his performance of "Fire" was later released as a music video. The following month he was in Paris, where his wife was shooting the film *Sweet Lies*; while there, on November 5, he attended a show by Huey Lewis and the News and ended up performing Robert Parker's "Barefootin'" along with Bob Geldof.

He returned to the United States on November 10, the date *Live/1975–85* was released. There was much excitement about the set (sold in five-LP, three-cassette, and three-CD versions), with fans lining up on November 9 to be the first to get a hold of it at midnight, when it officially went on sale. It debuted at No. 1 on the *Billboard* chart, a very impressive feat for a multialbum set. "War," the song that had inspired the set in the first place, was the first single, and reached No. 8 with a non-album live song, "Incident on 57th Street" as the B-side. A second single, "Fire," was released in January 1987 with another non-album live song, "For You," on the flip side; it reached No. 46. The singles were accompanied by videos, though the video for "Fire" showed Springsteen's performance of that song from his Bridge Show set.

At some point during 1986 he met up with his former manager again. Appel had called Landau during the year and suggested it was time for everyone to let bygones be bygones. Landau agreed and set up a lunch date at Anche Vivolo's in New York. "We hugged each other, went through things, and it was very, very warm," Appel recalled in his 1992 autobiography, *Down Thunder Road: The Making of Bruce Springsteen.* "It was almost as if there had never been any lawsuit. We couldn't understand how the three of us, having been through so much, could ever have allowed things to come down to lawsuits."

Springsteen was in no rush to get back into doing regular live shows, but he wound up making more live appearances in 1987 than he had the previous year. On January 21, 1987, he inducted Roy Orbison at the second annual Rock and Roll Hall of Fame ceremony, saying in part, "In 1975, when I went into the studio to record *Born to Run*, I wanted to make a record with words like Bob Dylan, that sounded like Phil Spector's productions, but most of all I wanted to sing like Roy Orbison. Now, everybody knows that nobody sings like Roy Orbison." During the all-star jam that followed he performed "Stand by Me" and "Oh, Pretty Woman" along with the other special guests, including Vini Lopez, whom he'd invited to the show along with George Theiss of the Castiles. Later that year, he participated in the concert film *Roy Orbison & Friends: A Black & White Night,* which featured Springsteen and such musicians as Elvis Costello, k. d. lang, Tom Waits, and Jennifer Warnes performing with Orbison at a special concert at the Cocoanut Grove, a club at the Ambassador Hotel in L.A., a program that became a perennial favorite on the PBS network.

Springsteen joined Van Zandt in the studio to contribute backing vocals to "Native American," a track on Van Zandt's third album, *Freedom—No Compromise,* released that May. He was also working on new material for his own album.

★ ★

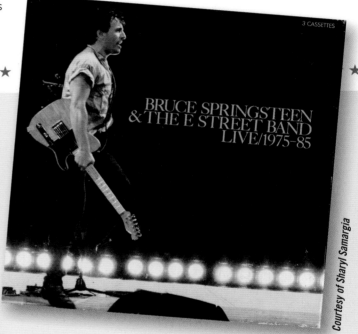

Courtesy of Sharyl Samargia

Live/1975–85

Springsteen's first live album was a multi-platinum success before it even was released. There were 1.5 million advance orders before the first copy was sold, which, since the set consisted of five albums, translated into 7.5 million records.

The earliest track on the set, "Thunder Road," was also the opening song, taken from an October 18, 1975, date at the Roxy Theatre. Of special interest to the fans were songs previously unreleased in either live or studio versions, including "Paradise by the 'C'" (July 7, 1978, Roxy Theatre), "Fire," the Elvis-inspired number that gave the Pointer Sisters a hit (December 16, 1978, Winterland), "Raise Your Hand" (July 7, 1978, Roxy Theatre), "Because the Night," Patti Smith's biggest single (December 28, 1980, Nassau Coliseum), and Edwin Starr's "War" (September 30, 1985, Los Angeles Coliseum). It was also his first release to have a recording of Woody Guthrie's "This Land Is Your Land."

Interestingly, the set ends not with one of his own songs, but with a cover of Tom Waits's "Jersey Girl," a low-key performance from a July 9, 1981, show at the Meadowlands Arena (in East Rutherford, New Jersey), though it's an appropriate number for the hometown crowd, who cheered at the first mention of the word Jersey. The release also marked the first time an album was credited to both Bruce Springsteen and the E Street Band on the front cover.

Since January he'd been recording songs at "Thrill Hill East," the name given to the studio at his home in New Jersey. Overdubbing with additional musicians was done in New York and L.A., and the album, *Tunnel of Love*, was completed by August. With such a quick turnaround, the backlog of unreleased material was smaller than what other albums produced: five songs from the sessions later appeared on *Tracks*, and another four remained unreleased.

Released on October 6, *Tunnel of Love* topped both the US and UK charts. In talking about the album to *Rolling Stone* in 1992, Springsteen explained, "I thought I had to reintroduce myself as a songwriter." But a number of those who listened to the album's lyrics got a message he might not have expected—that his marriage was in trouble.

October also saw the release of the album's first two singles, "Brilliant Disguise" (which reached No. 5) and the title track (which reached No. 10). But there was no announcement of a tour. He made a few guest appearances, performing "Stand by Me" during a U2 show in Philadelphia on September 25 and "Remember When the Music" at a Harry Chapin tribute concert on December 7 at Carnegie Hall in New York. On December 13 he joined a heady roster at Madison Square Garden in a benefit for homeless children, turning in a solo rendition of "Born to Run," gleefully backing Dion as he sang his classic, "Teenager in Love," and joining in an all-star rendition of "Rock and Roll Music" with Lou Reed, Debbie Harry, James Taylor, and Grace Jones, among others. On Halloween, Springsteen and most of the E Streeters (minus Clemons and Lofgren) played a surprise set at McLoone's Rum Runner in Sea Bright, New Jersey, taking the stage wearing masks. A more somber performance came on October 22, at the memorial service for John Hammond at Saint Peter's Church. Hammond had died on July 10, after suffering a number of strokes; Springsteen honored the man who had irrevocably changed his life by singing "Forever Young" at the service.

On January 20, 1988, Springsteen was once again in attendance at the Rock and Roll Hall of Fame induction ceremony, at the Waldorf Hotel. This ceremony was more contentious than usual. Both the Beatles and the Supremes were being inducted, but neither Paul McCartney or Diana Ross showed up, due to disputes with members of their respective groups. And when the Beach Boys were inducted, Mike Love went on a bizarre rant, stating that the group had performed 180 shows the previous year and going on to say, "I'd like to see the Mop Tops [the Beatles] match that! I'd like to see Mick Jagger get out on this stage and do 'I Get Around' versus 'Jumpin' Jack Flash,' any day now. And I'd like to see some people kick out the jams, and I challenge 'the Boss' to get up on stage and jam."

Springsteen made no reference to Love's comments when he inducted Dylan. "When I was fifteen years old and I heard 'Like a Rolling Stone,' I heard

Springsteen and Van Zandt prepare to hit the road in 1986. *Kevin Winter/DMI/The LIFE Picture Collection/ Getty Images*

a guy like I've never heard before or since," he said. "Who had the guts to take on the whole world and made me feel like I had to, too. . . . There isn't a soul in this room who does not owe you his thanks, and to steal a line from one of your songs—whether you like it or not—'You was the brother that I never had.'" But Dylan couldn't resist a remark about the preceding events when he made his speech: "I want to thank Mike Love for not mentioning me," he said, to laughter and applause. "I play a lot of dates every year too. Peace, love, and harmony is greatly important indeed, but so is forgiveness and we gotta have that too." And as it happened, Springsteen did get up and jam at the show's end, as the inductees and musician guests played "I Saw Her Standing There," "(I Can't Get No) Satisfaction," and "All Along the Watchtower," among others.

By then, a tour in support of *Tunnel of Love* had been announced. Springsteen had not wanted to do a large-scale tour for the album, but did add the Miami Horns to the lineup; previously, they'd only made occasional guest appearances during his shows. Rehearsals began in January, though Springsteen found time for one more side appearance prior to the tour,

THE ALBUMS

★★★★★★★ ★★★★★★ ★★★

TUNNEL OF LOVE

Released: October 1987
Chart Position: No. 1 (US), No. 1 (UK)

Tunnel of Love was released when Springsteen was on the verge of two breakups: the end of his first marriage and the (temporary) end of his partnership with the E Street Band.

It's not wise to read too much into a song; just because songwriters take personal perspectives doesn't mean they're singing about themselves. But in this case, the pervasive themes of disconnection and lack of trust can't be ignored. It surely is no coincidence that these songs are seldom performed in concert.

Nowhere are stories of secrets and lies better told than on the album's first single, "Brilliant Disguise." It's a startling depiction of two people who no longer recognize each other, or even themselves. The singer admits that both parties are hiding behind outer masks, and the subdued music only heightens the pensive mood. It's a similar tale on the title track, where the amusement park ride that once allowed couples to snuggle in the dark becomes a maze in which they lose sight of each other, less of a pleasure cruise and more a place where the "ride is rough."

That rough ride began on the opening track, the self-explanatory "Ain't Got You," a lively, gospel-infused number, with Springsteen singing the first verse a cappella. "Spare Parts" is a back-country stomper about a single mother forced to sell her wedding ring for "good cold cash" when she's abandoned by her baby's father. In "Two Faces," the singer acknowledges the two sides of his nature, unable to keep his darker personality at bay even when it endangers his relationship. In "When You're Alone," it's the man who is left behind, holding out the hope she'll return. And in "Walk Like a Man," the marriage feels like it's over before the happy couple has even exchanged vows.

There are also hints of the narrator's wandering eye: in the downbeat "Tougher Than the Rest," the singer seeks to drown his heartbreak in the arms of someone new; in "One Step Up" he escapes domestic discord for an evening out alone at the local bar, enjoying flirtatious glances from a comely stranger.

The album isn't entirely about broken relationships. "All That Heaven Will Allow" is a wistful number about yearning to attain the right woman. In "Cautious Man," the song's protagonist works past his fears for the sake of his relationship. In the closing track, "Valentine's Day," the singer drives home, anticipating a warm reunion with his loved one.

But the majority of the album is steeped in sadness. And instead of societal or political concerns, the disappointments are entirely personal. It's a mature work that confronts the realities of adult relationships; in the real world, it takes more than a song to wash away the pain.

performing some Woody Guthrie songs in February for the documentary *A Vision Shared: Tribute to Woody Guthrie and Leadbelly*, which was released later in the year. There was also a shoot for *Tunnel of Love*'s second video, "One Step Up," on February 15 at the Wonder Bar in Asbury Park; the single, released the same month, reached No. 13.

The *Tunnel of Love* tour began February 25, 1988, in Worcester, Massachusetts. Playing off the carnival theme of the album's title track, the band members made their stage entrance by getting tickets from a man in a ticket booth, as if they were boarding an actual "tunnel of love" amusement park ride. A sign was posted near the ticket booth reading "This is a dark ride," and Springsteen himself was more somberly attired, in a suit jacket and trousers and a white shirt. New to the set was a stark, stripped-down acoustic version of "Born to Run," which recast this celebratory song of escape into something quite different. The US leg ended on May 25, and there was a break of a few weeks before it resumed overseas on June 11 in Turin, Italy.

A few days later, Springsteen's private life became fodder for the gossip mill when he was photographed on a hotel balcony in Rome, in his underwear,

Springsteen and his wife in New York City on August 24, 1988; that evening, he made a guest appearance at a Sting concert at Madison Square Garden.
Ron Galella, Ltd./WireImage

Patti Scialfa

Patti Scialfa, Bruce's second wife, and Bruce attend the eighth annual "Stand Up for Heroes" benefit concert at Madison Square Garden on November 5, 2014. In addition to being a member of the E Street Band, Patti has released three solo albums. *Monica Schipper/Getty Images for New York Comedy Festival*

P atti Scialfa is best known as Springsteen's second wife. But she's also a recording artist in her own right and was inducted into the Rock and Roll Hall of Fame as a member of the E Street Band.

Vivienne Patricia Scialfa was born on July 29, 1953, and grew up in Deal, New Jersey, part of the same Jersey Shore scene where Springsteen was raised. She began writing songs at a young age and joined her first group, Ecstasy, when she was fourteen. After high school, she attended the Frost School of Music jazz conservatory at the University of Miami, later transferring to New York University and graduating with a degree in music. By that time, one of her song demos had attracted the attention of Jerry Wexler of Atlantic Records. He wanted to pass the song on to Aretha Franklin—if Scialfa would agree to change some of the lyrics. But Scialfa refused to compromise and, to Wexler's astonishment, said no.

Prior to joining the E Street Band, Scialfa provided vocals on albums by Don Cherry, Narada Michael Walden, David Johansen, and Southside Johnny & the Asbury Jukes. Her sultry voice was front and center on her own albums, *Rumble Doll* (1993), *23rd Street Lullaby* (2004), and *Play It*

as It Lays (2007), records well worth investigating if you're a Springsteen fan. (Springsteen makes appearances on the albums as well.)

Scialfa and Springsteen celebrated their twenty-fifth wedding anniversary in 2016.

with Patti Scialfa by his side. *Tunnel of Love* had provided strong lyrical clues that all was not well in Springsteen's marriage, and the onstage interaction between Springsteen and Scialfa during the current tour was noticeably steamy. Springsteen and Julianne had been seen less and less frequently in each other's company, and rumors flew that the two had decided to separate early in 1988, and Springsteen's relationship with Scialfa was the reason. But in fact, the marriage had been over for some time. "I didn't really know how to be a husband," Springsteen told *Rolling Stone* in looking back at his marriage in 1992. "She was a terrific person, but I just didn't know how to do it."

Typically, Springsteen played down the controversy, not doing any interviews addressing the matter at the time. He had a bit of fun in Rome when he stopped to play a handful of songs, including "Dancing in the Dark," with some street musicians he met while strolling around the city (he did the same while in Copenhagen in July). On June 18 he and Clemons made a guest appearance at an S.O.S. Racism concert in Paris. On July 3, during his show in Stockholm, Springsteen announced he planned to get even more involved with promoting a political agenda, signing on for Amnesty International's Human Rights Now! tour, set to begin on September 2. The *Tunnel of Love* tour ended a month later, in Barcelona, giving everyone a month's break before the Human Rights Now! tour began. Springsteen prepared for the upcoming tour by making a guest appearance with one of the other performers, Sting, at the latter's concert at Madison Square Garden on August 24.

Peter Gabriel, Tracy Chapman, and Youssou N'Dour were the other performers on the Human Rights Now! bill. The shows opened with everyone performing Bob Marley's "Get Up, Stand Up," and the musicians frequently guested during each other's sets; Sting joined Springsteen in performing "The River," and Springsteen returned the favor during Sting's set, performing "Every Breath You Take." There were twenty dates on the tour, in the United States, Canada, Europe, Costa Rica, India, Japan, Africa, and South America. The tour's last date was October 15 in Buenos Aires, Argentina. Springsteen also released an EP, *Chimes of Freedom*, in conjunction with the tour; it contained four live songs from the *Tunnel of Love* tour: "Tougher Than the Rest," "Be True," "Chimes of Freedom," and "Born to Run." The title track reached No. 16 on *Billboard*'s Mainstream Rock chart.

It would be four years before Springsteen toured again. And it would be another decade before he toured with the E Street Band again.

(opposite)
Springsteen during a June 19, 1988, show in Paris during the *Tunnel of Love* tour. *BERTRAND GUAY/AFP/ Getty Images*

(below)
The finale of the "Amnesty International: Human Rights Now!" show on September 19, 1988, at the John F. Kennedy Stadium in Philadelphia, when all the acts took the stage to sing "Get Up, Stand Up." *John Roca/ NY Daily News Archive via Getty Images*

LIVE
GIRL
DANCERS
WANTED
APPLY WITHIN
Tel: 768-2094
SALE
WaterPik

57

CHANNELS
(AND NOTHIN' ON)

I t was time for a break. A long one. The preceding four years had seen an enormous number of changes in Springsteen's life. He'd become a superstar. He'd gotten married. And he'd seen his marriage end—as the rest of the world watched from the sidelines.

He made only three more live appearances after the end of the Human Rights Now! tour in 1988, making a guest appearance with John Prine on November 11 in Tarrytown, New York, taking a fun swing through classics like "In the Midnight Hour" and "Keep a-Knockin'" with Southside Johnny in San Francisco on November 26, and a holiday drop-in at the Stone Pony on December 18, performing "Santa Claus Is Comin' to Town."

And so it went: for the next few years, Springsteen limited himself to guest appearances and drop-ins. He and Scialfa also spent a lot of time at his home in L.A., where, ironically, it was easier to keep out of the public eye than in the more rural setting of his home in Rumson, New Jersey. Not that he was a recluse: on January 18, 1989, he was once again at the Rock and Roll Hall of Fame induction ceremony, not inducting anyone, but joining the concluding all-star jam as usual, turning in an impressive performance on Roy Orbison's "Crying." When he and Patti returned to New Jersey for the summer, it wasn't unusual to find him hanging out at the Stone Pony.

On September 23, 1989, Springsteen turned forty. He hosted a birthday party at McLoone's Rum Runner in Sea Bright, New Jersey, with the E Street Band in attendance, as well as Van Zandt. But the next day, he headed west on his motorcycle, along with his friend Matty DiLea and Matty's brothers Tony and Eddie. Their most memorable stop came on September 29, when they arrived in Prescott, Arizona, and dropped in at a bar called Matt's Saloon. In talking to waitress Brenda "Bubbles" Pechanec, he learned that she'd been married eight times; later, when invited to join the Mile High Band onstage, he cracked "I'm here in Prescott to take Bubbles away and be her ninth!" He played with the band for about an hour, sticking to rock 'n' roll numbers, begging off playing "Pink Cadillac" by saying he didn't remember the words (though he did manage to recall the lyrics to "I'm on Fire"). He later surprised Bubbles by sending her a large check to help out with her medical expenses.

Springsteen was nearly always ready to play when the opportunity arose. But now he was having trouble writing his own music. He'd been reevaluating his life through intensive therapy, and in the fall of 1989 decided to make a break with his musical past. "That was just a moment when I didn't know where to go next and it needed to stop for a while," he later told *Mojo*. On October 18, he telephoned each member of the E Street Band and told them he wasn't planning on using the band on any of his upcoming projects. There had always been some downtime following Springsteen's tours before work on a new record began, so the band members were surprised to hear Springsteen had decided to change course completely. "I was shocked, hurt, angry, all at

Whether in a club or stadium, Springsteen always tried his best to get up close and personal with his fans.
The LIFE Picture Collection/Getty Images

once," Clemons later recalled in 1998. "Then after a while I thought, 'The man's gotta do what he's gotta do.'"

In fact, Springsteen had already made a recording without the E Streeters. In September he had recorded a cover of "Viva Las Vegas" for the UK charity album *The Last Temptation of Elvis*, using Bob Glaub on bass, the Small Faces' Ian McLagan on keyboards, and Jeff Porcaro, of Toto, on drums. The album was released in 1990; the song later appeared on *The Essential Bruce Springsteen*. Nor did he cut all ties with the band. While in L.A., he and Bittan began writing songs together and recording them at "Thrill Hill West," his home studio on the West Coast. Overdubbing on some tracks was done later, at more high-end studios; R&B singer Sam Moore (of the soul singing duo Sam & Dave) contributed backing vocals to "Real World," for example.

Springsteen continued steadily writing and recording throughout 1990, with former E Streeter Sancious also appearing on some recordings. But Springsteen was in no rush to finish an album. He did a handful of live performances that year, including another return to the Rock and Roll Hall of Fame induction ceremony on January 17, 1990; a private benefit for the Rainforest Foundation at the Beverly Hills home of movie producer Ted Field on February 12 (followed by an impromptu performance later the same evening, when the musicians, including Joe Walsh of the Eagles and Sting, along with Springsteen, dropped by the China Club in Hollywood); and guest appearances at shows by Dylan and Tom Waits, as well as with Tom Petty and the Heartbreakers on March 1 (performing "Travelin' Band" and "I'm Crying").

One reason for Springsteen's low profile was that he and Patti were preparing for the birth of their first child, Evan James Springsteen, born on July 25. Like most first-time parents, Springsteen found the event extraordinary: "I had this feeling of a kind of love that I hadn't experienced before," he later said.

Now, for the first time, his personal life took priority. His two remaining appearances of the year came on November 16 and 17, at benefit concerts for the Christic Institute (a law firm supportive of progressive causes) held at

Springsteen's love of live performance means that even when he's on tour, he'll drop into a local club for a quick jam. *The LIFE Picture Collection/Getty Images*

L.A.'s Shrine Auditorium; Jackson Browne and Bonnie Raitt were also on the bill. In December he joined Nils Lofgren in the studio and provided harmony vocals for the song "Valentine," released on Lofgren's album *Silver Lining* the following year.

But 1991 would be a quiet year for him as well. He sang on "Take a Look at My Heart" on John Prine's album *The Missing Years* and performed on two tracks on Southside Johnny's *Better Days* album, "All the Way Home," which he wrote, and "It's Been a Long Time"; both released in 1991. There was the obligatory Rock and Roll Hall of Fame appearance in January and some drop-ins at New Jersey clubs when Springsteen and his family headed back east for the summer. On June 8 he and Scialfa were married, and the birth of a second child, Jessica Rae Springsteen, followed on December 30.

Nonetheless, by early 1991 Springsteen had recorded around thirty songs, more than enough for an album. But, typically, he was unsatisfied with his work, and in the summer he recorded more songs at Thrill Hill West and A&M Studios in L.A. The end result was unexpected; instead of drawing on the wealth of material he'd recorded for one album, or even a double album, he decided to release two different records: *Human Touch* (drawn from the earlier sessions) and *Lucky Town* (drawn from the later 1991 sessions). Both albums were released on March 31, 1992.

Fans debate the wisdom of releasing two albums at once to this day. Some thought that doing so diminished the impact of each. *Human Touch* fared slightly better in the charts, reaching No. 2, while *Lucky Town* reached No. 3. The first single paired "Human Touch" with "Souls of the Departed" (from *Lucky Town*) and reached No. 16 (and No. 1 on *Billboard*'s Hot Mainstream Rock Tracks chart). The video for "Human Touch" was shot in New Orleans; during the week of filming, Springsteen and Scialfa made a surprise drop-in at the Maple Leaf Bar and played a few rock 'n' roll classics with the band playing there that night, the Iguanas. "Better Days," from *Lucky Town*, was released as a single in the United Kingdom and Europe, with a video for the song shot in March.

In preparation for the tour to promote the new albums, Springsteen and Bittan held auditions. On guitar they chose Shane Fontayne; born Mick Barakan, Fontayne was the guitarist with Lone Justice, among other credits, and Springsteen had first seen him when the band played *Saturday Night Live* in 1986. Tommy Sims, who had played with Amy Grant and the Divinyls, was on bass, with New York–based Zach Alford, who admitted he didn't own a single one of Springsteen's records, on drums.

There was a warm-up date May 6 at the Bottom Line in front of music industry VIPs, followed by a May 9 appearance on *Saturday Night Live*, Springsteen's first appearance on the long-running comedy show. The band first performed "Lucky Town." The second segment began with a reworked

HUMAN
TOUCH & LUCKY TOWN

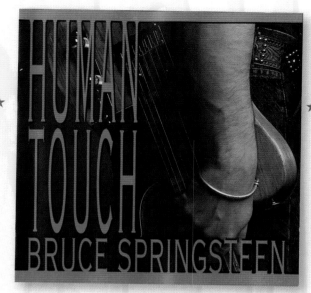

Released: March 1992
Chart Position: No. 2 (US), No. 1 (UK)

It had been four long years since Springsteen had released an album, so it was no surprise that he returned with not one, but two records to promote. But instead of releasing a set, he released them as two separate albums, citing Guns N' Roses' release of their 1991 albums *Use Your Illusion I* and *II* as inspiration.

After the gloomy outlook of *Tunnel of Love*, "Better Days," the lead track and first single from *Lucky Town*, showed Springsteen to be in a much more positive place. He sounds almost reborn on the midtempo rocker, looking ahead to the future with a new love by his side. Numerous songs reflect his new domestic bliss. "Living Proof" (*Lucky Town*) was inspired by the wonder he felt at the birth of his first son. The delicate "Pony Boy" (*Human Touch*) is a song Springsteen's grandmother used to sing, and that he also sang to his newborn son. "If I Should Fall Behind" (*Lucky Town*) is a lovely song about commitment, something Springsteen was now truly ready to embrace.

The desire to make a connection and the importance of reaching out to find one are underlying themes on both albums. In the title track of *Human Touch*, the narrator admits love comes with the risk of getting hurt—but it's a risk well worth taking. "Man's Job" (*Human Touch*) is about finding the strength to be vulnerable in a relationship, something also expressed in the synth-driven "Real Man" on the same album.

Other songs touched on Springsteen's real-life experiences as well. In "The Long Goodbye" (*Human Touch*) he bids farewell to the seductive lure of fame, while the wry "Local Hero" (*Lucky Town*) was based on seeing own his portrait painted on velvet. His playful side comes out in the light rock 'n' roll of "57 Channels (And Nothin' On)."

The records were the first "band" albums (as opposed to a solo work like *Nebraska*) Springsteen recorded without the E Streeters, which

Released: March 1992
Chart Position: No. 3 (US), No. 2 (UK)

gave them a different sound. There was a slickness, a studio perfection that some fans found off-putting, and there were no out-and-out rockers (though the songs did sound tougher when performed live). Springsteen himself, with typical self-deprecation, joked with audiences about *Human Touch* being considered "my weakest album."

They are both transitional works for Springsteen, revealing a man finally comfortable in his own skin. He'd survived the turbulence of worldwide fame and a failed marriage and was now back on track, ready to face whatever fate had in store for him next.

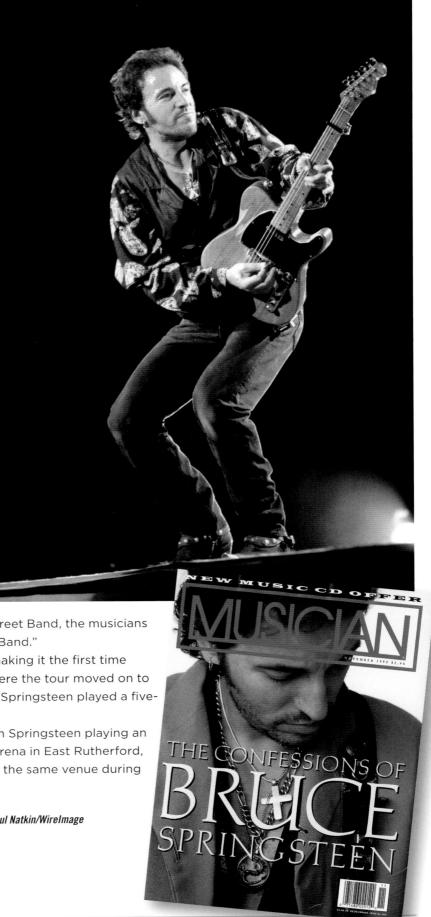

"57 Channels (And Nothin' On)." The song had a new, visceral introduction made up of soundbites drawn from news coverage of the riots that had broken out in Los Angeles in late April in the wake of the "not guilty" verdict in the trial of four police officers who had beaten Rodney King, who had been stopped for a traffic violation—riots that had broken out at the same time Springsteen was rehearsing with his new band. At the end, the song segued into "Living Proof," with Springsteen saying "See you in the summer!" at the song's end, a clear sign he was looking forward to hitting the road again.

But he planned to expand the lineup first. He added Crystal Taliefero, a veteran of John Mellencamp's band, who played guitar and sax and provided vocals. He added five additional backing vocalists as well: Gia Ciombotti, Carol Dennis, Bobby King, Cleopatra Kennedy, and Angel Rogers. "Throw in a Monopoly board, and you almost had Dr. Zoom and the Sonic Boom up there," writer Marc Dolan observed in his book on Springsteen. It was also the most ethnically diverse lineup Springsteen had ever put together: he, Bittan, and Cambotti were white; Fontayne was mixed race; and everyone else was African American. But to loyal fans of the E Street Band, the musicians would always be collectively known as the "Other Band."

The tour kicked off on June 15 in Stockholm, making it the first time Springsteen began a major tour overseas. From there the tour moved on to Italy, Germany, France, Spain, and England, where Springsteen played a five-night stand at Wembley Arena.

The North American leg began on July 23, with Springsteen playing an impressive eleven-night stand at Brendan Byrne Arena in East Rutherford, New Jersey, one night more than he'd managed at the same venue during

(right, above)
Springsteen circa 1992, during his first tour without the E Street Band. *Paul Natkin/WireImage*

(right)
November 1992 issue of *Musician* magazine

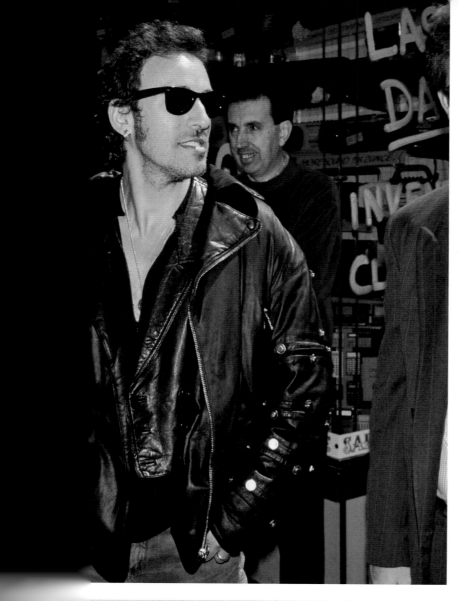

the *Born in the U.S.A.* tour. The same month, "57 Channels (And Nothin' On)" was released as a single from *Human Touch*, reaching No. 68.

One of the most memorable shows came on September 22, when Springsteen recorded an appearance for MTV's *Unplugged* show at Warner Hollywood Studios in L.A. After a solo acoustic performance of the racy "Red Headed Woman" (obviously inspired by Scialfa), the full band used electric instruments during the rest of the set. MTV's honchos didn't have a problem with Springsteen's decision to ditch the unplugged format: "When you have the chance to work with Springsteen, he can do what he wants," said the show's producer, Alex Coletti. The set featured every song on *Human Touch*, with Scialfa providing a guest vocal on the title track. An edited version of the full show was released the following April in Europe and the United Kingdom under the name *MTV Plugged* (or *MTV XXPlugged*, a reference to the *X*s over the "Un" in "Unplugged" on the cover). It reached the Top 20 in five different countries. A US release followed in 1997, but the album only hovered around the lower reaches of *Billboard*'s Top 200. The show was also released on VHS and later on DVD.

The tour ended in Lexington, Kentucky, on December 17, and Springsteen kicked back for the end of year, guesting with Southside Johnny & the Asbury Jukes at a December 27 show at the Stone Pony. Springsteen made a few guest appearances before the next leg of the tour began in 1993: backing John Fogerty for the induction of Creedence Clearwater Revival into the Rock and Roll Hall of Fame, and a performance in Red Bank, New Jersey, benefiting a local theater and food bank. The latter show featured a set list reaching all the way back to "Blinded by the Light" and saw Springsteen tearing off his shirt before playing a cover of Billy Ray Cyrus's hit "Achy Breaky Heart." "Everybody gets a giggle out of it, but that damn thing was good," he said of the song, to applause and laughter. Touring began again on March 31, 1993,

in Scotland, and closed on June 1 in Germany. A few hectic days in New York followed. On June 24, Springsteen was the star of "A Concert to Fight Hunger" at Meadowlands Arena in East Rutherford, with numerous special guests, including Scialfa, Southside Johnny, the Miami Horns, and his E Street buddies Van Zandt and Clemons. The next night he made a surprise appearance on *Late Night with David Letterman*, playing "Glory Days," and then on June 26 he played another benefit at Madison Square Garden for the Kristen Ann Carr Fund. Carr, the daughter of Springsteen's comanager Barbara Carr and stepdaughter of Dave Marsh, had also worked for Springsteen herself and died at age twenty-one of liposarcoma. Springsteen opened the show with Woody Guthrie's "You've Got to Walk That Lonesome Valley," Scialfa sang on a few numbers, and Joe Ely and Terence Trent D'Arby made guest appearances. D'Arby shared vocals with Springsteen on "My Hometown," but when he returned to sing solo on his own "I Have Faith in These Desolate Times," he was booed; "loud enough to be obnoxious," Marsh recalled. Angry, Springsteen told the crowd, "Need I remind some of you rude motherfuckers that everybody onstage is my guest?" before performing "Light of Day." The concert raised $1.5 million.

Springsteen and his family then returned to L.A. for the rest of the summer. Scialfa's solo debut album, *Rumble Doll*, came out in July. Springsteen coproduced it and also played on two tracks; E Streeters Bittan

1992–93 tour T-shirt. *Courtesy of Sharyl Samargia*

(opposite)
Springsteen in Berlin on May 14, 1993, during the *Human Touch/Lucky Town* **tour.** *POP-EYE/ullstein bild via Getty Images*

and Lofgren played on the album, as did Scialfa's Trickster bandmate Soozie Tyrell. In the early fall, Springsteen recorded the song "Gypsy Woman" for *A Tribute to Curtis Mayfield*, released the following year. But his next major work was the song "Streets of Philadelphia," written for Jonathan Demme's 1993 film *Philadelphia*, which starred Tom Hanks as a lawyer dying of AIDS. Springsteen played every instrument himself on the original recording; Demme said he cried on first listening to it. Springsteen then recorded a more fully fleshed-out version for use in the film, with Tommy Sims on bass, Ornette Coleman on sax, and Little Jimmy Scott joining the other two on backing vocals, and shot a video set to that version. But he then decided to use his original solo recording instead, adding some backing vocal overdubs from Sims; this version ultimately played over the film's opening credits.

The new year opened with the birth of Springsteen's third child, Sam Ryan Springsteen, on January 5, 1994. There were no major tours or records scheduled; 1994 would be one of Springsteen's more relaxed years. To a point. For, while he kicked back at that year's Rock and Roll Hall of Fame induction on January 20, performing an impromptu version of "Come Together" with Axl Rose of Guns n' Roses, he soon had a new hit of his own to promote when "Streets of Philadelphia" was released as a single on February 2. It reached No. 9 in the charts, and little more than a month later, on March 21, he performed it on the Academy Awards, taking home the Oscar for Best Original Song (beating Neil Young, whose song "Philadelphia" was also used in the film and had been nominated for the same award). When Springsteen accepted the award, he thanked Kristen Carr, "whose spirit is in this song." He also performed the song at that year's MTV Music Video Awards on September 8, winning the award for Best Video from a Film. More honors for the song were to come.

Springsteen credited the song with helping to broaden his audience. "The bonus I got out of writing 'Streets of Philadelphia' was that all of a sudden I could go out and meet some gay man somewhere and he wouldn't be afraid to talk to me and say, 'Hey, that song really meant something to me,'" he told national gay magazine *The Advocate*. "My image had always been very heterosexual, very straight. So it was a nice experience for me, a chance to clarify my own feelings about gay and lesbian civil rights."

The rest of 1994 saw scattered Springsteen sightings. He played at the private opening of L.A. club House of Blues in April 30 (backing James Brown on "Sex Machine"), with John Fogerty at House of Blues on September 20 (on "In the Midnight Hour"), and Bob Dylan at Roseland Ballroom on October 20 (on "Rainy Day Women #12 and 35" and "Highway 61 Revisited"). He was naturally on hand when the Stone Pony celebrated its twentieth anniversary

on July 16. He also produced and performed on Joe Grushecky's album *American Babylon*, released in 1995.

Meanwhile, Springsteen had been sporadically working on new material himself, sometimes working with Bittan and Other Band members Fontayne, Sims and Alford. One solo number, "Missing," ended up in the 1995 film *The Crossing Guard* after Sean Penn, the film's director, heard the song. But Springsteen had no new album of his own. At this point, Landau made a suggestion. Why not release a greatest hits package? And include a few new songs on it as well, as had become the practice with greatest hits sets? And, most audaciously of all—why not record those new songs with the E Street Band?

Springsteen thought about it and ultimately agreed. On January 5, 1995, his son Sam's first birthday, he called up the E Streeters, and a few days later everyone found themselves at the Hit Factory in New York. Springsteen

"Streets of Philadelphia"

"**B**orn to Run" might be Springsteen's signature song (with "Born in the U.S.A." another contender for that title), but "Streets of Philadelphia" is also one of his most notable works.

Springsteen wrote the song for Jonathan Demme's AIDS drama *Philadelphia*. As he had with the songs for *Nebraska*, Springsteen recorded what he thought was a demo, accompanying himself on guitar, bass, synthesizer, and a drum machine. Demme had wanted a more rousing number, but the song's restrained performance undeniably tugged on the heartstrings. Springsteen had vocalist Tommy Sims overdub some backing vocals, and the song was done.

"Streets of Philadelphia" has one of Springsteen's most evocative vocals. When he sings of feeling himself fading away, you believe him; unlike in his other songs, there's no hope of redemption at the end. Knowing it would be hard to lip sync convincingly to such an emotional song, Springsteen sang a live vocal in the song's video.

"Streets of Philadelphia" swiftly became one of Springsteen's most acclaimed numbers when released as

a single, hitting the Top 10 in the United States, United Kingdom, and Australia, and topping the charts in Canada, Austria, Germany, Norway, Italy, Ireland, and France. It also received a clutch of honors, from Grammys to an Oscar, and, as Springsteen said, introduced him to a whole new audience.

Be sure to seek out the original single version, which is longer than the version on *Greatest Hits* and *The Essential Bruce Springsteen*.

Leaping for glory during the *Human Touch/Lucky Town* tour in 1992. *Paul Natkin/WireImage/Getty Images*

brought out some numbers originally recorded during the *Born in the U.S.A.* sessions: "Murder Incorporated" (which he decided to not rerecord) and "This Hard Land" (which was rerecorded). These two songs, along with the new numbers "Secret Garden" and "Blood Brothers," appeared on *Greatest Hits*. Other songs recorded at the time included "Without You" and "High Hopes," which were later released on the 1996 *Blood Brothers* EP, released in conjunction with a documentary about the sessions of the same name, first aired on the Disney Channel and later released on video and DVD. "Back in Your Arms" later appeared on *Tracks*. "Waiting on the End of the World" and "By Your Side" remain officially unreleased.

Greatest Hits was released on February 28, 1995. Along with the new songs, and "Streets of Philadelphia," the album featured two tracks from *Born to Run*, one from *Darkness*, two from *The River*, one from *Nebraska*, four from *Born in the U.S.A.*, and one each from *Tunnel of Love*, *Human Touch*, and *Lucky Town*. It reached No. 1 in the United States, selling more than four million copies, and reached No. 1 in fifteen other countries as well. There was no full-fledged tour planned, but the reunited band did make a few promotional appearances. There was a club date at Tramps in New York, on February 21. On April 5, the band appeared on the *Late Show with David Letterman;* after reminding the audience the E Street Band was playing together for the first time in years, Letterman joked "Every member of that band had dental surgery today!" They then performed a private set in front of an invited audience that was edited down to an hour for television (a few songs from the set also appeared on the *Hungry Heart Berlin '95* CD single).

And that was it for the E Street reunion—for the time being, anyway. Springsteen had made other live appearances throughout the year. On February 15, he was a guest on Melissa Etheridge's *MTV Unplugged* show, performing "Thunder Road." He performed "Streets of Philadelphia" at the Grammys on March 1, scooping up four awards for Best Rock Song, Best Male Rock Vocal Performance, Best Song Written for a Motion Picture, and Song of the Year. On April 12 he was at Carnegie Hall, playing a Rock for the Rainforest benefit show with James Taylor (on "The River"), Elton John (on "Streets of Philadelphia"), and Sting (on "Guitar Man"; the set included a lot of Elvis numbers). He was a natural choice to play a September 2 show in Cleveland in conjunction with the grand opening of the Rock and Roll Hall of Fame museum, giving Springsteen the chance to play with some of his rock 'n' roll heroes, including Chuck Berry (on "Johnny B. Goode") and Jerry Lee Lewis (on "Great Balls of Fire"). And he honored an icon of a different sort, performing "Angel Eyes" at Frank Sinatra's eightieth birthday tribute concert on November 11.

He found time to work on other artists' projects too, performing on two tracks on Joe Ely's 1995 album *Letter to Laredo* and singing on one song on Elliott Murphy's 1995 *Selling the Gold* album. His work with Joe Grushecky led to a six-show tour with Grushecky in October, later released on the *A Good Life: The Joe Grushecky Story* DVD and the accompanying *October Assault* CD, as well as the album *Down the Road Apiece: Live.* Springsteen welcomed the chance to take a backseat in concert, without the responsibilities of being the star of the show.

After all this freelancing, he finally started work on his own album. He'd been writing and recording material at Thrill Hill West since the spring, both solo material and songs with other musicians. One song he had considered recording for *Greatest Hits* became the title track of the album: "The Ghost of Tom Joad" referred to the lead character in John Steinbeck's classic novel about the Great Depression, *The Grapes of Wrath,* which had a profound impact on Springsteen. During the sessions he also wrote the title song for Tim Robbins's film *Dead Man Walking* and another track, "Brothers Under the Bridge," that later appeared on *Tracks*; at least six further outtakes remain unreleased.

Greatest Hits, released February 27, 1995

"Blood Brothers"

Springsteen recorded "Blood Brothers" with the E Street Band in January 1995, his first reunion with the band since 1988. Like many of Springsteen's songs, it's open to different interpretations; the bittersweet lyric could refer to old army buddies. But anyone that knew Springsteen's history with the E Streeters couldn't miss the autobiographical elements of the song.

The first version of the song to be released appeared on the 1995 *Greatest Hits* set. It starts out acoustically, Springsteen accompanying himself on guitar, making it easy to hear the lines about one-time friends who were pulled apart by the forces of life: "work to do and bills to pay." Springsteen's ambivalence about the split is clear, though the final verse holds out the possibility of reconciliation as the narrator closes his eyes and imagines he's with his "blood brothers" once again.

A second, more rousing version was released on the *Blood Brothers* EP, which came out in 1996. This version starts out with Springsteen forcefully singing the first verse a cappella, after which the band joins in. It's a more robust performance, making the song more uplifting and less melancholy.

"Blood Brothers" was an appropriate closing number on the last night of the 1999–2000 reunion tour, and the last night of *The Rising* tour.

The Ghost of Tom Joad was an acoustic album, not a rock album, and Springsteen was determined to perform his next tour in that fashion. He warmed up with an acoustic performance at that year's Bridge School Benefit concert on October 28, but he played only a short, seven-song set; he'd never done an entire show acoustically before. The album was released on November 21 (reaching No. 11), the same day as his preview show for the tour in New Brunswick, New Jersey. The tour itself began the next night at the Count Basie Theatre in Red Bank, New Jersey, and continued into 1997 with a total of 127 shows.

The shows exposed Springsteen in a new way, completely by himself onstage (with Kevin Buell, stationed off stage, providing some keyboard accompaniment). It was something he had wanted to do for a while—he had considered doing a solo tour when *Tunnel of Love* was released—and *Tom Joad* was the perfect record to take on the road in a solo format. There was another *David Letterman* appearance on December 14, with the North American leg continuing through January 28, 1996. On January 14, the day after a show in Youngstown, Ohio, Springsteen met with author Dale Maharidge and photographer Michael Williamson, whose book, *Journey to Nowhere: The Saga of a New Underclass*, had inspired the songs "Youngstown" and "The New Timer" on *Tom Joad*. The two men were being filmed for a *CBS Morning News* segment on their book; Springsteen was also interviewed for the segment and later wrote forewords for a new edition of *Journey to Nowhere* and another of their books, *Someplace Like America: Tales from the New Great Depression*.

After the US leg ended, the tour headed to Europe, beginning with a February 12, 1996 date in Frankfurt, Germany. He mixed in television appearances along the way. While in San Remo, Italy, on February 20, he performed "The Ghost of Tom Joad" for Italian TV, at the same venue used for the San Remo Music Festival; three days later he performed the same song for French TV. On March 13, Bruce made his first appearance in Northern Ireland, with a show at King's Hall in Belfast. He also performed his first dates at London's prestigious Albert Hall, on April 16, 17, 22, and 27. The Euro/UK leg ended May 8. After another break, the tour picked up again stateside with a September 16 show in Pittsburgh. The most remarkable performance came on November 8, at a place Springsteen probably never expected he'd visit again: his elementary school, Saint Rose of Lima, where he'd last played in 1965 with the Castiles. Scialfa and Soozie Tyrell joined him on a number of songs, and Marion Vinyard, the wife of the Castiles' manager Tex Vinyard, was in the audience; Springsteen dedicated "This Hard Land" to her (Tex had died in 1988).

Another highlight that fall was Springsteen's appearance at a Woody Guthrie tribute concert on September 29 in Cleveland, marking the first time Springsteen performed with folk legend and activist Pete Seeger. The US leg came to an end on December 14 in Charlotte, North Carolina, and the tour continued in 1997 with a Pacific Rim tour that included four dates in Tokyo, Japan, and shows in Brisbane, Melbourne, and Sydney, Australia, from January 27 to February 17. There was also another trek through Europe, beginning with a May 6 show in Vienna, Austria. In addition to stops in familiar

Springsteen at the Wiltern Theatre in Los Angeles on November 26, 1995, during his first ever solo tour.
Bob Riha Jr/WireImage

THE GHOST OF TOM JOAD

Released: November 1995
Chart Position: No. 11 (US), No. 16 (UK)

Springsteen returned to the acoustic and thematic realms of *Nebraska* on *The Ghost of Tom Joad*. Taking up the torch from Woody Guthrie, he updated the trials and tribulations suffered by those living in Tom Joad's 1930s era of depression and brought them into the modern age, with searing results.

Tom Joad is, of course, the lead character in John Steinbeck's classic novel *The Grapes of Wrath*, and Springsteen was inspired by John Ford's 1940 film of the book as well. The album's title song is also the first track, paraphrasing Tom's famous speech to his mother about being there, in spirit, wherever people are fighting for justice. But the musical mood is somber, as it remains throughout the album.

Springsteen had never written about such desperate characters before, like Miguel and Louis in "Sinaloa Cowboys," two teenage Mexican immigrants who forgo working in the fields for the chance to make big bucks selling methamphetamine—with tragic results. "Balboa Park" also addresses the issue of immigration, this time of teenage boys whose dreams of a better life in the United States have crashed and burned, forcing them to turn to drug dealing and prostitution. At the time Springsteen was living in Los Angeles, where immigration was a hot topic in the media, and both songs were inspired by stories he read in newspapers and magazines. Balboa Park (now

named Lake Balboa Park) was just fifteen miles from where Springsteen lived a very different life in Beverly Hills. But he was also a storyteller, his songs always emphasizing the humanity of his subjects; thus, he hoped his songs of the downcast would generate empathy and compassion in the listener.

Springsteen also understood the role ambiguity plays in human nature. The ex-con in "Straight Line" toys with the idea of returning to his former criminal life but restrains himself—for now. In "Galveston Bay," an American considers killing a Vietnamese immigrant but at the last moment puts his knife away and goes home to his wife. In "The Line," two border patrol officers end up at odds when one takes up with an immigrant whose brother turns out to be a drug smuggler.

"My Best Was Never Good Enough" brings the album to a thoroughly dispirited close, with Springsteen casting feel-good homilies such as "every dog has his day" as taunts rather than inspirations. It's a kiss-off to a former love, but in this context it also comes across as a weary "goodbye and good riddance" to the sad world depicted on *Tom Joad*. Springsteen truly spoke from his heart on the album, which drove home the importance, as Joad himself would put it, of always extending that "helpin' hand."

countries like France and Italy, he also broke into new territories, playing his first shows in Poland (Warsaw, May 9) and the Czech Republic (Prague, May 12). The tour ended with a May 26 show in Paris. Bruce picked up a few more honors on the way as well, performing "The Ghost of Tom Joad" at the Grammy Awards on February 26 and taking home the Best Contemporary Folk Album award. And on May 5, while in Sweden, he received the country's Polar Music Prize from King Carl XVI Gustaf, performing "Tom Joad" and "Thunder Road" at the ceremony.

He wasn't always a winner. He attended that year's MTV Music Video Awards on September 4, 1997, at Radio City Music Hall; though "Secret Garden" lost out in the Best Video from a Film category (which went instead to Will Smith's "Men in Black"), he had a good time playing with the Wallflowers on their song "One Headlight." He was a special guest when Dylan received his Kennedy Center Honor on December 7, in Washington, DC, performing "The Times They Are a-Changin'," as Dylan looked on. Earlier in the day, he'd taken Scialfa to the Vietnam Memorial on the National Mall, where they saw the name of the Castiles' first drummer, Bart Haynes, etched into the wall.

Springsteen also made a good musical connection that would pay off in the future. For his birthday party that year, he hired a bluegrass group named the Gotham Playboys on Tyrell's recommendation. He later contacted the group about working with him on a recording of "We Shall Overcome" for the tribute album *Where Have All the Flowers Gone: The Songs of Pete Seeger*, released in 1998. It was the start of a musical collaboration that would bear more fruit in later years.

The year 1998 was also light on live performances. There were a handful of drop-ins: playing with Steve Earle and the Dukes in Sea Bright, New Jersey, on February 6; a show with Grushecky in Pittsburgh on March 2; a few songs with Clemons in West Palm Beach, Florida, on November 6. And there were other, more formal occasions. On January 22, 1998, he was filmed recording "Tom Joad" and "Across the Border" for the TV special *Where It's At: The Rolling State of the Union*, which aired on May 21.

There were various special performances as well. On January 21, Springsteen, Scialfa, and friends including Van Zandt, Southside Johnny, and Jon Bon Jovi played a benefit at the Count Basie Theatre in Red Bank, New Jersey, for the Sergeant Patrick King Memorial Fund, honoring a Long Branch police officer who had been killed the previous year. On February 7, Springsteen read a poem by Paul Lawrence Dunbar at the Count Basie Learning Center in honor of Black History Month. On April 4, he proudly performed "Oh, What a Beautiful Morning" and "Tom Joad" at a tribute show for Elaine Steinbeck, John Steinbeck's widow, at the Bay Street Theatre in Sag Harbor, New York.

Tracks

Springsteen unveiled a treasure trove of material to his fans on *Tracks*, a four-CD, sixty-six-song box set released in November 1998, with most of the material previously unreleased.

The songs go all the way back to before Springsteen even had a recording contract, beginning with four songs he recorded for an audition demo for Columbia in 1972. It's just Springsteen and his guitar; "It's Hard to Be a Saint in the City" is so compelling, you can understand why some wanted Springsteen to pursue the solo artist path and not use a rock band. Another interesting track from this early period was "Bishop Danced," from a January 31, 1973, show at Max's Kansas City.

The sprawling "Thundercrack" was originally recorded for *The Wild, the Innocent & the E Street Shuffle*. Though it didn't make the final cut, it became a live favorite, so it is fascinating to finally hear the studio version. There is also his demo for "Born in the U.S.A.," a taut and edgy number before it was transformed into a global anthem.

The following year saw the release of a sequel of sorts, *18 Tracks*, which featured three more songs not on the box. The most notable was "The Promise," a legendary outtake from *Darkness on the Edge of Town* inspired by Springsteen's lawsuit with Mike Appel. As Steve Van Zandt pointed out to *Rolling Stone*, "There's a lot going on in those lyrics. He's leaving it open as to who broke the promise."

That same month, Springsteen went through a new rite of passage when his father died, at the age of seventy-three. Father and son had long since made their peace, and Doug Springsteen lived long enough to see his grandchildren. His body was sent to his hometown of Freehold. Springsteen said in a statement, "I was lucky to have been so close to my dad as I became a man and a father myself."

Instead of releasing a new studio album, Springsteen decided to finally start going through his archive of unreleased material, which by this point in his career was huge; the website Brucebase stated that at the time it ran to more than three hundred and fifty songs—four times the number of songs that had been officially released.

So Springsteen and a team of recording engineers spent much of 1998 listening to the unreleased songs. He winnowed the songs down to sixty-six, enough for four CDs. Most tracks were simply remixed to sound a bit better, but he put on a few overdubs as well, bringing in Federici, Clemons, and even original drummer Lopez. The earliest songs were from 1972, demos of numbers that had later appeared on Springsteen's first album. There were outtakes from *The Wild, The Innocent & the E Street Shuffle, Born to Run, Darkness on the Edge of Town, The River, Nebraska, Born in the U.S.A., Tunnel of Love, Lucky Town, Human Touch,* and *Tom Joad,* as well as live songs. Songs such as "Thundercrack," which had only been performed live, were now presented in studio versions. Not all songs were previously unreleased; a number had seen official release as B-sides. The set, simply entitled *Tracks,* was released on November 10, 1998, and reached No. 27 (a follow up, *18 Tracks,* with three songs that hadn't appeared on *Tracks,* was released the following year and reached No. 64).

There was no tour in support of *Tracks.* In interviews at the time, Springsteen noted that he'd gained a new appreciation of songs he'd recorded over the years. "It was enjoyable to do now because at the time you're making those decisions, you're putting a lot of pressure on yourself," he explained when he appeared on *The Charlie Rose Show* promoting the album. "I think if you go back ten or twenty years later and you're free of that context, you can just hear the music. . . . So it was nice to go back and enjoy the stuff just for what it was."

The *Charlie Rose* appearance was one of a number of promotional appearances supporting the release of *Tracks.* In October he was filmed for a BBC documentary, *A Secret History,* which was broadcast in December. Stateside, he appeared on *Dateline* on November 19, taping the *Charlie Rose* interview the following day. In December he went overseas, appearing on a number of television shows in Europe. While in France, he also performed at an Amnesty International Foundation benefit in Paris on December 10, along with Peter Gabriel, Tracy Chapman, and Youssou N'Dour; footage from the show was later officially released, most recently in CD, DVD, and Blu-ray packages, as *Released: The Human Rights Concerts 1986–1998.*

Back home, he took part in a recording session with Mike Ness, of punk band Social Distortion, who was recording a solo album. Springsteen played guitar and provided backing vocals on the song "Misery Loves Company," which appeared on the album *Cheating at Solitaire,* released the next year.

By then, Springsteen's fans had something more exciting to anticipate. Springsteen himself had made the announcement during the *Tracks* promotional tour, on an appearance taped December 8 for the Swedish TV program *Sen kväll Med Luuk* ("Late Night with Luuk"), and confirmed it in a press release issued the same day. There was going to be a tour with Bruce Springsteen and the E Street Band.

7

THE
RISING

On March 15, 1999, Springsteen was once again in the audience at the annual Rock and Roll Hall of Fame induction ceremony, held that year at the Waldorf Astoria Hotel in New York. But this time he was the one being inducted. Bono, of U2, made the induction speech, lauding Springsteen for not behaving like a typical rock star ("He got rich and famous, but never embarrassed himself with all that success, did he?") and praising his work ethic ("Bruce has played every bar in the USA, and every stadium. Credibility—you couldn't have more, unless you were dead"). "We call him the Boss," Bono concluded. "Well, that's a bunch of crap. He's not the boss. He works *for* us. More than a boss, he's the owner, because more than anyone else, Bruce Springsteen owns America's heart."

Springsteen's own speech focused on thanking those who had played key roles in his life and career. His mother, for buying his first guitar. His father, for providing him with abundant source material. "What would I conceivably have written about without him?" Springsteen said in his speech. "I mean, you can imagine that if everything had gone great between us, we would've had disaster. I would have written just happy songs." Many from Springsteen's long career were in the audience: Marion Vinyard, who had supported Springsteen along with her husband in the days of the Castiles; Tinker West; and Mike Appel. He happily name-checked each member of the E Street Band. He played a short, four-song set with the band, unusual in that he skipped better-known songs in favor of "The Promised Land," "Backstreets," "Tenth Avenue Freeze-Out," and his perennial favorite, "In the Midnight Hour" (this time with the song's originator, Wilson Pickett, on vocals). He joined the closing all-star jam as well, alongside Paul McCartney and Billy Joel, among others, performing "What'd I Say," "People Get Ready," "Long Tall Sally," and McCartney's "Let It Be."

By the time of the induction ceremony, details of Springsteen's reunion tour with the E Street Band had been announced. The full lineup included Springsteen and Scialfa, Van Zandt, Lofgren, Clemons, Bittan, Federici, Tallent, and Weinberg. And he still managed to make time for a few outside projects before the tour began: in February, he made a video of "Give My Love to Rose" for the TV special *An All-Star Tribute to Johnny Cash* that aired on April 18 on TNT, and he sat in with the Max Weinberg 7, the house band on *Late Night with Conan O'Brien* on February 26 (Weinberg's last show before the tour). Then he dedicated himself to rehearsing with the reunited band. Two pretour rehearsals, on March 18 and 19 at Convention Hall in Asbury Park, New Jersey, were open to the public and benefitted local community centers.

The tour opened on April 9, in Barcelona, Spain, and ran for eighty-three shows. "I'm so glad to be here in your beautiful city," Springsteen told the expectant crowd. "But I want you to know that we're not here for a casual visit; we're here to rededicate you to the power, the passion, the mystery and

(previous spread)
Springsteen and Clemons during the opening night of the US leg of the "Reunion" tour on July 15, 1999, at the Continental Airlines Arena in East Rutherford, New Jersey. The "Reunion" tour reunited Springsteen with his most popular backing group, the E Street Band.
Mike Albans/NY Daily News Archive via Getty Images

the ministry of rock 'n' roll! I can't promise you life everlasting—but I can promise you life right now."

Opening the set with "My Love Will Not Let You Down," from *Tracks*, was a clear sign that Springsteen wasn't interested in basing the tour around his classics. "This tour is about rededication, rebirth," he told *Los Angeles Times* music critic Robert Hilburn at the time. "The only way we wanted to do this was to make everything feel current; to put all the music into the present to make the emotion true to right now." Hilburn, who was in the audience on opening night, felt that he'd succeeded, writing, "In a rock world filled with distasteful reunion tours, here's one that doesn't feel like a final payday, but the start of a shining new chapter." Springsteen's constant references to "rededication" and "rebirth" made it clear there would be more to come: the tour would not be a one-shot deal.

The first leg of the tour took the band around Europe and the United Kingdom. After Spain, the tour moved to Germany, then went to Italy, Austria, Switzerland, France, England, Ireland, Belgium, the Netherlands, Sweden and Denmark. A few guests dropped in, including Jon Bon Jovi, who performed "Hungry Heart" with the band during the April 28 show in Lyon, France, and Edwin Starr, who joined in on "War" during a May 16 show in Birmingham, England. Bruce's mother also came out to dance on stage when the band played Genoa,

Springsteen's 1999 "Reunion" tour began in Europe, not the United States. He's seen here in Lyon, France, on April 28, 1999. *Alexis ORAND/Gamma-Rapho via Getty Images*

Italy, on June 11. The leg ended on June 27 in Oslo, Norway. There was a two-and-a-half-week break, during which Springsteen shot a short cameo appearance for the film *High Fidelity*. The US leg began on July 15 with a record fifteen shows at Continental Airlines Arena in East Rutherford, New Jersey. On the final night in East Rutherford, Melissa Etheridge, Jon Bon Jovi, and Richie Sambora made guest appearances, and special guests turned up at a few other shows throughout the US tour as well, including Bonnie Raitt, Jackson Browne, Shawn Colvin, Mary Chapin Carpenter, Bruce Hornsby, and Sam Moore.

The US leg paused after a November 29 show in Minneapolis, Minnesota, and resumed on February 28, 2000, at Penn State University in State College, Pennsylvania. This leg of the tour found Springsteen embroiled in a controversy due to a new song he'd added to the set, "American Skin (41 Shots)." The song was about the death of Amadou Diallo, a twenty-two-year-old immigrant from the Republic of Guinea, who had been killed in New York City by the police; Diallo had been stopped because he matched the description of a rape suspect, and the police shot him when they mistook the wallet he pulled from his pocket for a gun. The four police officers, who fired a total of forty-one shots (nineteen of which hit Diallo), were charged with second-degree murder and reckless endangerment but ultimately found not guilty; the City of New York later paid the Diallo family a settlement of $3 million.

★ ★

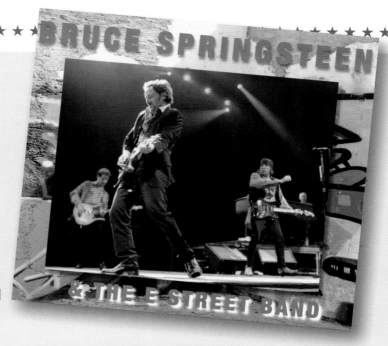

Opening Overseas

Most of Springsteen's tours opened in the United States, but on a few occasions a tour began outside of America. And one of those occasions was very special indeed.

April 9, 1999, was the first date of the E Street Band reunion tour, which Springsteen elected to kick off at Palau Sant Jordi in Barcelona, Spain (with a second show at the venue on April 11). Steve Knopper, writing in the *Journal Sentinel*, described the show as "low on experimentation and high on renewing old friendships. With Springsteen, the E Street Band's thunderous bar-and-arena rock was as tight as ever, especially on straight-forward anthems such as 'Badlands' and 'She's the One.'"

The twenty-five-song set also included "My Love Will Not Let You Down" (which opened the show), the band's origin story "Tenth Avenue Freeze-Out," "Streets of Philadelphia," and such live favorites as "Thunder Road" and "Born to Run."

Springsteen introduced the last song of the night by saying, "I want to thank everybody for coming down tonight while we got our legs underneath us tonight for the first time. This is a special night for us, these first few nights; we haven't played together in a long time. This is a rededication of our band, and the re-birth of our band, and we're here to serve you." The band then went into "Land of Hope and Dreams." For the fans who'd wondered if they'd ever see the E Streeters playing with Springsteen again, it was a night when dreams came true.

If you can't see the Boss in person, you can always see his effigy in wax. Here, a 1984-era Springsteen is seen at Madame Tussaud's Wax Museum in New York City.
Stan Godlewski/Liaison

Springsteen debuted the song at a June 4 concert in Atlanta. "I was just setting out to basically continue writing about things that I'd written about for a long period of time, which is 'Who are we? What's it mean to be an American? What's going on in the country we live in?'" Springsteen told the *Oakland Press*. In concert, the song was intense and moving, opening with each member of the band singing the line "41 shots," against a moody, subdued backing of keyboards, until Springsteen came in with the lead vocal. But when the live recording was posted online by concertgoers who had illicitly recorded the show, and the lyrics were printed in the newspapers, a furor broke out among those who felt the song was unduly critical of the police. Yet the song addressed both sides of the issue, the first verse depicting a police officer praying over Diallo's fallen body, while a later verse has a mother warning her son to watch his behavior around the police. The chorus makes the stark observation, "You can get killed just for living in your American skin."

Springsteen was on the verge of winding up the reunion tour with a ten-night stand at Madison Square Garden. But in the wake of "American Skin," Patrick Lynch, president of the Patrolman's Benevolent Association in New York, urged his fellow officers to not work security at any of the shows. Bob Lucente, president of the New York chapter of the Fraternal Order of Police,

Springsteen performing "The Rising" during the album's tour in 2002. The album was inspired by the events of 9/11. *Michael Williamson/The Washington Post/Getty Images*

declared, "Springsteen has turned into some type of fucking dirtbag. He goes on the boycott list. He has all these good songs and everything, American-flag songs and all that stuff, and now he's a floating fag, and you can quote me on that." (If nothing else, it seemed clear that Lucente had never read the lyrics of "Born in the U.S.A.") New York mayor Rudolph Giuliani stated he didn't like the implication that the police had been in the wrong, when they'd just been acquitted at trial. Dave Marsh, who attended the first concert on June 12, wrote of the show, "The Garden felt close to the edge of real violence. I was scared as hell. I don't know how Springsteen or the band felt, but when your opponents are armed and angry, just singing the song takes some guts." Springsteen, of course, had the guts, and Diallo's parents were also in attendance for that first Garden performance. Those who felt Springsteen was becoming too "politicized" were sure to be disappointed in the years ahead, as he became increasingly outspoken.

"Basically, I have faith in the songs," Springsteen said about his more controversial material in 2004. "And I also surrender to the reality that once your songs are out there, that you're simply another voice in the ongoing discussion to define them. That's just the way it plays. And that's okay—I think they're out there to be debated, some of them."

At the tour's final show, on July 1, the last song was a revamped "Blood Brothers," Springsteen adding a new final verse that looked back with gratitude at all he had shared with the E Street Band over the years. Not that he was planning to break up the brotherhood now—there would be new recording sessions with the band the following year.

But there wouldn't be many shows for a while. For the rest of 2000, Springsteen stuck close to home, performing two benefit concerts and two Christmas shows in New Jersey. The next year was the same, with a handful of drop-ins, including an unannounced appearance at Asbury Park's annual Clearwater Festival on August 18, 2001. Springsteen just showed up and asked if he could play a few songs—who was going to say no? Those who missed the festival might have been able to catch him that night, sitting in with Lofgren's band at the Stone Pony.

And then came the events of September 11. After watching the World Trade Center towers collapse on TV, Springsteen drove out to the Rumson–Sea Bright Bridge and looked across the water toward Manhattan in shock and sadness at the huge emptiness where the towers once stood. Just days later he received an unexpected appeal; after visiting the beach at Sea Bright, he returned to his car to hear a man driving by call out to him, "We need you—now!" The tragedy had hit home for Springsteen especially hard, given that a large number of the nearly three thousand people who died when the World Trade Center towers were brought down were from New Jersey.

So, fittingly, Springsteen was chosen to be the first performer on the telethon *America: A Tribute to Heroes,* which aired on September 21 (and was quickly released on CD and DVD) and raised money for victims of the disaster, and their families. The words to the song he sang, "My City of Ruins," were especially appropriate to the occasion—eerily so, considering that Springsteen had

The events of 9/11 had a profound effect on Springsteen, and he spoke with numerous people who lost loved ones on that day. *The Kansas City Star/MCT via Getty Images*

September 11, 2001

The events of September 11 had a profound impact on Springsteen. His New Jersey home was five minutes from the Rumson-Sea Bright Bridge, which offered a commanding view of the Manhattan skyline. Now that view had been changed forever. He later described how the smoke from the fallen towers remained in the sky for days.

In Monmouth County, where he lived, around one hundred and fifty people died in the attacks. "In the following weeks if you were driving towards the beach or something, if you drove by the Catholic church there was a funeral every day," he told Uncut. "I don't know what it was like in the middle of the country or on the West Coast, but here it was very real."

Springsteen played a number of benefit concerts in the wake of the tragedy. He also reached out in a more personal way. When he would read in an obituary that a person who had died in the attacks was a Springsteen fan, he made a point of calling their family, a gesture that was greatly appreciated. One of those who received a call was Stacey Farrelly, whose husband, Joe, was a captain for the New York Fire Department. "I got through Joe's memorial and a good month and a half on that call," she told *Time* magazine.

written the song in 2000 as a reflection on the deterioration of Asbury Park. (He first performed it at his two Christmas shows in Asbury Park the previous December.) On October 18 and 19 he performed at two more 9/11 benefits at the Count Basie Theatre in Red Bank, New Jersey. "This was a song that I wrote for Asbury Park," he said by way of introducing "My City of Ruins." "Songs have a way of—they go out in the world and they hopefully end up where people need them. So, I guess, this is a gift from Asbury Park to New York City in its time of need." He closed out 2001 with five Christmas shows at Convention Hall.

On January 12, 2002, Springsteen joined Clemons at his sixtieth birthday party, held at B.B. King's Night Club at the Foxwoods Resort Casino in Mashantucket, Connecticut; King himself gave the Big Man his birthday cake. Springsteen went onstage and played four songs, and King joined in on "Glory Days."

Springsteen kicking off *The Rising* tour on August 7, 2002, at the Continental Airlines Arena in East Rutherford, New Jersey. He's performed at the venue, which opened in 1981 as the Brendan Byrne Arena, more than fifty times. *Frank Micelotta/ImageDirect*

Springsteen already had more plans for the E Streeters. He had always intended to follow the tour with new studio recordings, and in the spring of 2001, Springsteen and the band recorded a number of songs, coproduced with Chuck Plotkin. But after listening to them, Springsteen decided he wanted the songs to have a more contemporary sound. Don Ienner, then chairman of Sony Music (which had purchased CBS Records in 1987), suggested Springsteen consider working with Brendan O'Brien, known for his work with Pearl Jam, Neil Young, and Rage Against the Machine, as coproducer. Springsteen agreed, and by the end of January 2002, everyone reconvened at Southern Track Studios in Atlanta, Georgia.

Springsteen worked fast; the sessions were completed by March, and O'Brien even performed on the album, playing glockenspiel and hurdy-gurdy. Springsteen had written a number of songs in the wake of 9/11, including the album's title track, "The Rising." Springsteen addressed the tragedy in human terms; "The Rising" was sung from the perspective of a firefighter arriving at the scene of the disaster, looking for a way to come to terms with the situation.

(opposite)
Springsteen with Clemons and Weinberg on December 2, 2002, at the Phillips Arena in Atlanta, Georgia, during *The Rising* tour. *Rick Diamond/WireImage*

The album was set for release in the summer, giving Springsteen time to squeeze in a few side endeavors. There was a session with Philadelphia rock band Marah in February, with Springsteen performing on the song "Float Away" for the band's *Float Away with the Friday Night Gods* album, released in June. In April, there were two benefit performances for the Rumson Country Day School at the Stone Pony. He recorded parts for two tracks on Soozie Tyrell's debut solo album, *White Lines* (2003) in May. Tyrell had played violin on *The Rising* and would be joining the E Street Band for the first time on the upcoming tour, eventually become a regular touring member.

Promotion for *The Rising* began in July 2002. Springsteen taped a performance of "Empty Sky" at his home in Colts Neck, New Jersey, for *Nightline*, which aired on July 30, the day of the album's release. He also made a live appearance on the *Today* show July 30, performing four songs with the band. August 1 saw a return to *David Letterman*, with a performance of "The Rising" shown that day and "Lonesome Day" broadcast the day after. A number of rehearsals were also open to the public before the tour officially began on August 7, in East Rutherford, New Jersey.

The Rising topped the chart in the United States, as well as the United Kingdom and Canada. The singles didn't perform as strongly; the title track, released in mid-July, reached No. 52, and "Lonesome Day," released in early December, only charted on *Billboard*'s Adult Top 40 chart at No. 36 (a third single, "Waitin' on a Sunny Day," was only released overseas). But the album nonetheless went on to sell three million copies.

The tour continued for over a year, with a total of 120 shows—one of Springsteen's longest tours. First came the US leg, which included a stop on August 29 for an appearance on the MTV Video Music Awards, held at the Hayden Planetarium in New York. The band played a ten-song set outside, despite the rain. On October 4, Springsteen spoke at the dedication ceremony of a bridge in Boston named after civil rights activist Lenny Zakim and performed an acoustic version of "Thunder Road." He dedicated "My Hometown" to Zakim at his show at the Fleet Center that night and later welcomed Peter Wolf as a special guest for an encore performance of the Standells' "Dirty Water." The following evening, Springsteen and the band performed "Lonesome Day" and "You're Missing" on *Saturday Night Live*.

The US leg ended two nights later in Buffalo. After a week's break, a short European and UK tour began on October 14 in Paris. The October 16 show in Barcelona was broadcast live on VH1 in Europe and later released on the DVD *Live in Barcelona*. Springsteen was back in the States by the end of the month, working in an appearance at the third annual Light of Day benefit concert for the Parkinson's Disease

2002 *Springsteen: Troubadour of the Highway* traveling exhibit, program, curated by the Weisman Art Museum, Minneapolis, Minnesota

THE
RISING

Released: July 2002
Chart Position: No. 1 (US), No. 1 (UK)

The Rising was a highly emotional album for Springsteen. It was not only the first studio album he had recorded with the full E Street Band since *Tunnel of Love*, over a decade earlier, but also his response to the events of September 11, 2001.

Not all of the songs were written after the attacks. "My City of Ruins," which Springsteen performed on the *America: A Tribute to Heroes* telethon, was written the previous year about hard economic times in Asbury Park. But the lyrics, about the "blood red circle" on the "cold dark ground," now had a new resonance. One could easily imagine Springsteen performing it in the solo acoustic fashion of *Nebraska* or *The Ghost of Tom Joad*. But the use of the full band (and, as on this song, a choir) gave a greater richness to the material.

Some songs were written in direct response to the tragedy, but they weren't specific to September 11; they had a universal appeal. The opening track, "Lonesome Day," touches on the new emptiness in your life when a loved one is gone, as does "You're Missing," with its heartbreaking lines about there being "too much room in my bed." "Empty Sky" follows the same lines. The songs reflect the spirit of the 9/11 event but invite anyone who has suffered loss inside too.

"Into the Fire" was inspired by the firefighters and emergency workers who arrived at Ground Zero and fearlessly entered the inferno to help others. Its stirring musical backing builds up the nobility of the impending sacrifice. The edgy "The Fuse" evokes the tense days after the attacks.

One of the most intriguing songs is "Paradise," sung from the perspective of a suicide bomber. This dreamy number could almost be a love song, were it not for the references to backpacks, plastic, and wire. "Worlds Apart" is an attempt at building bridges, using a guest performance from Pakistani musician Asif Ali Khan and his band as a backdrop for the story of an interfaith couple.

There are some lighter moments on the album. The singer of the upbeat "Waitin' on a Sunny Day" misses his loved one and awaits her return; its bright beat made it a live favorite. The soulful "Let's Be Friends (Skin to Skin)," a plea to a prospective new love, has a lazy swing that makes it a natural for the dance floor. And "Further On (Up the Road")" is a raver tailor-made for the reformed E Street Band (not to mention a promise of future touring).

The album's title track is a majestic piece of work. The song's narrator is a firefighter climbing the stairs of one of the towers—or is he rising into heaven? Is the Mary he sees in the garden a loved one on earth or a vision of the Blessed Virgin? Whatever you conclude, the chorus swelling at the end makes this a song about rising above the most difficult of circumstances.

Springsteen, Scialfa, and Van Zandt rehearsing for the Grammy Awards on February 23, 2003, at Madison Square Garden. He'd win three Grammys during the ceremony, including Best Rock Album for *The Rising*. *KMazur/WireImage*

Foundation on November 2 at the Tradewinds in Sea Bright, New Jersey, before a second US leg began the following night in Dallas. There was a tense moment at a November 16 concert in Greensboro, North Carolina, when Springsteen fell on a ramp onstage and cut his arm, but he recovered quickly and continued the show; a few other dates were rescheduled when Clemons needed emergency eye surgery. Emmylou Harris turned up for the November 19 date in Birmingham, Alabama, to sing "My Hometown" with Springsteen, while Bono and Eurythmics' Dave Stewart were brought on during the November 23 show in Miami to join in on "Because the Night." There was a holiday break after a December 17 show in Indianapolis. Springsteen also found time during the month to contribute to "Disorder in the House" and "Prison Grove," two tracks on Warren Zevon's last album, *The Wind* (2003).

Springsteen's first shows of 2003 were benefit performances for *Double Take* magazine on February 19 and 20 at the Somerville Theatre in Somerville, Massachusetts. In a show billed as an "Intimate Evening of Conversation and Music," he shared stories about how he wrote his songs and took questions from the audience—"like hearing Springsteen interviewed by himself," in Dave Marsh's words. February 23 was Grammy night, at Madison Square Garden, and Springsteen performed the Clash's "London Calling" with Van Zandt, Foo Fighters lead singer/guitarist (and former Nirvana drummer) Dave Grohl, and Elvis Costello, in tribute to the band's lead singer and guitarist, Joe Strummer, who had died the previous December. He also performed "The Rising," which ended up winning Grammys for Best Rock Song and Best Male Rock Vocal Performance, while the album itself won Best Rock Album.

Bruce Springsteen and the E Street Band Summer Tour 2003, pennant

By the time *The Rising* tour resumed on February 28, 2003, in Duluth, Georgia, the United States was on the verge of war with Iraq; the invasion officially began on March 19. Springsteen had regularly addressed the topic during his shows, as when he introduced "Born in the U.S.A." by stating, "I originally wrote this song about the Vietnam War. I want to play it tonight as a prayer for peace." He later began opening shows with an acoustic version of the song to make its antiwar message more explicit. And he took pains to talk about a line in the *Rising* song "Empty Sky" that went "I want an eye for an eye," which he felt was being misinterpreted. "I wrote that phrase as an expression of the character's anger and confusion and grief," he said during a show in Atlantic City on March 7. "It was never written to be a call for blind revenge or bloodlust. . . . Living in a time when there's real lives on the line and there's enough destructive posing going on out there as it is, I wanted to make sure that that line was clearly understood."

The second US leg ended March 11 in Rochester, New York, after which the band headed down under for five dates in Australia and New Zealand, beginning March 20. During a break before the next European tour, Springsteen fit in a handful of side performances. On April 29, the Count Basie Theatre in Red Bank, New Jersey, hosted the "The Hope Concert," benefiting Robert Bandiera Jr., the son of its house band leader, local musician Bobby Bandiera, a friend of Springsteen's. Jon Bon Jovi (another friend of Bandiera's), Southside Johnny, and Gary U.S. Bonds performed as well. On April 30, Springsteen and Scialfa were among the performers at a Rumson Country Day School benefit at the Stone Pony, an event they'd regularly return to in the coming years. They returned to the Pony on May 2 for the record release party of Tyrell's solo album, *White Lines*, which Springsteen and Scialfa had each performed on, and they joined Tyrell onstage for two songs.

Another European leg began on May 6 in Rotterdam, the Netherlands, taking in Germany, Belgium, Spain, France, England, Ireland, Denmark,

Norway, and Sweden, as well as Bruce's first dates in Finland, with shows in Helsinki on June 16 and 17. Throughout the tour Jon Landau displayed his own heretofore undiscovered musical abilities by coming out on occasion to play guitar. There were a few personal moments; while in Florence, Italy, on June 8, "Tougher than the Rest" was played in honor of Bruce and Patti's anniversary, and Nils Lofgren got a surprise during a Gothenburg, Sweden, show on June 21 when the audience began singing "Happy Birthday" to him. Part of the June 25 show in Vienna, Austria, was also broadcast on TV. The leg's final date was June 28 in Milan, Italy. After a few weeks, the final US leg began on July 15, starting with a seven-night stand at Giants Stadium in East Rutherford. Springsteen's former drummer, Vini Lopez, met with him prior to the show on the July 21. Lopez had formed a band called Steel Mill Retro and was shopping a new demo of songs; as the songs had all been written by Springsteen, he wanted to get his approval. Meeting Springsteen backstage, Lopez got a hug from his former bandleader and a thumbs-up on the demo. Then came a surprise. "Hey, I've got a question I want to ask you," Springsteen said. "Are you ready to play one tonight?" A stunned Lopez agreed and later played on "Spirit in the Night." "That was something, going back to play," he told the *New York Times.* "Giants Stadium, never expected that. All those years, that was the first time I played with them in 30 years."

That wasn't the only run of shows at Giants Stadium that summer. Springsteen returned to the venue on August 28 for another three shows, with Emmylou Harris a special guest on August 30, singing "Across the Border." The tour closed with three nights, October 1, 3, and 4, at Shea Stadium in New York. The final night was the longest show of the tour and featured a number of special guests. First, Dylan came out to sing "Highway 61 Revisited." "When I was growing up in my little town, he just made me think big thoughts," Springsteen said afterward. "His music really empowered me and got me thinking about the world outside of my own little town." Gary U.S. Bonds was on hand for "Quarter to Three," joined by Landau, producer Brendan O'Brien, and even Sony Music VP Don Ienner on a medley of "Twist and Shout"/"La Bamba."

Springsteen had been making more political statements during his shows, and this night was no exception. In dedicating "Land of Hope and Dreams" to Dylan, Springsteen went on to say, "It's a time right now in our country when there's a lot of questions in the air about the forthrightness of our government. Playing with the truth during wartime has been a part of both Democratic and Republican administrations in the past, and once again the lives of our sons and our daughters are on the line. So it's a good time to be good, vigilant citizens, and protecting the democracy we ask our sons and our daughters to die for is our sacred trust. Demanding accountability from our leaders, and taking our time to search out the truth, that's the American way."

(opposite)
Springsteen in front of a Union Jack during rehearsals for the Grammy Awards on February 23, 2003. The British flag was in reference to a special segment honoring the British punk musician Joe Strummer, who'd died the previous year. *M. Caulfield/WireImage*

DEVILS
&DUST

Released: April 2005
Chart Position: No. 1 (US), No. 1 (UK)

"These are all songs about people whose souls are in danger, or at risk, through where they are in the world and what the world is bringing to them," was Springsteen's description of his thirteenth album. The record was seen as a response to George W. Bush's reelection in 2004, a bitter disappointment to Springsteen, who had endorsed Democratic candidate Senator John Kerry. However, most of the songs were written and recorded back in the 1990s, with new overdubs giving them a more modern punch.

It's another largely acoustic album, closer to The Ghost of Tom Joad than Nebraska in its instrumentation (the only E Streeters on the album are Danny Federici and Patti Scialfa). The opening song is the title track, a newer number updating Springsteen's catalog of songs about soldiers at war with a reflective piece inspired by America's conflict in Iraq (which began in March 2003). The soldier in the song wrestles with a troubling question: what if a war, however righteous, taints your soul forever?

"All the Way Home" is Springsteen's rollicking take on a number he originally gave to Southside Johnny. Its sweet sentiments are thrown into sharp relief by the next number, "Reno," in which the narrator recounts a sexual encounter with a prostitute, ending with a world-weary "It wasn't the best I ever had."

"Long Time Comin'" lightens the mood, its bright beat underscoring the happiness of the narrator as he heads home to his loved one. The theme of life's gifts is also key to "Maria's Bed," the gentle "Leah," and the pulsating swing of "All I'm Thinkin' About."

For a change, this album looks at relationships between mothers and sons: the disintegrating connection in "Black Cowboys" (with its subtle oedipal undercurrent), the poignant separation of "Silver Palomino," and the sorrow of Mary in the resonant hymn "Jesus Was an Only Son."

Springsteen's songs often have a cinematic quality, and that's certainly true of "The Hitter," a story of a failed boxer who returns home, begging his mother for a place to "lie down for a while"; it reads like a draft for an independent movie.

The album ends with the striking "Matamoras Banks." It's the story of a man who drowns trying to cross the Rio Grande, told in reverse, opening with the description of his floating body and then working back to his farewells to his loved one prior to her successful crossing of the river. It's a fitting conclusion for an album depicting human struggles in troubled times, balanced by a few moments of hope poking through. The album was also released in a dual-disc format, with an audio CD on one side and a DVD featuring performances of five songs on the other.

The night ended on an emotional note with the same closing song as the last E Street Band tour, "Blood Brothers."

Springsteen kicked back for the rest of the year. He joined Grushecky's band for another Light of Day benefit, at the Stone Pony on November 1, and played a benefit for the Muscular Dystrophy Association on November 8 in Aberdeen, New Jersey. Three Christmas shows at Convention Hall in Asbury Park, on December 5, 7, and 8, benefited the Asbury Park High School band and featured plenty of guests, from regulars such as Southside Johnny and Van Zandt, to Bandiera, Moore, Jesse Malin, and the Asbury Park–based Victorious Gospel Choir.

Springsteen also had an album out in time for the holidays: the three-CD compilation *The Essential Bruce Springsteen*. In a nice bonus for the fans, the third disc compiled rarities and live tracks. Springsteen also did recording sessions—for other people. He contributed backing vocals to Jerry Lee Lewis's cover of "Pink Cadillac," which later appeared on the terrific duets album *Last Man Standing* (2006). In 2004, he worked on Scialfa's second solo album,

The Rising tour ended with three shows at Shea Stadium in October 2003. *Mark Von Holden/FilmMagic*

The Essential Bruce Springsteen, released
November 11, 2003

23rd Street Lullaby, as well as on tracks for Gary U.S. Bonds's *Back in 20* album, both records released later in the year. There were two prerelease shows for Scialfa's album at the Hit Factory in New York on April 18, with Springsteen joining his wife on two numbers: a live recording of "As Long As I (Can Be With You)" appeared on initial pressings of her album.

Springsteen had few other performances during the first part of the year. During Jackson Browne's show at the Beacon Theatre in New York on March 16 he performed "Take It Easy," and he played another Rumson Country Day School benefit at the Stone Pony on April 25. In September, he made guest appearances at three of Scialfa's shows promoting her album, including one at the Roxy in L.A., where he hadn't played since 1978.

He also began work on his next album, *Devils & Dust*, which was largely drawn from previously recorded material in his archives, given new overdubs and polished up by O'Brien. Springsteen later revealed that after the *Rising* tour he had begun taking antidepressants and found them hugely beneficial. It certainly increased his productivity; over the next five years, he would release four studio albums, something he hadn't managed since the 1970s. But *Devils & Dust* was not released until the next year, for Springsteen had another item on his agenda in 2004: the presidential election.

Taking a bigger step into politics than he had before, Springsteen agreed to sign on for the Vote for Change tour, which ran October 1 through 13. Instead of a single roster of artists going out on tour, different packages of acts performed in different cities: Bruce Springsteen and the E Street Band shared the bill with R.E.M., John Fogerty, and indie band Bright Eyes. Other artists on Vote for Change tours included Bonnie Raitt, Pearl Jam, the Dixie Chicks, and Neil Young.

Springsteen was the headliner, but he was involved throughout the show, introducing the bands and joining R.E.M. in performing "Man on the Moon" and other songs during their set. Springsteen's own set began with "The Star Spangled Banner," played on acoustic guitar, followed by an equally stripped-down "Born in the U.S.A." Fogerty came out to sing during the set, including on his own, pointed song "Fortunate Son," and R.E.M.'s Michael Stipe sang "Because the Night" with the band. At the set's end, all the performers came out to sing "(What's So Funny 'bout) Peace Love and Understanding" and Patti Smith's call to arms, "People Have the Power."

Springsteen's seven dates closed on October 13 at the Continental Airlines Arena in East Rutherford, New Jersey, with Scialfa doing a solo set and Jackson Browne and Pearl Jam performing during Springsteen's set. With New Jersey considered a swing state, Springsteen teased the audience about their supposed indecision: "If you're swinging, if you're swanging, if you're sweeping, if you're swooping, if you're switching, if you just can't decide—if you wanna be even temporarily released from the burdens of the Republicanism, you can be saved right now!"

The Vote for Change tour wasn't meant to be strictly partisan, as the main intention was getting people registered to vote. However, given that the tour was put together by progressive advocacy group MoveOn.org, and that people were encouraged to vote for "change" instead of supporting the incumbent, President George W. Bush, it was decidedly left-leaning. Springsteen's own comments during the shows made that clear, and he decided to taken an even bigger step by publicly endorsing the Democratic contender, Senator John Kerry, whom he had first met when playing a Vietnam Veterans of America benefit in L.A. back in 1981.

It marked the first time Springsteen had endorsed a presidential candidate. "I stayed a step away from partisan politics because I felt it was always important to have an independent voice," he had told Ted Koppel during his *Nightline* appearance in August. "I wanted my fans to feel like they could trust that. But you build up credibility. And you build it up for a reason over a long period of time. And hopefully, we've built up that credibility with our audience. And there comes a time when you feel, all right, I've built this up and it's time to spend some of this." He didn't mind that his new outspokenness might cost him fans, telling Koppel that people would sometimes boo when he played "American Skin." "The audience aren't lemmings," he said. "They come to you for resource and inspiration. And sometimes they'll come and maybe you'll make them angry or you'll disappoint them or you'll excite them. And that's how I see my job."

He also told *Rolling Stone* publisher Jann Wenner that the Iraq war had been the tipping point for his involvement in the election: "I felt we had been misled. I felt [the Bush administration] had been fundamentally dishonest and had frightened and manipulated the American people into war." He felt the

Springsteen in Washington, DC, on October 11, 2004, during the "Vote for Change" tour. His involvement in the tour was the first step in his becoming more politically outspoken. *Theo Wargo/WireImage*

issue of war more keenly now that his own children were old enough to serve in the military.

Springsteen appeared at four of Kerry's rallies, starting on October 28 in Madison, Wisconsin, and continuing to Columbus, Ohio; Miami, Florida; and, on the eve of the election, Cleveland, Ohio. In Cleveland he performed "The Promised Land" and "No Surrender," which was also the theme song for Kerry's campaign. At the last rally he added "Thunder Road" to the set list, dedicating it to Kristen Breitweiser, a fellow New Jerseyite and a 9/11 widow, whom he'd met that night. He gave a short stump speech of his own at each rally before Kerry was brought on, making Springsteen's dreams for America explicit in a way he'd never done before:

I've written about America for thirty years. I've tried to write about who we are, what we stand for, what we fight for, and I believe that these essential ideals of American identity are what's at stake on November second: the human principles of economic justice, just healing the sick, health care, feeding the hungry, housing the homeless, a living wage so folks don't have to break their backs and still not make ends meet, the protection of our environment, a sane and responsible foreign policy, civil rights and the protection and safeguarding of our precious democracy here at home. And I believe that Senator Kerry honors these ideals.

President Bush was reelected on November 2, but Springsteen didn't have time to get too discouraged; he was back at the Stone Pony on November 6, performing at the annual Light of Day benefit concert as a member of Grushecky's band. On December 12 he teamed up with Grushecky again at the Concert for Flood Aid in Pittsburgh, Pennsylvania, benefiting victims of Hurricane Ivan. On December 19 he held two Christmas shows at Harry's Roadhouse in Asbury Park, with speakers set up outside the venue to allow the overflow crowds to hear the fun.

In 2005, Springsteen planned to take another break from the E Street Band. But it was not long before he was in front of an audience again. He had finished

Springsteen had never endorsed a presidential candidate before 2004, when he came out in support of Senator John Kerry. He joined Kerry at a number of rallies during his campaign, including one at Ohio State University on October 28 in Columbus, Ohio. *Justin Sullivan/Getty Images*

most of the work on *Devils & Dust* before heading out on the Vote for Change tour. In January 2005, after a few final touches, the album was ready to go. The title track was the most recent, a somber depiction of the Iraq war. Other songs were drawn from the archives. "Long Time Coming" and "It's the Little Things That Count" were originally recorded for *Tom Joad*. "Reno," "The Hitter," and "All I'm Thinkin' About" were from the 1990s. "All the Way Home" dated from 1990; Springsteen had first given it to Southside Johnny, who recorded it for his 1991 album *Better Days*, and then made his own recording in the late 1990s. Despite the songs' decade-long span, *Rolling Stone* found the album "as immediate and troubling as this morning's paper."

It was also a solo album after the fashion of *Nebraska* and *Tom Joad*, albeit with more instrumentation. After initially rehearsing with more musicians, Springsteen decided to go out as he had on the *Tom Joad* tour, performing alone onstage while Buell (percussion) and Alan Fitzgerald (piano, synthesizer) played their parts offstage. Springsteen also showed off his multi-instrumental skills by playing not just acoustic and electric guitar, but also harmonica, piano (including electric piano), pump organ, and the ukulele.

Springsteen at the Fox Theater in Detroit, Michigan, on April 25, 2005, on the *Devils & Dust* solo tour. He'd been nervous on his first solo tour, but found he enjoyed the experience and didn't hesitate to tour solo again. *Robert Gauthier/Los Angeles Times via Getty Images*

(opposite)
Springsteen played two nights at London's historic Royal Albert Hall during the *Devils & Dust* solo tour, in May 2005. © *Brandon/Redferns*

Springsteen spent most of the first part of the year in rehearsal. But there was always time for the Rock and Roll Hall of Fame induction appearance, this year at the Waldorf Astoria on March 5. Springsteen inducted U2, saying of the band, "They are both a step forward and direct descendants of the great bands who believed rock music could shake things up in the world, dared to have faith in their audience, who believed if they played their best it would bring out the best in you." He later joined them onstage, performing "I Still Haven't Found What I'm Looking For."

On April 4 he taped a show for *VH1 Storytellers* before a live audience at the Rechnitz Theater in Red Bank, with a Q&A session following the eight-song set. (Scialfa joined him on "Brilliant Disguise.") And then it was time for Springsteen to take the stage as a headliner once again.

8

JESUS
WAS
AN ONLY
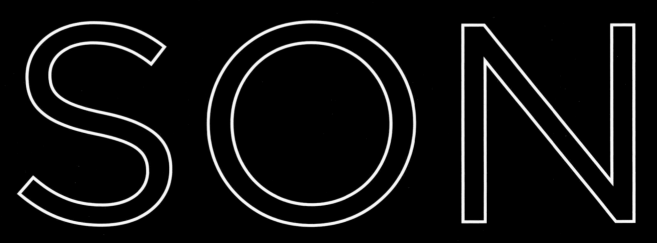

The first single issued from *Devils & Dust* was the title track, released on March 28, 2005, which peaked at a lowly No. 72. The album followed on April 25 and topped the charts. There was some controversy after the album was pulled from the shelves of Starbucks coffee stores, ostensibly due to its profanity, though sources told *Newsweek* the real reason was that the coffee chain had hoped to do a promotional tie-in with Springsteen and were turned down. Either way, the ban had little effect, as the album eventually sold more than a million copies.

After two public rehearsals on April 21 and 22 at Asbury Park's Paramount Theatre (benefiting World Hunger Year and assorted local charities), the *Devils & Dust* tour proper began on April 25, at the Fox Theatre in Detroit, Michigan, the first of seventy-two shows. The stage had a minimal set, decorated with a carpet, a lamp, and two chandeliers, with subdued lighting. A handout distributed to attendees emphasized the formal nature of the performance: it gave notice that latecomers would not be seated while the songs were being played and the concessions stand would be closed ten minutes before the concert, among other deviations from the rock norm. Although the handout stated that the show was a "solo acoustic performance," that wasn't strictly the case—performances included electric guitar, electric piano, and synthesizer. Springsteen also injected a new sonic quality into his music by using a special "bullet" microphone to distort his vocal on songs such as "Reason to Believe." As usual, he reached deep into his catalog, performing not only reworked versions of well-known songs such as "The River" and "Backstreets," but also such rarities as "Zero and Blind Terry" and "Song for

(previous spread)
Springsteen on the *Today* show on September 28, 2007, promoting his latest album, *Magic. Al Pereira/ WireImage/Getty Images*

The opening night of the "Vote for Change" tour, October 1, 2004, at the Wachovia Center in Philadelphia. The shows ended with all the acts coming onstage to sing a cover of Patti Smith's "People Have the Power." *Scott Gries/Getty Images*

Orphans," neither of which had been performed live for more than thirty years. Many shows closed with a most unusual choice: Springsteen accompanying himself on pump organ in a cover of Suicide's "Dream Baby Dream," a ghostly number that wouldn't have been out of place in David Lynch's *Twin Peaks.*

The first US leg ended May 20 in Boston; four days later, the UK/European leg began with a performance in Dublin, Ireland. That was followed by two shows at the Royal Albert Hall in London, as well as shows in Madrid, Spain; Rome, Italy; Copenhagen, Denmark, and Paris, France, among other places. The final date was a June 28 show in Berlin, Germany. During the show, a young girl came onstage to give Bruce some flowers; "I owe the little girl 20 dollars now," he joked. After Springsteen's first-ever appearance in Iceland on June 30, there was a two-week break before arena leg of the tour picked up in North America on July 13 with a date in Ottawa, Ontario. On a night off, Springsteen and Scialfa joined U2's show on October 17 in Philadelphia, coming onstage to perform "People Get Ready" with the band. Bruce Hornsby was a guest on "Across the Border" at Springsteen's November 11 show in Norfolk, Virginia, and Van Zandt and Clemens joined Springsteen on a few numbers when the tour hit Hollywood, Florida. The tour's final date was a November 11 show in Trenton, New Jersey, with Springsteen's family, wearing Santa hats, joining him in singing "Santa Claus Is Comin' to Town."

There were no more shows for the rest of the year. Springsteen would be back with a new album less than a year later, the shortest time between studio releases since his first and second albums. In the meantime, for the holiday season, a thirtieth-anniversary edition of *Born to Run* was released, including a remastered version of the album and two DVDs, one with a documentary on the making of the album and the second featuring his November 18, 1975, concert debut in London (the latter DVD was released on its own the following year). November also saw the launch of the program *E Street Radio* on the Sirius Satellite Radio network, broadcasting interviews and rarities through the end of January 2006.

At London's Royal Albert Hall during the *Devils & Dust* solo tour. The shows ended with a riveting cover of Suicide's "Dream Baby Dream." *Jo Hale/Getty Images*

By then, Springsteen had nearly finalized his upcoming album, *We Shall Overcome: The Seeger Sessions*. The seed for the album had been planted in 1997 when he worked with the Gotham Playboys on a track for the Seeger tribute album *Where Have All the Flowers Gone.* "We Shall Overcome" was the track that was ultimately chosen, but Springsteen had recorded five other songs with the musicians as well. In 2004, while considering putting out another collection of unreleased songs, he listened again to the Gotham Playboys session for possible material for that project. As he and Landau played the songs, they came up with another idea: create a full album along the same lines.

Springsteen got in touch with the Gotham Playboys, and two further sessions were held (and filmed) on March 19, 2005, and January 21, 2006. The album was to feature songs popularized by Seeger. "I don't know any other single performer who has put his hands on so many disparate kinds of music," Springsteen told Marsh. He was also keen that the songs not be presented as museum pieces. "It was: how do I make this very, very present?" he explained. "How do I make these characters leap off the record and make them sit, or dance, or sing in your living room? . . . what's gonna be exciting to play, and fun to sing and to people cut loose on, you know? That was my main criteria."

There was time for a few performances and other projects before the album's tour began. On February 6 Springsteen performed at an L.A. benefit for MusiCares, the charity arm of the National Academy of Recording Arts and Sciences, the organization that puts on the Grammy Awards. Two days later Springsteen appeared at the Grammy ceremony at the Staples Center, performing "Devils & Dust" and joining in an all-star rendition of "In the Midnight Hour" with Bonnie Raitt, Sam Moore, and Elvis Costello, among others, in honor of Wilson Pickett, who had died in January. That same month, Springsteen recorded vocals and guitar for the track "Better to Have and Not Need," which would appear on Moore's *Overnight Sensation* album, and worked with Grushecky on his album *A Good Life*, both records released later in the year.

Springsteen then began rehearsing for the upcoming tour. Nearly all of the musicians who performed on the Seeger album became members of what was dubbed "the Sessions Band," embellished by additional horns. The touring group also featured both of Scialfa's former Trickster bandmates, Tyrell on violin and backing vocals and Lowell on backing vocals. The album was released on April 25 and reached No. 3, though sales were slow and it failed to reach platinum status on its initial release. A later edition of the album featured live versions of "Bring 'Em Home" (with new lyrics by Springsteen), "How Can a Poor Man Stand Such Times," and "American Land."

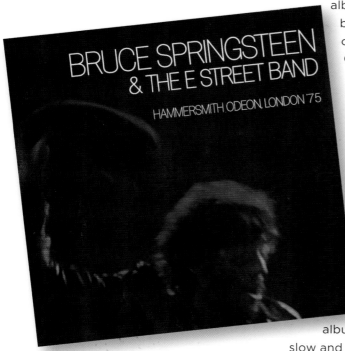

Hammersmith Odeon London '75, released
February 28, 2006

WE SHALL OVERCOME

THE SEEGER SESSIONS

Released: April 2006
Chart Position: No. 3 (US), No. 3 (UK)

W*e Shall Overcome* is, hands down, the most joyous record Springsteen has ever made. As he himself put it in the album's liner notes, "I counted off the opening chords to 'Jesse James' and away we went."

The album's title refers to Pete Seeger, the legendary folk musician and political activist. As a member of the politically progressive folk act the Weavers and as a solo artist, Pete reintroduced America to its musical heritage, popularizing the work of musicians such as Lead Belly and Woody Guthrie.

"We Shall Overcome" was strongly associated with the Civil Rights movement of the 1960s, and in that sense the album could be considered a "political" record. But it was hardly a dry and earnest one; Springsteen wasn't interested in delivering a history lesson. The lively "Jesse James" recasts the famed outlaw as a Robin Hood–esque hero, shamefully gunned down by "that dirty little coward" Robert Ford. "John Henry," the story of a man fighting against being replaced by a machine, is far more raucous than the version you sang around the fire at summer camp. And Springsteen's hearty take on "Froggie Went a-Courtin'" will have you wishing he would attempt a full-length children's record.

Sadly, war-themed songs have been relevant throughout human history, and the Irish-influenced "Mrs. McGrath" recounts the high cost of war when a wounded son is brought home to his mother. "Pay Me My Money Down" and "Erie Canal" are songs of labor and toil, about the kind of steadfast work ethic—and its accompanying challenges—that helped build the United States.

Having used biblical imagery in his own songs, it's no surprise that Springsteen was drawn to similar folk numbers. "O Mary Don't You Weep," which opens with a violin line before the horns come in, is a jazzy celebration of Moses vanquishing Egypt's Pharaoh that can be read as conquering any kind of hardship. Similarly, "Jacob's Ladder" refers to the ladder bridging heaven and earth, emphasizing the strength one gains in rising to meet a challenge. "Eyes on the Prize" is another call to keep fighting the good fight, with a promise of heaven in the last verse.

"My Oklahoma Home" could be a prequel to *The Grapes of Wrath*, a surprisingly upbeat song about why the "Okies" had to strike out for fresh territory. "Shenandoah," the album's most languid track, tells how a sailing captain spirited away a Native American chief's daughter. And "Old Dan Tucker" is just for fun, a terrific toe-tapper that sets the mood for the rest of the album. On the whole, Springsteen just kicks back and has fun, making these folk numbers as vibrant as any rock 'n' roll song.

Be sure to pick up the "American Land" edition of the album, released in October 2006, which has five bonus tracks.

Springsteen in Paris on May 10, 2006, during the *Seeger Sessions* tour. *JEAN AYISSI/AFP/Getty Images*

(opposite)
A dramatically lit Springsteen during the Grammy Awards on February 8, 2006. Springsteen performed "Devils & Dust" and joined in an all-star rendition of "In the Midnight Hour," honoring the late Wilson Pickett. *TIMOTHY A. CLARY/AFP/Getty Images*

The outtake "Hobo's Lullaby" was given to Seeger, who recorded a new vocal and banjo for the track, and later released on the charity compilation *Give US Your Poor* (2007); Seeger also added vocals to a new version of "Tom Joad" that Springsteen recorded in 2006; it later appeared on the charity compilation *Sowing the Seeds* (2007).

There were four public rehearsals at Convention Hall in Asbury Park, on April 20 and 24 through 26; on April 25, the band appeared on *Good Morning America*. The tour's opening date was a set at the New Orleans Jazz & Heritage Festival on April 30, 2006. The city was still recovering from the devastation of Hurricane Katrina the previous August, and Springsteen noted during the show that he'd taken a tour of the city the previous day. "I think I saw sights I never thought I'd see in an American city," he told the crowd. "The criminal ineptitude makes you feel furious; this is what happens when political cronyism cuts the very agencies that are supposed to serve American citizens in times of trial and hardship. This is what happens when people play political games with other people's lives." He went on to introduce his next song, Blind Alfred Reed's "How Can a Poor Man Stand Such Times and Live?," by explaining that Reed "recorded it the week after the stock market crash that preceded the Great Depression. I kept the first verse and I wrote three

Performing "Devils & Dust" at the Grammy Awards on February 8, 2006. *L. Cohen/WireImage for The Recording Academy/Getty Images*

more. This is for New Orleans tonight—dedicated to President 'Bystander'"—a scathing reference to President Bush.

"Perhaps no song was as bittersweet as 'We Shall Overcome,'" an Associated Press reporter wrote of the show. "As Springsteen somberly performed the tune, some people embraced each other, others dabbed their eyes. Another emotional moment came as he dedicated one of his old tunes to New Orleans: 'My City in Ruins' [*sic*]. Though he wrote it for his favorite town of Asbury Park, N.J., its lyrics resonated with the crowd." The reviewer also noted that not all of the show was as "downbeat; his huge band at times sounded like a boisterous New Orleans brass band, with its booming horn system, while he later injected some boogie and swing."

Springsteen made a quick detour back to the Stone Pony on May 2 for the annual Rumson Country Day School benefit (backed by Bobby Bandiera's band) before the Sessions Tour headed overseas for a May 5 show in Dublin. After dates in England (with part of a May 9 show broadcast on television), the tour moved to the continent, with shows in Milan, Italy (May 12), Amsterdam, Netherlands (May 16), Frankfurt, Germany (May 17), and closing in Stockholm, Sweden, on May 21. A full US leg began on May 27 in Mansfield, Massachusetts, and ended on June 25 in Holmdel, New Jersey. While in Oslo, Norway, on May 18, Springsteen recorded a new vocal for the track "Bring 'Em Home," which was released as a download single in June.

Springsteen took most of the summer off. He participated in a benefit for the Ranney School (based in Tinton Falls, New Jersey), at the Stone Pony, and contributed to the track "Broken Radio" on Jesse Malin's album *Glitter in the Gutter* (2007); he also appeared in the song's video. At his home studio he recorded a track, "Once Upon a Time in the West," that later appeared on the 2007 compilation *We All Love Ennio Morricone*. Touring recommenced on October 1, with a date in Bologna, Italy. Songs from his three-night return to Dublin, November 17 through 19, were compiled into the CD and DVD releases *Live in Dublin* and released the following year. After fifty-six shows, the tour came to an end on November 21 in Belfast, Northern Ireland. That left just two more performances in 2006, a December 2 appearance with Grushecky at that year's Light of Day benefit concert in Sayreville, New Jersey, and Bandiera's All-Star Holiday Concert at the Count Basie Theatre on December 12.

Live performances were also rare in 2007. Springsteen was guest of honor at a Music for Youth benefit, "Celebrating the Music of Bruce Springsteen," held at Carnegie Hall on April 5; Jewel, Steve Earle, and Pete Zorn were among those on the bill, and Springsteen himself performed a few songs. There was another Ranney School benefit on April 29 at the Stone Pony. On May 5, he sat in with Brian Wilson, who was headlining a Count Basie Theatre Foundation benefit in Red Bank, New Jersey, playing guitar on "Barbara Ann"

In Manheim, Germany, on December 2, 2007, during the European leg of the *Magic* tour. Though Springsteen initially made few overseas appearances, by the twenty-first century he regularly scheduled plenty of foreign tours. *THOMAS LOHNES/AFP/Getty Images*

and contributing backing vocals on "Love and Mercy." He also made a guest appearance at a Jackson Browne concert on June 12 at the Rechnitz Theater in Red Bank, a benefit raising funds to fight ALS.

But most of his time went to his next album—a rock album this time, with the E Streeters. Springsteen and O'Brien had been listening to songs he had written since late December 2006, and in February 2007 work on the album, which would be called *Magic*, began at Southern Tracks in Atlanta. The album was largely completed by June; Springsteen added "Terry's Song" in August, after a longtime friend, Terry Magovern, died in July.

Springsteen's fans had *Magic* in their hands before the end of the year—another fast album turnaround. The release date was September 25, with the

MAGIC

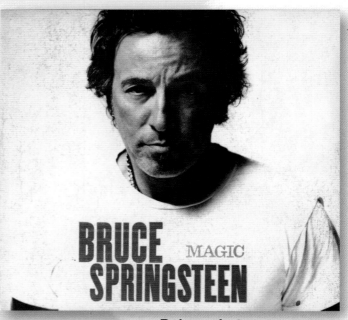

Released: October 2007
Chart Position: No. 1 (US), No. 1 (UK)

Fans of the E Street Band had waited a long time for Springsteen to record with the E Streeters again. Finally, their patience was rewarded with *Magic*, a rich, full-bodied record that showed Springsteen was ready to rock out once again.

"I would say on this record I got re-infatuated with pop music," Springsteen told *Rolling Stone*. That's more than evident on the album's opening track, "Radio Nowhere," which bursts out of the starting gate in full-throttled glory; when Clemons's sax blares out during the instrumental break, you know you're home free.

Yet the robust melodies mask a sense of impending doom. The opening track bemoans the state of a world with no soul; "You'll Be Comin' Down" seems to foretell the economic crisis that would grip the world in the following year. "Livin' in the Future" imagines a time of "somethin' righteous goin' under"—but hey, we're not there yet, so let's revel in another solo by the Big Man.

"Your Own Worst Enemy" (which could be about a divided personality or a divided country) boasts lush harmonies worthy of the Beach Boys. The bittersweet "Gypsy Biker" is the first song on the album to make that divide more explicit; it's about a solider being sent home for burial. The song poses the query "Which side are you on?"—in this case a sad question that matters only to the living, and not the dead.

"Girls in Their Summer Clothes" is another unabashed pop song, but with a sad undercurrent as the narrator sits on the sidelines, watching the girls—and, it's suggested, life itself—pass him by. Ostensibly a love song, "I'll Work for Your Love" is a skillful lyrical mix of the sacred and the profane, rooted in Springsteen's Catholic school childhood.

The mood then turns very dark for the rest of the album. On the title track, Springsteen sings of a con man's tricks with a sinister cool; in the Bush era, it's not hard to figure out who he thinks the bad guys are. "Last to Die" is another war lament, the powerfully surging music underscoring the fear and resignation in the narrator's voice as he wonders if he'll survive. "Long Walk Home" is a predeployment number, a man taking a last look around his hometown before heading to the hell that awaits him in "Devil's Arcade." It's the album's longest song, starting out quietly and rising in intensity as you pass through a landscape littered with metal, plastic, and buried guns, with a "thick desert dust on your skin."

Yet despite the tragedies, large and small, in the album's final number, "Terry's Song" (a tribute to a close friend who died shortly before the album's completion), Springsteen acknowledges that love's power is stronger than death. As always, the challenge is not to give in to despair.

band playing the second of two public rehearsal shows at Convention Hall in Asbury Park the same day. The first single, "Radio Nowhere," had been released the previous month; though it failed to break into the US chart, it did better overseas, peaking at No. 2 in Ireland and Norway.

On September 28 Springsteen performed a number of songs throughout the broadcast of NBC's *Today* show, with another public rehearsal show held that evening at the Continental Airlines Arena in East Rutherford, New Jersey. The tour proper began on October 2, 2007, in Hartford, Connecticut, with the same musicians who had gone out on the *Rising* tour; there would be one hundred shows. Springsteen also found time to play two benefits during the first leg of the tour, joining drummer Weinberg's band, the Max Weinberg 7, at a fundraiser for the Monmouth County SPCA held at the Weinbergs' home on October 13 in Atlantic Highlands, New Jersey, and giving a solo performance at "Stand Up for Heroes: A Benefit for the Bob Woodruff Family Fund," on November 7 at Town Hall in New York City.

The E Street Band hadn't toured with Springsteen since 2004, and the passage of time was evident. The sight of Clemons resting on a chair when not playing was the clearest indication that this was no longer a group of young men with the energy to leap around the stage, cutting up. Nor were the shows as long; they ended well before midnight. The most profound change came on November 19, when the band played the TD Banknorth Garden in Boston. Peter Wolf made a guest appearance during "Tenth Avenue Freeze-Out," but the show was remembered as the last full concert Federici played with Springsteen and the E Street Band. The keyboardist had been diagnosed with melanoma in 2005; the cancer was in remission after treatment, but it returned, forcing him to bow out for the rest of the tour. Federici's last show was also the last concert on the US leg, and when the tour recommenced on November 25 in Madrid, Spain, Charles Giordano, who had played with Springsteen as a member of the Sessions Band, was in his place. The European leg primarily stuck to familiar locales on the Continent: Bilbao, Spain (November 26), Copenhagen, Denmark (December 8), Cologne, Germany (December 13), and Paris, France (December 17). The final night was a December 19 show at the O2 Arena in London, the show closing with "Santa Claus is Comin' to Town." Following a break for the holidays, the second US leg began on February 28, 2008; interestingly, it began at the same place the tour had first started, the Hartford Civic Center in Hartford, Connecticut.

On March 8, between shows in Buffalo, New York, and Uniondale, New York, Springsteen made a guest appearance, playing "Glory Days" at

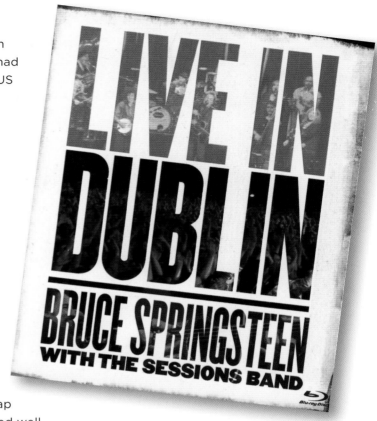

Live in Dublin, Blu-ray disc, released June 5, 2007

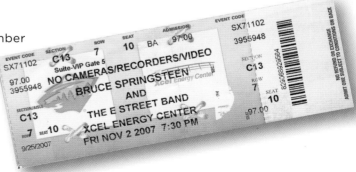

November 2, 2007, concert ticket, Xcel Energy Center, Saint Paul, Minnesota. *Courtesy of Scott Woitaszewski*

the 21st Annual RSPA Panther Ball, benefiting the Ranney School, held at the Eagle Oaks Country Club in Farmingdale, New Jersey. Twelve days later he welcomed Federici back to the E Street Band when the tour reached Indianapolis. Federici came on halfway through the set; "American Land" was the last song he played with his longtime friends. He died on April 17, and three shows were canceled to allow Springsteen and the E Streeters to attend his funeral. It was a poignant moment: the first time Springsteen's band of "blood brothers" had been permanently broken. When the tour began again on April 22 in Tampa, Florida, the show opened with a short tribute film about Federici.

July saw the release of the *Magic Tour Highlights* EP, a digital download featuring a performance of "4th of July, Asbury Park (Sandy)" from Federici's last full show with the band on November 19. All proceeds went to the Danny Federici Melanoma Fund.

After a May 2 show in Sunrise, Florida, there was a break. Of course, Springsteen always had time to squeeze in a few personal appearances. On May 4 he was inducted into the New Jersey Hall of Fame, at the Performing Arts Center in Newark, with his mother watching proudly from the audience (May 4 happened to be her birthday, too). In his acceptance speech, Springsteen paid homage to his home state, calling it "a repository of my time on Earth. My memory, the music I've made, my friendships, my life—it's all buried here in a box somewhere in the sand down along the Central Jersey coast. I can't imagine having it any other way." On May 7 he performed at a benefit for the Count Basie Theatre in Red Bank, the first in a series of shows in which he performed an album in its entirety; on this night, Springsteen and the band played *Darkness on the Edge of Town* and *Born to Run*. On May 13 there was another benefit for the Ranney School at the Stone Pony, with Springsteen returning to the venue on May 17 to sit in with Mike Ness for a few songs.

The *Magic* tour continued on May 22, with the first of two shows in Dublin, Ireland. The UK and European leg ended on July 20 with a show in Barcelona, Spain; from there it was back to the States for the final leg, which began July 27 in East Rutherford, New Jersey. Shows were gradually becoming longer, and now the audience had a hand in determining the set lists, holding up signs with songs they wanted Springsteen to sing. During the show, Springsteen would ask for the signs to be passed up to the stage, and he'd flip through them, deciding which songs to do. It was another way of adding some spontaneity to an arena show.

The final show came in Milwaukee, Wisconsin, where the band played Harley Davidson's 105th Anniversary Festival, with Federici's son Jason joining the band during "4th of July, Asbury Park (Sandy)," playing the accordion. And after the tour's end, Springsteen became a man with a mission. It was another presidential election year, and Springsteen was heading out to stump for the Democratic candidate, Senator Barack Obama.

(opposite)
More *Magic* in Milan, Italy, on June 25, 2008. The show opened and closed with rock 'n' roll classics, "Summertime Blues," and "Twist and Shout," respectively. *Morena Brengola/Redferns/Getty Images*

Back at home, at Giants Stadium in East Rutherford, New Jersey, on July 27, 2008, the start of the third US leg of the *Magic* tour. *Larry Busacca/WireImage/Getty Images*

Springsteen had declared his support for Obama the previous spring, before the senator had even secured the nomination. On April 24, 2008, Springsteen had posted a special message on his website:

Like most of you, I've been following the campaign and I have now seen and heard enough to know where I stand. Senator Obama, in my view, is head and shoulders above the rest. He has the depth, the reflectiveness, and the resilience to be our next President. He speaks to the America I've envisioned in my music for the past 35 years, a generous nation with a citizenry willing to tackle nuanced and complex problems, a country that's interested in its collective destiny and in the potential of its gathered spirit. A place where ". . . nobody crowds you, and nobody goes it alone" [a lyric from Springsteen's song "Long Walk Home"]. After the terrible damage done over the past eight years, a great American reclamation project needs to be undertaken. I believe that Senator Obama is the best candidate to lead that project and to lead us into the 21st Century with a renewed sense of moral purpose and of ourselves as Americans. Over here on E Street, we're proud to support Obama for President.

The announcement caught Senator Obama's campaign staff by surprise; Springsteen hadn't informed them he was going to make a statement. The senator spoke with Springsteen that afternoon, and by fall Springsteen was—as one of Obama's campaign slogans put it—"fired up, ready to go." Springsteen performed short solo sets at three rallies from October 4 to 6, and then signed on for a "Change Rocks" fundraiser at the Hammerstein Ballroom in New York, playing solo as well as with Billy Joel and his band ("The reason I'm running for president is I can't be Bruce Springsteen," Obama cracked at the show).

Springsteen at the Fox Theatre in Atlanta, Georgia, on September 30, 1978. The show was broadcast over radio and quickly released as a bootleg.
Tom Hill/WireImage

On November 2, two days before the election, Springsteen appeared at a "Change We Need" rally. His remarks at the show touched on his own dreams for America, calling himself, "an advocate for a set of ideas; economic and social justice, America as a positive influence around the world, truth, transparency and integrity in government, the right of every American to have a job, a living wage, to be educated in a decent school, and to have a life filled with the dignity of work, promise and the sanctity of home. These are the things that make a life." While praising Obama for his "understanding, his temperateness, his deliberativeness, his maturity, his pragmatism, his toughness," he stressed that everyone needed to play a role in creating the kind of society in which they wished to live: "all that a nation has that keeps it from coming apart is the social contract between us, between its citizens."

"So I don't know about you, but I know I want my country back," he said in conclusion. "I want my dream back. I want my America back! Now is the time to stand with Barack Obama and Joe Biden, roll up our sleeves, and come on up for the rising." Two nights later, after Obama made his victory speech at Grant Park in Chicago, the first song that came booming out of the speakers was "The Rising."

The song Springsteen debuted at the November 2 show could have served as a campaign slogan: "Working on a Dream." It was destined to be the title track of his next album. Work on the album began toward the end of the *Magic* sessions, when Springsteen recorded the song "What Love Can Do." He didn't see it as a song that would fit on *Magic*, and O'Brien agreed, suggesting that Springsteen instead use it as the jumping-off point to write more songs. The music came easily, and within a week, Springsteen had five more numbers written. *Magic* hadn't even been released, but *Working on a Dream* had already begun.

Sessions were fit in around the *Magic* tour, not only at Southern Tracks Studios in Atlanta, Georgia, but also studios in New York and L.A., in addition to Springsteen's own Thrill Hill Recording home studio. It was the last album of Springsteen's to involve Federici; Jason Federici recorded an accordion part for the song "The Last Carnival," written in his father's memory, and the album itself was dedicated to Federici. The raw, bluesy "A Night with the Jersey Devil," a "prerelease" single of sorts, appeared as a free download on Springsteen's website on Halloween. "If you grew up in central or south Jersey, you grew up with the 'Jersey Devil,'" Springsteen explained. "Here's a little musical Halloween treat. Have fun!"

The album's title track was the first official single, released to radio on November 21 and then as a free download on November 24 (a physical CD single was available as well); though it did not crack the main *Billboard* singles chart, it did reach No. 2 on *Billboard*'s Adult Alternative Songs chart. The next single, "My Lucky Day," arrived a week later, reaching No. 18 in the Adult Alternative Songs chart. The single that received the most acclaim was "The Wrestler," the title song to the film of the same name, starring Mickey Rourke as the titular wrestler past his prime. The song dropped on December 16 as a download-only release, though a promo single was made for members of the Academy of Motion Picture Arts and Sciences in hopes of getting the song an Oscar nomination; collectors noted that the promo featured a longer, unedited version of the number. "Life Itself" was another download-only release, coming out at the end of December.

After the Obama campaign gigs, Springsteen only did two shows for the remainder of 2008: another "Stand Up for Heroes" benefit at Town Hall in New York on November 5, and an appearance at Bandiera's Hope Concert on December 22 at the Count Basie Theatre, a show featuring local legends Southside Johnny and Jon Bon Jovi, as well as Gary U.S. Bonds. But there was a lot more yet to come. The next year was gearing up to be very big, something of a victory lap for Springsteen.

On January 11, 2009, Springsteen attended the Golden Globe Awards at the Beverly Hilton in Beverly Hills, where "The Wrestler," newly released, won an honor for Best Original Song. On January 18 came an especially proud moment, when he appeared at "We Are One: The Obama Inaugural Celebration at the Lincoln Memorial," a concert held two days before President Obama's inauguration. The event drew nearly half a million attendees. Springsteen first performed "The Rising," accompanied by the Joyce Garrett Singers, and returned later to sing Woody Guthrie's "This Land Is Your Land" with Pete Seeger and Seeger's grandson, Tao Rodríguez-Seeger. Seeger insisted that they sing all the song's verses, not just the most

WORKING
ON A
DREAM

Released: January 2009
Chart Position: No. 1 (US), No. 1 (UK)

Working on a Dream was written on the run, with recording sessions on both coasts fitted in around tour dates. As such, the music has a freshness and urgency about it, as if Springsteen couldn't wait to start working with his band again.

The album opens with "Outlaw Pete," the story of an infant bandit who never quite outgrows his bad side; a fun romp with a little moral at the end. But in contrast to the decidedly downbeat atmosphere of Magic, the themes of Working on a Dream are much more optimistic.

Many of the numbers are love songs, like "My Lucky Day," a buoyant tune about the fortuitous day the singer met his loved one. It's as irresistibly catchy as anything the E Street Band has done. There's a hint of Pet Sounds–era Beach Boys on the celebratory "This Life," depicting a couple literally counting their lucky stars on one glorious night. The expansive "Kingdom of Days" is the daytime counterpart: a couple still delighting in each other over the passing years, and not a single cloud on the horizon. The album's laid-back title song is a hopeful vision of the future that could refer to a relationship or just to better days in general. (Springsteen drove the meaning home when he performed it at Senator Obama's 2008 presidential campaign rallies.)

The sweet pop of "Surprise, Surprise" is another straightforward love song. And Springsteen has some fun on "Queen of the

Supermarket," which harkens back to the character studies he did in the Greetings from Asbury Park, N.J. era, the narrator longing for a checker at the local grocery store, insisting he can see the beauty underneath her uniform. Even "Good Eye," a song of loss, takes the sting out of a less-than-happy situation with its bluesy swing and clever lyrics.

But the album's sunny spirits are balanced by shadow, as in the nuance of "Tomorrow Never Knows." A scratchy guitar opening sets a brisk pace for this country-flavored number with hints of discord in its swaying melody. "What Love Can Do" is a plea to hold on, even when everything seems to have turned to "ashes and dust"; love, Springsteen sings, can provide salvation. Though even he concedes, in "Life Itself," that you can't pull everyone back from the brink; in this sad observation of a life gone off the rails, the narrator seems to have given up hope for his loved one.

"The Last Carnival" is the most personal song for Springsteen and the band. It's a farewell to the circus that has packed up and moved on, and it's also a farewell to the E Street Band's keyboardist, Danny Federici, who had died the previous year. "The Wrestler" brings the album to a somber close with a poignant lyric of a man trying his best to overcome the odds, hanging on to the bitter end.

well-known ones, and as they did so, Springsteen later recalled, "I realized that sometimes things that come from the outside, they make their way in, to become a part of the beating heart of the nation. And on that day, when we sung that song, Americans—young and old, black and white, of all religious and political beliefs—were united, for a brief moment, by Woody's poetry."

Working on a Dream was released on January 27, 2009, topping the album charts in the United States, United Kingdom, and seventeen other countries. Two days before the album's release, Springsteen shot a moody, atmospheric video for "The Wrestler" at the New Brunswick Boxing Gym. The video premiered on Springsteen's MySpace page the following month, and the single reached No. 20.

Then came an event he had long been asked to do: the Super Bowl halftime show. Springsteen had been turning down invitations to play one of the biggest entertainment events in America for a decade. The tipping point came in 2008, when Landau watched Tom Petty perform during that year's halftime show and realized, "That could be *us*." Springsteen agreed, and a deal was quickly struck for the following year's game, set for February 1, 2009, at the Raymond James Stadium in Tampa, Florida.

Springsteen turned in a terrific halftime performance during the Super Bowl at the Raymond James Stadium in Tampa, Florida, on February 1, 2009; "Put the chicken wings down!" he told the audience before the first number. *Rob Tringali/Sportschrome/Getty Images*

The game (in which the Pittsburgh Steelers beat the Arizona Cardinals 27 to 23) drew an estimated viewing audience of more than 151 million. The show began with Springsteen and Clemons seen in silhouette; Springsteen then tossed his guitar aside and grabbed the mic to proclaim, "Ladies and gentlemen, for the next twelve minutes we're going to bring the righteous and mighty power of the E Street Band into your beautiful home!" He was in a playful mood; after demanding that the viewers "put the chicken wings *down!*" and turn their TV volume up, he climbed on the piano to yell, "And what I wanna know is—*is there anybody alive out there?*" As fireworks went off and Springsteen bent backwards until he was nearly on his knees, the band then went into an abbreviated "Tenth Avenue Freeze-Out," followed by shortened versions of "Born to Run," "Working on a Dream" (accompanied by the Joyce Garrett Singers), and "Glory Days." Springsteen was in his element, pacing the stage, sliding on his knees, slapping the hands of the eager fans down front. For weeks afterward, Springsteen said, people he encountered on the street came up to say how much they'd enjoyed his set: "It was quite wonderful and meant quite a bit to all of us."

The performance made a great trailer for the upcoming tour, still two months out. Springsteen took his time warming up, making an appearance on *The Daily Show* on March 19 (performing an acoustic version of "Working on a Dream"), then performing at another Ranney School benefit in Long Branch on March 21. There were two public rehearsal shows, held March 23 and 24 at Convention Hall in Asbury Park, before the tour began April 1 in San Jose, California. When drummer Weinberg missed a few of the eighty-three shows, his son Jay filled in for him.

As usual, Springsteen squeezed in a few extra performances along the way. On April 27, he and Scialfa performed "Streets of Philadelphia" at a "Tribute to Tom Hanks" gala held at Lincoln Center. On May 3, a very special concert was held at Madison Square Garden in celebration of Pete Seeger's ninetieth birthday. An array of musicians gathered to honor Seeger and his wife Toshi, including not only Springsteen and Scialfa, but also Arlo Guthrie, Emmylou Harris, Ramblin' Jack Elliott, and Ani DiFranco, among many others. In addition to "When the Saints Go Marching In" and "Goodnight Irene" (and "Happy Birthday," of course), Springsteen performed an acoustic version of "Tom Joad" with Tom Morello.

The first North American leg ended on May 23 in East Rutherford, New Jersey, with a short break before picking up overseas with a May 30 date in Landgraaf, Netherlands. There was a quick detour back to Manchester, Tennessee, where Springsteen appeared at the Bonnaroo Music and Arts Festival on June 13 and 14, then he headed overseas again for an appearance at the Glastonbury Festival on June 27. The festival was held just outside Pilton, England, a three-hour drive west of London. Springsteen had some fun before his set, making a surprise appearance with the band Gaslight Anthem. The next day, he headlined the "Hard Rock Calling" concert in London's Hyde Park, a performance later released on the 2010 DVD *London Calling: Live in Hyde Park*.

The European leg ended August 2 in Santiago de Compostela, Spain, and the final US leg began August 19 in Hartford, Connecticut. The following month, Springsteen began regularly performing an entire album during each show, beginning with a September 20 performance in Chicago, when the audience was treated to the complete *Born to Run*. On subsequent dates, the band performed *The Wild, the Innocent & the E Street Shuffle, Darkness on the Edge of Town*, and *Born in the U.S.A.*

On a jaunt up to the Apollo Theater on September 25, Springsteen taped an appearance for Elvis Costello's TV series *Spectacle*, backed by Lofgren and Bittan on some numbers and joined by Costello's band on others. The show

★ ★

Glastonbury Festival

Part of Springsteen's performance at the Glastonbury Festival in England on June 27, 2009, was broadcast on the BBC. *Jim Dyson/Getty Images*

Springsteen has never played too many festivals, making his 2009 appearance at the Glastonbury Festival especially notable.

The Glastonbury Festival, which began in 1970, is held in Pilton, England. The festival runs for a number of days (five days in 2009), and is so popular that tickets sell out before the lineup is even announced.

Springsteen was scheduled to play on June 27. Impatient for his own set to begin, he dropped by early to see the Gaslight Anthem (a fellow New Jersey act, based in New Brunswick) and joined them on the song "The '59 Sound."

Springsteen's twenty-five-song set opened with Joe Strummer's "Coma Girl," the first (and so far the only) time he played the song live. Part of the show was broadcast on the BBC, and the band's performance of "The River" turned up as a bonus feature on *London Calling: Live in Hyde Park*. The Gaslight Anthem's Brian Fallon made a guest appearance on "No Surrender."

"Bruce Springsteen and the E Street Band put on a show so good it's quasi-religious," the *Guardian* later wrote.

"Springsteen is perhaps the finest practitioner of gig-as-religious-event, a huge communion between performer and audience. His ability to render such vast spaces intimate is unrivalled, effortlessly bridging the gap between band and audience—sometimes strutting down to the front and making brief attempts at crowd-surfing. It's an orchestrated routine, certainly, but it's hard to deny the Boss's sheer passion and conviction."

In addition to performing his own set, Springsteen was a special guest during Phish's set at the annual Bonnaroo Festival, in Manchester, Tennessee, on June 13, 2009. *C. Taylor Crothers/FilmMagic/Getty Images*

was broadcast in two parts on January 20 and 27, 2010, and later released on DVD.

Back on familiar ground, Springsteen fronted Bandiera's band again on October 17, with Scialfa and Southside Johnny taking lead vocals on a number of songs in a school-benefit performance at the Stone Pony. A five-night stand at Giants Stadium in East Rutherford, New Jersey, followed. Springsteen's mother attended the October 20 show in Philadelphia, the last night of three nights in that city, coming onstage for "Dancing in the Dark," and drummer Lopez made a guest appearance on "Spirit in the Night."

On October 29, at Madison Square Garden, Springsteen headlined the first night of a two-concert series celebrating the twenty-fifth anniversary of the Rock and Roll Hall of Fame. He brought plenty of guest vocalists, including Sam Moore ("Soul Man"), John Fogerty ("Proud Mary"), Darlene Love ("A Fine Fine Boy"), and Billy Joel ("Only the Good Die Young"). U2 headlined the next night, and Springsteen was still on hand, sharing vocals with Patti Smith on "Because the Night," as well as "I Still Haven't Found What I'm Looking For." Some of the performances were later released on CD and DVD.

The tour drew to a close in November, but there was always time for side performances, such as Springsteen's appearance at another "Stand Up for

Heroes" show on November 4. As an extra treat, after the set, Springsteen's guitar and four tickets to one of his upcoming Madison Square Garden concerts on November 7 and 8 were put up for auction; the winning bidder was actress Mariska Hargitay, who ponied up $50,000. For yet another benefit performance, this one on November 17 at Carnegie Hall, benefiting Autism Speaks, Springsteen performed a four-song set opening for comedian Jerry Seinfeld.

It all finally came to an end on November 11 in at the HSBC Arena in Buffalo, New York, with a monumental show that lasted three and a half hours. Springsteen planned to perform his very first album, *Greetings from Asbury Park, N.J.* during the show, and he wanted Mike Appel to be there. He gave his former manager a call and invited him. Appel, who was out at a restaurant, was amazed: "Bruce—it's twelve noon now. How am I gonna be there?" "Don't worry 'bout a thing," Springsteen told him. "Go to your house. I'll arrange everything." Appel returned home, and in due course, a limo arrived and ferried him to the airport, where he flew to the show on the band's jet. Springsteen unveiled a wealth of anecdotes during the show, recalling how he met Clemons during "Growin' Up," and the two men then delighted the crowd by striking the *Born to Run* cover pose. Van Zandt requested a rare performance of "Restless Nights," an outtake from *The River,* because it was his birthday. The night came to an end with "Rockin' All over the World"—something Springsteen had certainly done that year. There would be more to come.

Backstage in Baltimore on November 20, 2009, waiting for the show to begin. *The Washington Post/ Getty Images*

(opposite)
While performing "Hungry Heart" at during a November 20, 2009, show at the 1st Mariner Arena in Baltimore, Springsteen indulged in a little crowd surfing. *Michael Williamson/The Washington Post/Getty Images*

LAND OF
HOPE
AND DREAMS

Springsteen had welcomed President Obama to his new job in January 2009; he received the prestigious Kennedy Center Honor from the new president on December 5, 2009 (along with actor Robert De Niro, film director Mel Brooks, jazz musician Dave Brubeck, and opera singer Grace Bumbry). There was a reception at the White House, and a dinner at the John F. Kennedy Center for the Performing Arts, followed by live performances. Jon Stewart introduced Springsteen during the performance segment, stating,

I am not a music critic. Nor historian, nor archivist. I cannot tell you where Bruce Springsteen falls in the pantheon of the American songbook. I cannot illuminate the context of his work or his roots in the folk and oral history traditions of our great nation. But I am from New Jersey, and so I can tell you what I believe, and what I believe is this: I believe that Bob Dylan and James Brown had a baby. And they abandoned this child on the side of the road, between the exit interchanges of 8A and 9 on the New Jersey Turnpike. That child is Bruce Springsteen."

Springsteen, sitting in the audience, laughed in delight.

Springsteen didn't perform at the event, instead sitting next to the president and his wife, watching as other performers sang a selection of his greatest hits. John Mellencamp opened with "Born in the U.S.A.," Ben Harper and Jennifer Nettles performed "I'm on Fire," Melissa Etheridge took on "Born to Run," Eddie Vedder brought on a gospel choir to join him in "My City of Ruins," and Sting closed with "The Rising."

It was a remarkable ending to a remarkable year. Springsteen wouldn't release a new album or tour again for another two years. As 2010 began, most of his performances were benefits: as part of Joe Grushecky's band at "Light of Day 10," on January 16 at the Paramount Theatre in Asbury Park (where he also guested during sets by Willie Nile and Jesse Malin); performing "We Shall Overcome" at the "Hope for Haiti Now" telethon benefiting victims of the January 12 Haiti earthquake, held at MTV Studios in New York on January 22; at a

(previous spread)
Springsteen has made regular appearances at the Rock and Roll Hall of Fame induction ceremonies over the years. On March 14, 2011, he backed vocalist Darlene Love, who was inducted that year. *Dimitrios Kambouris/ Getty Images*

Springsteen campaigned for Senator Barack Obama in 2008. On December 5, 2009, President Obama awarded Springsteen with a Kennedy Center Honor; fellow honoree actor Robert De Niro is next to Springsteen. *MANDEL NGAN/AFP/Getty Images*

Ranney School benefit on January 23 at the Stone Pony. And so it went for the rest of the year, with appearances supporting a wide range of causes, including the Kristen Ann Carr Fund (April 24 at the Tribeca Grill in New York); Sting's annual Rainforest Foundation benefit (May 13 at Carnegie Hall); and another "Stand Up for Heroes" benefit (November 3 at Beacon Theatre in New York, which also saw Springsteen's guitar auctioned off for $140,000).

As always, there were drop-in performances as well. At Roseanne Cash's April 15 performance at Duke University, Springsteen joined her to perform "Sea of Heartbreak." He had a great time when Danny DeVito was inducted into the New Jersey Hall of Fame on May 2, the two of them jousting on "Glory Days." Four days later he was at Fairleigh Dickinson University in Madison, New Jersey, a guest at the WAMFest, the Words and Music Festival. He appeared with John Wesley Harding and Robert Pinsky at an event where he read poetry and performed a short set, with Harding and Pinsky joining him in a performance of "The Promised Land." Stone Pony regulars were pleased by his appearance at Alejandro Escovedo's show at the club on July 23. And he was always ready to sit in with his friend Joe Grushecky, appearing at two shows on November 4 and 5 at the Soldiers & Sailors Memorial Hall and Museum in Pittsburgh, celebrating the fifteenth anniversary of Grushecky's *American Babylon* album. He even gave brother-in-law Mike Scialfa a hand, sitting in on "Mustang Sally" when Mike's band, Timepiece, played a show at Woody's Roadside Tavern in Farmingdale, New Jersey.

Springsteen's own big project for the year was preparing the release of *The Promise: The Darkness on the Edge of Town Story*. The album's thirtieth anniversary had actually been in 2008, but Springsteen was too busy to put it together. *The Promise* was a double album featuring twenty-two tracks, spruced up with a few overdubs. There was also a lavish box set featuring three CDs (the original album and the new double album), and three DVDs. The DVDs featured a performance by the musicians who had appeared on the original album (with Giodano sitting in for Federici), filmed the previous December at the Paramount Theatre in Asbury Park, and a documentary about the making of the album. Released on November 16, 2010, the album reached No. 16 in the United States (and topped the charts in Germany, Spain, and Sweden), while the box reached No. 27. The documentary had its world premiere at the Toronto International Film Festival on September 14, with Springsteen in attendance; prior to the film's premiere, Springsteen was interviewed onstage by actor and director Ed Norton, a personal friend. Springsteen also made a promotional appearance in support of the album on *Late Night with Jimmy Fallon* on November 16. The band did a show

The Promise: Darkness on the Edge of Town, box set, released November 16, 2010

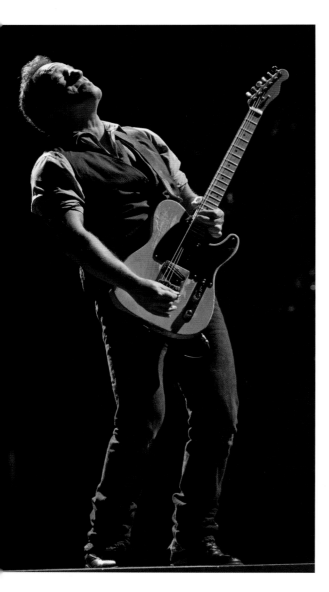

At Nationals Park in Washington, DC, on September 14, 2011. The show saw the live debut of the song "Blinded by the Light," from Springsteen's first album. *Tracy A. Woodward/The Washington Post via Getty Images*

before an invited audience on December 7 at the Carousel House in Asbury Park, and the performance was broadcast online later in month; it was also used as bonus material when the documentary *The Promise* was released on its own the following year. Two tracks from it, "Gotta Get That Feeling" and "Racing in the Street," appeared as a vinyl single for Record Store Day on April 16, 2011.

Benefit performances and drop-ins filled 2011. Springsteen made return appearances at the Light of Day benefit (January 15, Paramount Theatre, Asbury Park); the Ranney School benefit (January 29, Stone Pony, Asbury Park); and the "Stand Up for Heroes" benefit (November 9, Beacon Theatre, New York City), along with appearances at Sting's sixtieth birthday concert, which raised funds for the Robin Hood Foundation (October 1, Beacon Theatre, New York), and a benefit for Boston College (October 22 at the Stone Pony).

Springsteen also took the time for a few guest appearances. He was in his element at the Rock and Roll Hall of Fame induction ceremony, March 14 at the Waldorf Astoria Hotel in New York, backing inductee Darlene Love on three songs. He unexpectedly took the stage during a Dropkick Murphys show on March 18 at the House of Blues in Boston, after showing up with Max Weinberg to watch the opening act, Against Me!, whose drummer was Max's son Jay. The next month found him joining friends Southside Johnny and Vini Lopez at the "Nicky Addeo and Friends Celebrate the Music of Asbury Park's Westside" concert on April 2 at the Wonder Bar in Asbury Park. He played another two shows with Joe Grushecky and the Houserockers at the Soldiers & Sailors Memorial Hall & Museum in Pittsburgh, on November 3 and 4. And he rounded out the year by guesting at Bob Seger's December 1 show at Madison Square Garden, contributing guitar and vocals on Seger's classic "Old Time Rock and Roll," and joining the Gaslight Anthem on "American Slang" when they turned up at Convention Hall in Asbury Park on December 9.

He was also preparing his next album. But there was one player who wouldn't be making as many contributions to the record as Springsteen had hoped: Clarence Clemons. The Big Man had been plagued by health problems in previous years, having two different knee replacements, hip replacements, and spinal fusion surgery. A cart took him to and from the stage when he performed, and he had to sit on a stool during the shows. He had last played with Springsteen and the E Streeters on November 22, 2009, and he was determined to be ready for the next tour, telling *Rolling Stone*, "As long as my mouth, hands and brain still work I'll be out there doing it. I'm going to keep going 'til I'm not there anymore. This is what's keeping me alive and feeling young and inspired." But on June 12, 2011, he was felled by a stroke at his home in Palm Beach, Florida, and rushed to the hospital.

Springsteen and Scialfa were in France, and they interrupted their twentieth wedding anniversary celebrations to fly to Palm Beach and be at his side. Clarence died on June 18, at the age of sixty-nine.

Clarence's memorial service was held on June 21 at the Royal Poinciana Chapel in Palm Beach. Springsteen performed "Tenth Avenue Freeze-Out" and then spoke at length about his friend. "Standing next to Clarence was like standing next to the baddest ass on the planet," he said.

★ ★

Clarence Clemons

Clarence Clemons, AKA the Big Man, served as the perfect on stage foil for Springsteen. *Michael Ochs Archives/Getty Images*

Clarence Clemons was a larger-than-life character and the perfect onstage foil for Springsteen, matching him in exuberance and frequently delighting the crowd by sweeping Springsteen up in a big bear hug (sometimes topping it off with a kiss).

Clarence Anicholas Clemons Jr. was born on January 11, 1942, in Norfolk County, Virginia. He received his first saxophone at the age of nine, as a Christmas present. He grew up steeped in the gospel music of the Baptist church and then discovered the blues and R & B. He joined his first band, a jazz group, while he was in high school.

He attended Maryland State College on a football scholarship, where he attracted attention from the Dallas Cowboys and Cleveland Browns. But a car accident scuttled his pro bowl dreams, and he pursued music instead.

He made his first studio recordings in 1960, with Tyrone Ashley's Funky Music Machine, and while in college had been a member of the Vibratones. By the late 1960s, he was immersed in the Jersey Shore scene, playing with numerous bands until he signed on with Springsteen.

When he wasn't busy with the Boss, Clarence released records of his own, both solo albums and recordings as Clarence Clemons & the Red Bank Robbers, Aja and the Big Man, and Clarence Clemons & Temple of Soul. He recorded with numerous other artists as well, from Aretha Franklin to Todd Rundgren to Lady Gaga. He also established himself as an actor, appearing in such films as *Bill & Ted's Excellent Adventure* and *Fatal Instinct* and making guest appearances on the TV shows *Nash Bridges* and *The Simpsons*.

The Big Man was married five times and had four sons. He died on June 18, 2011, at the age of sixty-nine.

You were proud, you were strong, you were excited and laughing with what might happen, with what together you might be able to do. You felt like no matter what the day or the night brought, nothing was going to touch you. . . . And we were coming to your town to shake you and to wake you up. Together, we told an older, richer story about the possibilities of friendship that transcended those I'd written in my songs and in my music. . . . And that's what I'm gonna miss. The chance to renew that vow and double down on that story on a nightly basis, because that is something, that is the thing that we did together, the two of us. Clarence was big, and he made me feel, and think, and love, and dream big. How big was the Big Man? Too fucking big to die.

"Clarence doesn't leave the E Street Band when *he* dies," Springsteen said at another point. "He leaves when *we* die." At the conclusion of the ceremony, Springsteen, Jackson Browne, and the E Streeters performed a heartfelt rendition of "You're a Friend of Mine." The following month, Springsteen sat in with J. T. Bowen & the Sensational Soul Cruisers when they played a tribute show to Clarence on July 17 at the Wonder Bar in Asbury Park. In his eulogy, Springsteen also referred to his hopes that he'd work again with Clarence "in the next life." But for now, he would have to go on without him.

He played another Light of Day benefit at Asbury Park's Paramount Theatre on January 14, 2012, but devoted most of the year to a tour in support of his latest album, *Wrecking Ball*. Springsteen had worked on a number of songs after the *Working on a Dream* tour, finally getting together with producer Ron Aniello in 2011. Unusually, he worked with a wide variety of musicians on the album, drawing from both the E Street Band and the Sessions Band (Clarence was featured on two songs, the title track and "Land of Hope and Dreams"). There were two outtakes, "American Man" and "American Skin."

The album's first single, "We Take Care of Our Own," was released on January 19, 2012, reaching No. 11 in *Billboard*'s Adult Alternative Songs chart. Springsteen first performed the song live on February 12 at the Grammy Awards, held at the Staples Center in L.A.; it opened the show, with Springsteen and the band augmented by a string section. *The Promise* box set won a Grammy for Best Boxed or Special Limited Edition Package. The show closed with an all-star lineup, including Springsteen and Dave Grohl, performing a medley from the Beatles' *Abbey Road*, "Golden Slumber"/"Carry That Weight"/"The End," with Paul McCartney's touring band.

After a day in Paris doing overseas promotion for *Wrecking Ball*, Springsteen made two appearances on *Late Night with Jimmy Fallon* on February 27 and March 2. During the latter appearance, he poked fun at his 1980s-era image, donning a headband and sleeveless top while singing a boisterous "Sexy and I Know It" with Fallon dressed as Neil Young. He also dropped in at a show at the Press Room in Asbury Park on February 25, commemorating the life of his personal trainer, Tony Strollo, who had died earlier in the month. Springsteen played a song with Tony's brother, Michael, and then sat in with Boccigalupe and the Badboys for a few numbers.

Wrecking Ball was released on March 5, 2012; it topped the charts in the United States and fifteen other countries. March 9 saw a pretour warm-up show of sorts when Springsteen played a show at the Apollo Theater celebrating the ten-year anniversary of SiriusXM Radio; the show was broadcast live on the network's *E Street Radio* program. Then it was off to Austin, Texas, for his very first appearance at the South by Southwest music conference, where Springsteen had been chosen to give the keynote

Springsteen and the E Street band opened the 54th Grammy Awards, held February 12, 2012, at the Staples Center in Los Angeles, with "We Take Care of Our Own," from *Wrecking Ball. Kevin Winter/Getty Images*

address. On March 14, the day before his speech, he couldn't resist dropping in on the Austin Music Awards, held at Austin Music Hall, for Alejandro Escovedo's set. He was over a half hour late for his speech the next day, arriving at 12:35 p.m. and joking about the early time slot: "How important can this speech be if we're giving it at noon? It can't be that important. Every decent musician in town is asleep—or they will be before I'm done with this thing, I guarantee you."

After acknowledging the wide diversity of music the conference encompassed, Springsteen talked about his own wide-ranging musical inspirations: Elvis, doo-wop, the Beatles, Bob Dylan, Hank Williams. He rhapsodized about the Animals' music—"The first records with full blown class consciousness that I had ever heard"—and sang part of "We Gotta Get Out of This Place" to make his point. "That's every song I've ever written. Yeah. That's all of them. I'm not kidding, either. That's 'Born to Run,' 'Born in the U.S.A.,' everything I've done for the past forty years, including all the new ones. . . . And the other thing that was great about the Animals was there were

WRECKING BALL

Released: March 2012
Chart Position: No. 1 (US), No. 1 (UK)

Springsteen came out swinging on this album, which charted the painful aftermath of the recession that hit the world in 2008. *Rolling Stone* called it "the most despairing, confrontational and musically turbulent album Bruce Springsteen has ever made." "Despairing" is a bit strong; the music is far too robust for that. But the anger is unmistakable.

The opening track, "We Take Care of Our Own," has the anthemic sweep of "Born in the U.S.A."—and lyrics just as open to misinterpretation. As the bitter verses make clear, this is a country where we don't always take care of our own; in fact, that promise is routinely broken (making it all the more curious that President Obama chose to use this song during his 2012 reelection campaign).

Never before had Springsteen attacked economic injustice so fiercely. "Easy Money" lambasts the "fat cats" whose money allows them to ride out hard times. "Shackled and Drawn" is the kind of rousing lament one could imagine Woody Guthrie performing, with Springsteen pulling off the neat trick of making the narrator's impoverished circumstances ring out like a stirring call to arms. It stands in stark contrast to the mournful "Jack of All Trades," in which the narrator sees no respite from a world in which bankers get fatter while the working man gets thin—at least until the song's shocking punch line, which threatens a violent revenge.

"Death to My Hometown" is an obvious successor to "My Hometown" (from *Born in the U.S.A.*). An upbeat Irish folk–infused melody provides the stirring background for this depiction of a town where the factories haven't just closed, they've been razed to the ground.

The aptly named "This Depression" asks how you can find hope after losing everything; as in so many of Springsteen's songs, relationships are key to hanging on. "Wrecking Ball" is another song of destruction, in this case the 2010 demolition of Giants Stadium in East Rutherford, New Jersey. But it's also a song of defiance, with Springsteen daring those who turn "victories and glories . . . into parking lots" to bring it on. As a eulogy, it's a terrific sendoff.

Politics are laid aside in "You've Got It," a straightforward declaration of love. The record's mood then shifts to determined optimism. There's a gospel feel to "Rocky Ground" (with a touch of hip-hop during the spoken-word interlude), which, despite its title, makes the steadfast assertion "There's a new day coming." "Land of Hope and Dreams" also offers succor, a journey to a place where dreams survive and hopes thrive (there's a great solo from Clemons as well). "We Are Alive" brings the album to a powerful close, as the souls of those who have lost their lives in search of justice rise to give solace to those still living. It ends with jaunty whistle, emphasizing that a good song can always help lighten the load.

no good-looking members. There were none. They were considered to be one of the ugliest groups in all of rock 'n' roll. And that was good. That was good for me, because I considered myself hideous at the time!" He went on to demonstrate with his guitar how "Don't Let Me Be Misunderstood" had influenced the writing of "Badlands." "When you walk onstage tonight to bring the noise, treat it like it's all we have," he said in conclusion. "And then remember, it's only rock and roll."

After the speech, Springsteen performed at the Moody Theater (where the TV program *Austin City Limits* is filmed). Reggae musician Jimmy Cliff guested on three songs, including his signature song "The Harder They Come." The Animals' Eric Burdon was another special guest, coming on to sing "We Gotta Get Out of This Place" with Springsteen. The show concluded with a triumphant "This Land Is Your Land," Springsteen accompanied by Joe Ely, Escovedo, and members of Arcade Fire, among others.

The Wrecking Ball tour kicked off on March 18, 2012, in Atlanta and ran for 133 shows; in the horn section was Clemons's nephew, Jake Clemons, who played sax and sang backing vocals. The first US leg ran through May 2, after which the tour headed to Europe, beginning with a May 13 date in Seville, Spain. There was an unexpected "curfew" moment when Springsteen played Hyde Park on July 14. Paul McCartney had come at the show's end to join Springsteen in "I Saw Her Standing There," and "Twist and Shout," but when the show ran over its 10:30 p.m. closing time, the power was cut during the latter song. Springsteen sang a brief a cappella version of "Goodnight Irene" before leaving the stage.

Van Zandt took to Twitter, ranting in a series of tweets, "The cops got nothing more important to do? How about they go catch some criminals instead of fucking with 80,000 people having a good time? English cops may be the only individuals left on earth that wouldn't want to hear one more from Bruce Springsteen and Paul McCartney!" But Springsteen was quicker to laugh it off. At the next performance, on July 17 in Dublin, he opened the show by playing the end of "Twist and Shout," followed by "I Fought the Law." When he played "Twist and Shout" again at the show's conclusion, two men came out, one posing as a police officer, the other a city official, and jokingly tried to stop the show. Springsteen prevailed this time.

Springsteen and Scialfa performing during a concert celebrating satellite radio station SiriusXM's tenth anniversary. The concert was held on March 9, 2012, at the Apollo Theater in New York. *Kevin Mazur/WireImage for SiriusXM*

The tour was in Norway on July 22, when a shocking terrorist attack was carried out in the country by Anders Breivik, who killed seventy-seven people with guns and a bomb. Springsteen and Van Zandt appeared at a memorial concert that night in Oslo. "Steve and I are honored to be included here tonight," Springsteen told the crowd. "For all of us who love democracy and tolerance, this was an international tragedy. I want to send this out as a prayer for a peaceful future for Norway and dedicate it to the families that lost their loved ones." The two musicians then performed a heartfelt acoustic version of "We Shall Overcome."

The European leg ended July 31 in Helsinki, Finland, with the tour continuing stateside on August 14 in Boston. The shows on September 19, 21, and 22 took place at East Rutherford's new venue, Metlife Stadium, with Lopez guesting on the first night and Gary U.S. Bonds guesting on the latter two. The final show started two hours late, due to the thunderstorms raging through the area, which meant that the audience was still there when the clock stuck midnight and it became Springsteen's sixty-third birthday. The crowd spontaneously began singing "Happy Birthday," and members of Springsteen's family came out onstage with his birthday cake.

On October 16, Springsteen appeared at a "Right to Rock" benefit at the Hammerstein Ballroom in New York, a fundraiser for Little Kids Rock, an organization promoting music education in public schools. Van Zandt received the group's Big Man of the Year Award, and Springsteen joined him to perform three songs. With 2012 another presidential election year, Springsteen began mixing in a few appearances for President Obama's reelection campaign, beginning October 18 in Parma, Ohio. (He played other Obama rallies in Iowa, Virginia, Pennsylvania, and Wisconsin.)

And then Hurricane Sandy struck, causing billions of dollars' worth of damage to the East Coast. An October 30 date in Rochester, New York, was postponed until the following evening. "My City of Ruins" was added to the set list, and on November 2, Springsteen and the band performed at a telethon held to raise funds. Springsteen first performed "Under the Boardwalk" with Billy Joel and his band, along with guest vocalists Jimmy Fallon and Steven Tyler, and then returned to close the show with the E Streeters, performing "Land of Hope and Dreams." A second fundraising event for Hurricane Sandy victims was held on December 12, "12-12-12: The Concert for Sandy Relief," with Springsteen and the band playing a short set. Springsteen also fit in another charity appearance at the annual "Stand Up for Heroes" benefit on November 8.

There was a tour break after a December 10 show in Mexico City. Springsteen's final performance of the year was a guest appearance with the Rolling Stones, joining the band on "Tumbling Dice" when they played Newark on December 15. Before the tour continued, Springsteen was honored as the MusiCares Person of the Year in a ceremony held on February 8,

Springsteen campaigned for President Obama's reelection, appearing at rallies like this one, on November 5, 2012, in Madison, Wisconsin. *Chip Somodevilla/Getty Images*

Springsteen meets the press prior to his show in Oslo, Norway, on April 29, 2013, the first date of the second European leg of the *Wrecking Ball* tour. *Solum, Stian Lysberg/AFP/Getty Images*

(below)
This show in Paris on June 29, 2013, saw Springsteen and the band perform *Born in the U.S.A.* in its entirety. *David Wolff - Patrick/Redferns via Getty Images*

2013, in Los Angeles. Springsteen saw his own songs performed by other musicians, including Patti Smith ("Because the Night"), Elton John ("Streets of Philadelphia"), Emmylou Harris ("My Hometown"), and Neil Young ("Born in the U.S.A."), and then stepped up to perform four songs himself, with everyone joining for the final number, "Glory Days." The performance was later released on the DVD *A MusiCares Tribute to Bruce Springsteen*.

On March 14, Springsteen began a ten-date Australian tour, the first time he'd visited the country in ten years (Van Zandt, busy with his TV show *Lilyhammer*, missed this tour leg; Tom Morello of Rage Against the Machine filled in for him). The tour closed in the state of Victoria, with two outdoor gigs in the shadow of Hanging Rock, a mysterious volcanic formation immortalized in the novel *Picnic at Hanging Rock* and the 1975 film of the same name. After a month's break, the globetrotting resumed with another European leg beginning April 29 in Norway and ending on July 28 in Ireland. After another break, the tour continued in South America, beginning with Springsteen's first-ever appearance in Chile on September 12, then going on to Argentina and Brazil, and closing on September 21 in Rio de Janeiro, with an appearance at the Rock in Rio festival. Springsteen's last appearance of 2013 was at the annual "Stand Up for Heroes" benefit in New York on November 8.

But plans were already in the works for his next album and tour. Since his 2012 meeting with producer Ron Aniello, he had wanted to pull out material from his archives and flesh it out for release with new overdubs, rescuing songs that might otherwise be lost. "This is music I always felt needed to be released," he later explained. The only problem was that Springsteen was still on tour promoting *Wrecking Ball*. That meant sessions were squeezed in during tour breaks in 2012 and 2013, and a total of sixteen studios—in New

In Rome, Italy, on July 11, 2013, headlining the Rock in Roma festival. *Ernesto Ruscio/Redferns via Getty Images*

York, L.A., Atlanta, and Australia, not to mention Springsteen's home studio—were used in the making of the album.

It was during the Australian tour that a cover of "High Hopes," by L.A.-based band Havalinas, had been added to the band's live set, at Tom Morello's suggestion. Springsteen had previously recorded the song in the 1990s and released it on the *Blood Brothers* EP; now the band recorded a new version in Australia, and it became the album's title track. "The Wall," which Springsteen had originally recorded in late 1990s, was inspired by a fellow musician and acquaintance of Springsteen's, Walter Cichon, a member of the Jersey Shore band the Motifs, who went missing in action in Vietnam in March 1968. "He was the first person I ever stood in the presence of who was filled with the mystique of the true rock star," Springsteen wrote in the album's liner notes. The band also recorded new versions of "American Skin" and "Ghost of Tom Joad."

Out of twenty tracks recorded, twelve appeared on the album. Four more ("American Beauty," "Mary Mary," "Hurry Up Sundown," and "Hey Blue Eyes") later appeared on the EP *American Beauty*, released on Record Store Day, April 19, 2014. *High Hopes* also featured some previously recorded contributions from Clarence Clemons (on "Harry's Place" and "Down in the Hole") and Danny Federici ("Down in the Hole" and "The Wall").

With the album ready to go, the band would be back on the road just four months after the *Wrecking Ball* tour had ended. They appeared on *Late Night with Jimmy Fallon* on January 14, 2014, one day before *High Hopes* was released, and performed "High Hopes," "Heaven's Wall," and "Just Like Fire Would" (the latter performance was only available to view online). Springsteen

HIGH HOPES

BRUCE SPRINGSTEEN
HIGH HOPES

Released: January 2014
Chart Position: No. 1 (US), No. 1 (UK)

On his eighteenth studio album, Springsteen decided to dig into his archives, retrieving previously recorded songs and giving them a new buff and shine. He also rerecorded songs from previous albums and threw in some cover songs. The album was recorded in sixteen different studios and featured nearly thirty different musicians, including his three children (who provided backing vocals on "Down in the Hole") and posthumous appearances by Clemons and Federici. It made *High Hopes* one of Springsteen's most unique releases.

The album's three cover songs included the title track, written by Tim Scott McConnell (recorded by both McConnell and his band, the Havalinas). Springsteen himself had first released the song on the 1996 *Blood Brothers* EP. The new version is fleshed out with more instrumentation, giving a sharper edge to a song that looks toward better times in the face of adversity. Springsteen had performed Suicide's "Dream Baby Dream" as a stunning conclusion to his *Devils & Dust* tour; the studio version can't quite match it in intensity. "Just Like Fire Would" is a fine, passionate performance of a song originally recorded by Australian band the Saints.

The new version "The Ghost of Tom Joad" differs substantially from the cut on the album of that name, with more instrumentation and Springsteen trading lyrics with Tom Morello; it's not nearly as poignant as the haunting original. He had also recorded "American Skin (41 Shots)" before, but had released that version only to radio stations; this version finally gave the song its due, injecting new energy into a song that sadly remains all too relevant.

The rest of the album serves up a variety of material, giving *High Hopes* more of a freewheeling feeling than Springsteen's other albums. Sinister characters inhabit "Harry's Place." The industrial banging that opens "Down in the Hole" makes you expect a song about miners, but the lyric reveals a song about heartbreak. The rousing salvation of "Heaven's Wall" follows, complete with gospel choir and a repeated call to "raise your hand" in hope.

"Frankie Fell in Love" is just what its title implies: a rollicking, warm-hearted celebration of new love. The stirring anthem "This Is Your Sword" uses the instruments of war—a sword and a shield—as a metaphor for getting through the battles of life (with love conquering all, naturally); love also lies at the heart of the low-key "Hunter of Invisible Game."

The structure in "The Wall" is the Vietnam Veterans Memorial in Washington, DC. Springsteen had visited the memorial and seen the names of people he knew on the wall and later wrote this tribute to a fellow musician, Walter Cichon, making the sad observation that apologies cannot compensate those who lost their lives.

Was *High Hopes* a means of clearing the decks to inspire a round of new work? Time will tell, though Springsteen's extensive archives could result in another album cobbled together from his past as well.

and Jimmy Fallon also did a parody version of "Born to Run."

"High Hopes" had been released as a single at the end of November 2013, reaching No. 15 in the Adult Alternative Songs chart; now the album topped both *Billboard*'s Top 200 and Top Rock Albums charts, and it hit No. 1 in fourteen other countries as well. A deluxe edition of the album was also available, featuring an exclusive DVD of Springsteen's performance of the *Born in the U.S.A.* album from a June 30, 2013, show in London. A documentary about the making of the album aired on HBO in April.

After another Light of Day benefit, on January 18 at the Paramount Theatre in Asbury Park, Springsteen was off to South Africa, where the *High Hopes* tour opened on January 26 in Cape Town. It was the first of four dates in the region. The tour continued to Australia and New Zealand, with the US tour beginning April 6 in Dallas and closing on May 18, for a total of thirty-four shows. A documentary about the tour was released in Netherlands in May.

Keeping up with the changing technology, the shows were made available for download. Springsteen entered another new realm in fall 2014 when he released a children's book, *Outlaw Pete*, based on his song of the same name from *Working on a Dream*. The project came about when illustrator Frank Caruso was inspired by the song to make some sketches of the action. Caruso and Springsteen had a mutual friend in Dave Marsh, who agreed to pass Frank's work on to Springsteen. A year and a half later, Springsteen called Caruso, intrigued about working on something so different. In the book's afterword, Springsteen stated that the song's influences dated "probably all the way back to the bedtime story 'Brave Cowboy Bill' my mom used to recite from memory to me as a child." Of the depiction of Outlaw Pete's pistol-wielding

The *High Hopes* tour also saw Springsteen heading down under, performing in Australia and New Zealand. This shot is from a February 19, 2014, date in Sydney. *Mark Metcalfe/Getty Images*

(opposite)
The *High Hopes* tour opened with Springsteen's first ever date in South Africa, in Cape Town, on January 26, 2014. *Halden Krog/AFP/Getty Images*

antics as a youngster, he jokingly noted, "A six-month-old, bank-robbing baby is a pretty good protagonist."

"It's a very human story," he told the *Washington Post* when the book was published. "We start carrying some of the baggage of our past as small children. And then at some point we either try to sort it out or outrun it. You can't outrun it, which is what this character tries to do. And it's very difficult to sort it out. But it's the only way to go." Nor did he feel the darker aspects of the story would be off-putting: "The characters are outlandish. They're not real. They're mythical. The tale is a fable. . . . If Bambi is for kids, this is fine. If 'Lion King' is for kids, this will be fine also."

Since the end of the *High Hopes* tour, Springsteen's schedule had encompassed the usual mix of charity shows, drop-ins, and guest appearances. He played with Grushecky on May 22 and 23 in Pittsburgh, and on May 29 with the Rolling Stones in Lisbon, Portugal, for another go-round with "Tumbling Dice." After taking the summer off, he appeared at the annual "Stand Up for Heroes" benefit November 5 at Madison Square Garden, not only playing but also auctioning off two special packages, with the winners receiving a personal guitar lesson from Springsteen, dinner at his home, and

Springsteen inducted the E Street Band himself during the Rock and Roll Hall of Fame induction ceremony on April 10, 2014. *Dimitrios Kambouris/WireImage for Rock and Roll Hall of Fame*

a ride on his motorcycle. On November 11 he performed at "The Concert for Valor," a Veteran's Day show on the National Mall in Washington, DC, playing "Born in the U.S.A." to an audience estimated to be one million strong. He subbed for Bono when U2 was scheduled to play a World AIDS Day concert on December 1 in New York and the band's frontman was still recovering from a bike accident. A week later, on December 7, he was in Washington, DC, at the Kennedy Center Honors , where Sting was one of the recipients and Springsteen was among those who performed his songs in tribute, choosing "I Hung My Head."

There was no tour in 2015. Most of Springsteen's appearances were charity gigs: the annual Light of Day benefit (January 17, Paramount Theatre, Asbury Park); MusiCares' Person of the Year show (February 6, Los Angeles Convention Center), with Springsteen performing "Knockin' on Heaven's Door" in tribute to that year's honoree, Bob Dylan; "A Night to Remember," a fundraiser for the Kristen Ann Carr Fund (May 16, Tribeca Grill, New York City), which saw Springsteen playing with the Sessions Band once again; and the

The Boss isn't the only one who makes appearances at charity events; on October 22, 2014, Van Zandt spoke at the 6th Annual Little Kids Rock Benefit at the Hammerstein Ballroom in New York City, giving the audience the thumbs up afterwards. *Mike Coppola/ Getty Images for Little Kids Rock*

11th Annual MAP Fund Concert (May 28, Best Buy Theater, New York City), honoring Pete Townshend and The Who manager Bill Curbishley for their work with the MusiCares MAP Fund, which provides assistance for musicians recovering from substance abuse.

Springsteen gave a speech at the latter event. "I wouldn't be windmilling a Fender Telecaster if it weren't for Pete Townshend," he stated in his opening remarks, going on to recall how, after first seeing The Who, he'd been inspired to wreak a little havoc at his next gig with the Castiles at Saint Rose of Lima School, bringing a smoke bomb and strobe light and smashing a vase of flowers on the floor "as the nuns looked on in horror." He cited Townshend's influence in his own songwriting as well: "'The Seeker' is the guy in 'Born to Run.' There'd be no 'Down in Jungleland' without Pete's slashing bloody attack on his instrument. . . . Pete managed to take the dirty business of rock 'n' roll and somehow make it spiritual and turn it into a quest. He may hate this, but he identified the place where it was noble, and he wasn't afraid to go there."

You could say much the same thing about Springsteen's own work: he was never afraid to go wherever his muse might take him. *Born to Run* celebrated its fortieth anniversary in 2015. The song and the album had irrevocably changed the course of his career, for himself and for the E Street Band. There was no anniversary reissue of the album that year, though it was the last number performed on the final broadcast of *The Daily Show* on August 6, 2015, with host Jon Stewart asking the band to perform "Land of Hope and Dreams," which segued into the last verse of "Born to Run."

Bruce had also never hesitated to share credit with those who had helped him on his musical journey. On April 10, 2014, at the Barclays Center in Brooklyn, he'd finally had the pleasure of welcoming the E Street Band into the Rock and Roll Hall of Fame; the musicians received the Rock Hall's Award for Musical Excellence. It had been a long time coming—fifteen years since Springsteen himself was inducted—and there had been some hard feelings that the E Street Band wasn't inducted at the same time. Van Zandt had even asked Springsteen to see about getting the E Streeters in that year, telling him that the whole was greater than the sum of its parts: "Bruce Springsteen *and* the E Street Band—that's the legend." And Clarence Clemons had complained to Peter Carlin, "They have a saxophone of mine in the Hall of Fame. . . . But *I'm* still not in there. My fuckin' *saxophone* is in there, but I'm not. And I'm the one who fuckin' *played* it."

Now he'd finally made it, along with Vini Lopez, Danny Federici, Garry Tallent, David Sancious, Roy Bittan, Max Weinberg, Steve Van Zandt, Nils Lofgren, and Patti Scialfa. Clemons's widow, Victoria, accepted the award on her husband's behalf; Jason Federici was there in his father's place.

Springsteen spoke with affection about each of the E Streeters, recalling the days when he first met the musicians: "I was the new kid in a new town and these were the guys who owned the place. They sat back and looked at me like, 'Come on, come on, punk. Bring it; let's see what you got.'" He gave the audience a little trivia, reminding them that David Sancious was the only member of the band who actually lived on E Street. He spoke of Van Zandt, "My consigliere, my dependable devil's advocate whenever I need one," and of having Clemons play with him for the first time, unleashing "the force of nature that was the sound and the soul of the Big Man. In that moment, I knew that my life had changed."

He called Lofgren "one of the world's great, great rock guitarists, with a choir boy's voice," and heralded his wife's singing as "full of a little Ronnie Spector, a little Dusty Springfield and a lot of something that was her very, very own." And he sent out a thank you to Ernie "Boom" Carter, who had only been in the band for five and a half months and wasn't among the inductees, but had made one key appearance on record with Springsteen, on the song "Born to Run."

"I told a story with the E Street Band that was, and is, bigger than I ever could have told on my own," Springsteen said, adding, "that is the hallmark of a rock and roll band—the narrative you tell together is bigger than any one could have told on your own." And then it was time for what Springsteen proudly called "the heart-stopping, pants-dropping, hard-rocking, booty-shaking, love-making, earth-quaking, Viagra-taking, justifying, death-defying, legendary E Street Band" to do what they did best. A short set followed Springsteen's speech: "The E Street Shuffle," "The River," and "Kitty's Back," with both Lopez and Weinberg on drums.

It was a night of triumph for all concerned—another chapter in a story that wasn't close to being over. For Springsteen, whose rock 'n' roll dreams had taken him so far, was as devoted to music as he'd ever been.

"What else would I do?" he responded when, during a 2007 interview for *60 Minutes*, reporter Scott Pelley asked him why he continued to tour. "I mean, am I going to garden? Why would you stop? I mean, you know, you play the music and grown men cry and women dance, and . . . that's why you do it."

Whether with the E Street Band or other musicians, or as a solo act, there is still much more Bruce Springsteen wants to do. "I want to sing about who I am now," he once told *Rolling Stone*. "When I was young, I always said I didn't want to end up being 45 or 50 and pretending I was 15 or 16 or 20. That just didn't interest me. I'm a lifetime musician; I'm going to be playing music forever."

The Ties That Bind: The River Collection, box set, released December 4, 2015

SELECTED
DISCOGRAPHY

NOTE: This selected discography is not exhaustive, as compiling a complete and factually accurate list of Springsteen releases in all countries is nearly impossible. All known major releases from Springsteen are included, and variations and rereleases are noted whenever possible.

STUDIO ALBUMS ★★★★★★★★★

GREETINGS FROM ASBURY PARK, N.J.
Released: Columbia, January 5, 1973; reissued in 1975, 1979, and 1990
Recorded: 914 Sound Studios, Blauvelt, New York (June to October 1972)
Producers: Mike Appel and Jim Cretecos
Musicians: Bruce Springsteen , Clarence Clemons, Richard Davis, Vini Lopez, David Sancious, Garry Tallent, Steve Van Zandt, Harold Wheeler
All songs written by Bruce Springsteen
Tracks: "Blinded by the Light," "Growin' Up," "Mary Queen of Arkansas," "Does This Bus Stop at 82nd Street?," "Lost in the Flood," "The Angel," "For You," "Spirit in the Night," "It's Hard to Be a Saint in the City"

THE WILD, THE INNOCENT & THE E STREET SHUFFLE
Released: Columbia, November 5, 1973; reissued 1975, 1977, and 1990
Recorded: 914 Sound Studios, Blauvelt, New York (May to September 1973)
Producers: Mike Appel and Jim Cretecos
Musicians: Bruce Springsteen, Richard Blackwell, Clarence Clemons, Danny Federici, Suki Lahav, Vini Lopez, David Sancious, Garry Tallent, and Albany "Al" Tellone
All songs written by Bruce Springsteen
Tracks: "The E Street Shuffle," "4th of July, Asbury Park (Sandy)," "Kitty's Back," "Incident on 57th Street," "New York City Serenade," "Rosalita (Come Out Tonight)"

BORN TO RUN
Released: Columbia, September 1, 1975; reissued 1977, 1980, 1993, and 2005
Recorded: Record Plant, New York City; and 914 Sound Studios, Blauvelt, New York (May 1974 to July 1975)
Producers: Bruce Springsteen, Jon Landau, and Mike Appel
Musicians: Bruce Springsteen, Wayne Andre, Mike Appel, Roy Bittan, Michael Brecker, Randy Brecker, Charles Calello, Ernest "Boom" Carter, Clarence Clemons, Richard Davis, Danny Federici, Suki Lahav, David Sanborn, David Sancious, Garry Tallent, Steve Van Zandt, and Max Weinberg
All songs written by Bruce Springsteen
Tracks: "Thunder Road," "Tenth Avenue Freeze-Out," "Night," "Backstreets," "Born to Run," "She's the One," "Meeting Across the River," "Jungleland"

DARKNESS ON THE EDGE OF TOWN
Released: Columbia, June 2, 1978; reissued in 1982 and 1990
Recorded: Record Plant, New York City (June 1977 to January 1978)
Producers: Jon Landau and Bruce Springsteen
Musicians: Bruce Springsteen, Roy Bittan, Clarence Clemons, Danny Federici, Garry Tallent, Steve Van Zandt, and Max Weinberg
All songs written by Bruce Springsteen
Tracks: "Badlands," "Adam Raised a Cain," "Something in the Night," "Candy's Room," "Racing in the Street," "The Promised Land," "Factory," "Streets of Fire," "Prove It All Night," "Darkness on the Edge of Town"

THE RIVER
Released: Columbia, October 17, 1980; reissued in 1978 and 1990
Recorded: Power Station, New York City (March 1979 to May 1980)
Producers: Bruce Springsteen, Jon Landau, and Steve Van Zandt
Musicians: Bruce Springsteen, Roy Bittan, Clarence Clemons, Danny Federici, Flo and Eddie (Howard Kaylan and Mark Volman), Garry Tallent, Steve Van Zandt, and Max Weinberg
All songs written by Bruce Springsteen
Tracks: "The Ties That Bind," "Sherry Darling," "Jackson Cage," "Two Hearts," "Independence Day," "Hungry Heart," "Out in the Street," "Crush on You," "You Can Look (But You Better Not Touch)," "I Wanna Marry You," "The River," "Point Blank," "Cadillac Ranch," "I'm a Rocker," "Fade Away," "Stolen Car," "Ramrod," "The Price You Pay," "Drive All Night," "Wreck on the Highway"

NEBRASKA
Released: Columbia, September 20, 1982; reissued in 1985 (Japan only) and 1990
Recorded: Springsteen's Colts Neck, New Jersey, home (January 1982)
Producer: Bruce Springsteen
Musician: Bruce Springsteen
All songs written by Bruce Springsteen
Tracks: "Nebraska," "Atlantic City," "Mansion on the Hill," "Johnny 99," "Highway Patrolman," "State Trooper," "Used Cars," "Open All Night," "My Father's House," "Reason to Believe"

BORN IN THE U.S.A.
Released: Columbia, June 4, 1984
Recorded: Power Station, New York City; The Hit Factory, New York City; and Thrill Hill West (Springsteen's Beverly Hills, California, home recording studio), Los Angeles (January 1982 to May 1984)
Producers: Bruce Springsteen, Jon Landau, Chuck Plotkin, and Steve Van Zandt

Musicians: Bruce Springsteen, Roy Bittan, Clarence Clemons, Danny Federici, Ruth Jackson, Richie "La Bamba" Rosenberg, Garry Tallent, Steve Van Zandt, and Max Weinberg

All songs written by Bruce Springsteen

Tracks: "Born in the U.S.A.," "Cover Me," "Darlington County," "Working on the Highway," "Downbound Train," "I'm on Fire," "No Surrender," "Bobby Jean," "I'm Goin' Down," "Glory Days," "Dancing in the Dark," "My Hometown"

TUNNEL OF LOVE

Released: Columbia, October 6, 1987; reissued in 2003 in Europe

Recorded: Thrill Hill East (Springsteen's Rumson, New Jersey, home recording studio); Hit Factory, New York City; and A&M Studios, Los Angeles (January to July 1987)

Producers: Bruce Springsteen, Jon Landau, and Chuck Plotkin

Musicians: Bruce Springsteen, Roy Bittan, Clarence Clemons, Danny Federici, Nils Lofgren, The Schiffer Family, Patti Scialfa, Garry Tallent, Steve Van Zandt, Max Weinberg, and James Wood

All songs written by Bruce Springsteen

Tracks: "Ain't Got You," "Tougher Than the Rest," "All That Heaven Will Allow," "Spare Parts," "Cautious Man," "Walk Like a Man," "Tunnel of Love," "Two Faces," "Brilliant Disguise," "One Step Up," "When You're Alone," "Valentine's Day"

HUMAN TOUCH

Released: Columbia, March 31, 1992; issued in Europe in 1992 with *Lucky Town* in a limited-edition mahogany casket

Recorded: A&M Studios, Los Angeles; Soundworks West, Los Angeles; Oceanway Studios, Los Angeles; One On One Studio, Hollywood, California; The Record Plant, Los Angeles; Westlake Studios, Los Angeles; and Thrill Hill West (September 1989 to March 1991)

Producers: Bruce Springsteen, Jon Landau, Chuck Plotkin, and Roy Bittan

Musicians: Bruce Springsteen, Roy Bittan, Michael Fisher, Bobby Hatfield, Mark Isham, Randy Jackson, Bobby King, Douglas Lunn, Ian McLagan, Sam Moore, Tim Pierce, Jeff Porcaro, David Sancious, Patti Scialfa, and Kurt Wortman

All songs written by Bruce Springsteen, except "Cross My Heart" (Springsteen and Sonny Boy Williamson), "Roll of the Dice" and "Real World" (Springsteen and Roy Bittan), and "Pony Boy" (traditional)

Tracks: "Human Touch," "Soul Driver," "57 Channels (and Nothin' On)," "Cross My Heart," "Gloria's Eyes," "With Every Wish," "Roll of the Dice," "Real World," "All or Nothin' at All," "Man's Job," "I Wish I Were Blind," "The Long Goodbye," "Real Man," "Pony Boy"

LUCKY TOWN

Released: Columbia, March 31, 1992; issued in Europe in 1992 with *Human Touch* in a limited-edition mahogany casket

Recorded: Thrill Hill West (Springsteen's Beverly Hills, California, home recording studio); and A&M Studios, Los Angeles (July 1991 to January 1992)

Producers: Bruce Springsteen, Jon Landau, and Chuck Plotkin

Musicians: Bruce Springsteen, Roy Bittan, Randy Jackson, Lisa Lowell, Gary Mallabar, Ian McLagan, Patti Scialfa, and Soozie Tyrell

All songs written by Bruce Springsteen

Tracks: "Better Days," "Lucky Town," "Local Hero," "If I Should Fall Behind," "Leap of Faith," "The Big Muddy," "Living Proof," "Book of Dreams," "Souls of the Departed," "My Beautiful Reward"

THE GHOST OF TOM JOAD

Released: Columbia, November 21, 1995

Recorded: Thrill Hill West (Springsteen's Beverly Hills, California, home recording studio) (March to September 1995)

Producers: Bruce Springsteen and Chuck Plotkin

Musicians: Bruce Springsteen, Jennifer Condos, Danny Federici, Jim Hanson, Lisa Lowell, Gary Mallabar, Chuck Plotkin, Marty Rifkin, Patti Scialfa, Garry Tallent, and Soozie Tyrell

All songs written by Bruce Springsteen

Tracks: "The Ghost of Tom Joad," "Straight Time," "Highway 29," "Youngstown," "Sinaloa Cowboys," "The Line," "Balboa Park," "Dry Lightning," "The New Timer," "Across the Border," "Galveston Bay," "My Best Was Never Good Enough"

THE RISING

Released: Columbia, July 30, 2002

Recorded: Southern Tracks, Atlanta, Georgia (January to March 2002)

Producer: Brendan O'Brien

Musicians: Bruce Springsteen, Alliance Singers (choir), Asif Ali Khan and Group, Roy Bittan, Clarence Clemons, Danny Federici, Jerry Flint, Larry Lemaster, Nils Lofgren, Ed Manion, Nashville String Machine, Brendan O'Brien, Mark Pender, Rich Rosenberg, Jane Scarpantoni, Patti Scialfa, Mike Spengler, Garry Tallent, Soozie Tyrell, Steve Van Zandt, Jerry Vivino, and Max Weinberg

All songs written by Bruce Springsteen

Tracks: "Lonesome Day," "Into the Fire," "Waitin' on a Sunny Day," "Nothing Man," "Countin' on a Miracle," "Empty Sky," "Worlds Apart," "Let's Be Friends (Skin to Skin)," "Further On (Down the Road)," "The Fuse," "Mary's Place," "You're Missing," "The Rising," "Paradise," "My City of Ruins"

DEVILS & DUST

Released: Columbia, April 25, 2005

Recorded: Thrill Hill East (Springsteen's Rumson, New Jersey, home recording studio) and Thrill Hill West (his Beverly Hills, California, home recording studio) (March to August 2004)

Producer: Brendan O'Brien

Musicians: Bruce Springsteen, Brice Andrus, Danny Federici, Steve Jordan, Lisa Lowell, Nashville String Machine, Brendan O'Brien, Mark Pender, Chuck Plotkin, Marty Rifkin, Patti Scialfa, Donald Strand, Soozie Tyrell, Susan Welty, and Thomas Witte

All songs written by Bruce Springsteen

Tracks: "Devils & Dust," "All the Way Home," "Reno," "Long Time Comin'," "Black Cowboys," "Maria's Bed," "Silver Palomino," "Jesus Was an Only Son," "Leah," "The Hitter," "All I'm Thinkin' About," "Matamoros Banks"

WE SHALL OVERCOME: THE SEEGER SESSIONS

Released: Columbia, April 24, 2006
Recorded: Thrill Hill East (Springsteen's Rumson, New Jersey, home recording studio) (November 1997, March 2005, and January 2006)
Producer: Bruce Springsteen
Musicians: Bruce Springsteen, Sam Bardfield, Art Baron, Frank Bruno, Jeremy Chatzky, Mark Clifford, Larry Eagle, Charles Giordano, Lisa Lowell, Ed Manion, Mark Pender, Richie "La Bamba" Rosenberg, Patti Scialfa, and Soozie Tyrell
All songs traditional, except "Jesse James" by Billy Gashade; "Erie Canal" by Thomas S. Allen; "My Oklahoma Home" by Bill and Agnes "Sis" Cunningham; and "We Shall Overcome," adapted by Guy Carawan, Frank Hamilton, Zilphia Horton, and Pete Seeger.
Tracks: "Old Dan Tucker," "Jesse James," "Mrs. McGrath," "O Mary Don't You Weep," "John Henry," "Erie Canal," "Jacob's Ladder," "My Oklahoma Home," "Eyes on the Prize," "Shenandoah," "Pay Me My Money Down," "We Shall Overcome," "Froggie Went a-Courtin'"

MAGIC

Released: Columbia, October 2, 2007
Recorded: Southern Tracks, Atlanta, Georgia (February to June 2007)
Producer: Brendan O'Brien
Musicians: Bruce Springsteen, Roy Bittan, Justin Bruns, Amy Chang, Jeremy Chatzky, Jay Christy, Tania Maxwell Clements, Clarence Clemons, Danny Federici, Karen Freer, Charae Kruege, Daniel Laufer, Nils Lofgren, Sheila Lyengar, Lachlan McBane, John Meisner, Christopher Pulgram, Patti Scialfa, Olga Shpitko, Garry Tallent, Soozie Tyrell, Steve Van Zandt, Kenn Wagner, Patrick Warren, and Max Weinberg
All songs written by Bruce Springsteen
Tracks: "Radio Nowhere," "You'll Be Comin' Down," "Livin' in the Future," "Your Own Worst Enemy," "Gypsy Biker," "Girls in Their Summer Clothes," "I'll Work for Your Love," "Magic," "Last to Die," "Long Walk Home," "Devil's Arcade," "Terry's Song"

WORKING ON A DREAM

Released: Columbia, January 27, 2009
Recorded: Southern Tracks, Atlanta, Georgia (2007–2008)
Producer: Brendan O'Brien
Musicians: Bruce Springsteen, Roy Bittan, Clarence Clemons, Danny Federici, Jason Federici, Eddie Horst, Nils Lofgren, Patti Scialfa, Garry Tallent, Soozie Tyrell, Steve Van Zandt, Patrick Warren, and Max Weinberg
All songs written by Bruce Springsteen
Tracks: "Outlaw Pete," "My Lucky Day," "Working on a Dream," "Queen of the Supermarket," "What Love Can Do," "This Life," "Good Eye," "Tomorrow Never Knows," "Life Itself," "Kingdom of Days," "Surprise, Surprise," "The Last Track," "The Wrestler"

WRECKING BALL

Released: Columbia, March 6, 2012
Recorded: Stone Hill Studio (another name for Springsteen's Rumson, New Jersey, home recording studio) (recording dates unknown)

Producers: Ron Aniello and Bruce Springsteen
Musicians: Bruce Springsteen, Tiffany Andrews, Ron Aniello, Art Baron, Lilly Brown, Kevin Buell, Corinda Carford, Matt Chamberlain, Clarence Clemons, Soloman Cobbs, Clark Gayton, Charles Giordano, Stan Harrison, Steve Jordan, Rob Lebret, Greg Leisz, Darrell Leonard, Dan Levine, Lisa Lowell, Ed Manion, Cindy Mizelle, Michelle Moore, Tom Morello, Marc Muller, New York Chamber Consort, Clif Norrell, Ross Peterson, Curt Ramm, Antoinette Savage, Patti Scialfa, Soozie Tyrell, Victorious Gospel Choir, and Max Weinberg
All songs written by Bruce Springsteen
Tracks: "We Take Care of Our Own," "Easy Money," "Shackled and Drawn," "Jack of All Trades," "Death to My Hometown," "This Depression," "Wrecking Ball," "You've Got It," "Rocky Ground," "Land of Hopes and Dreams"

HIGH HOPES

Released: Columbia, January 13, 2014
Recorded: Between 2002 and 2013 at sixteen different studios across the United States and in Australia; see the notes on the album on brucebase.wikispaces.com for a full recounting of the recordings and studios used.
Producers: Ron Aniello and Bruce Springsteen
Musicians: Bruce Springsteen, Tawatha Agee, Ron Aniello, Atlanta Strings, Sam Bardfeld, Roy Bittan, Everett Bradley, Clarence Clemons, Jake Clemons, Barry Danielian, Danny Federici, Keith Fluitt, Josh Freese, Clark Gayton, Charles Giordano, Stan Harrison, John James, Jeff Kievit, Curtis King, Nils Lofgren, Ed Manion, Cindy Mizelle, Michelle Moore, Tom Morello, New York Chamber Consort Strings, Curt Ramm, Patti Scialfa, Evan Springsteen, Jessie Springsteen, Sam Springsteen, Garry Tallent, Al Thornton, Scott Tibbs, Soozie Tyrell, Cillian Vallely, Steve Van Zandt, Brenda White, and Max Weinberg
All songs written by Bruce Springsteen, except "Cross My Heart" by Bruce Springsteen and Sonny Boy Williamson; "Roll of the Dice" by Bruce Springsteen and Roy Bittan; and "Pony Boy" (traditional)
Tracks: "Human Touch," "Soul Driver," "57 Channels (and Nothin' On)," "Cross My Heart," "Gloria's Eyes," "With Every Wish," "Roll of the Dice," "Real World," "All or Nothin' at All," "Man's Job," "I Wish I Were Blind," "The Long Goodbye," "Real Man," "Pony Boy"

LIVE ALBUMS ★ ★ ★ ★ ★ ★ ★ ★ ★ ★

LIVE/1975–85

Released: Columbia, November 10, 1986; reissued in 1997 and 2002
Producers: Jon Landau, Chuck Plotkin, and Bruce Springsteen
Musicians: Bruce Springsteen, Roy Bittan, Clarence Clemons, Danny Federici, Flo and Eddie (Howard Kaylan and Mark Volman), Nils Lofgren, The Miami Horns, Patti Scialfa, Garry Tallent, Steve Van Zandt, and Max Weinberg
All songs written by Bruce Springsteen, except "Raise Your Hand" by Steve Cropper, Eddie Floyd, and Alvertis Isbell; "Because the Night" by Bruce Springsteen and Patti Smith; "This Land Is Your Land" by Woody Guthrie; "War" by Barrett Strong and Norman Whitfield; and "Jersey Girl" by Tom Waits
Tracks: "Thunder Road," "Adam Raised a Cain," "Spirit in the Night," "4th of July, Asbury Park (Sandy)," "Paradise by the 'C'," "Fire," "Growin' Up," "It's Hard to Be a Saint in the City," "Backstreets," "Rosalita (Come Out Tonight)," "Raise Your

Hand," "Hungry Heart," "Two Hearts," "Cadillac Ranch," "You Can Look (But You Better Not Touch)," "Independence Day," "Badlands," "Because the Night," "Candy's Room," "Darkness on the Edge of Town," "Racing in the Street," "This Land Is Your Land," "Nebraska," "Johnny 99," "Reason to Believe," "Born in the U.S.A." "Seeds," "The River," "War," "Darlington County," "Working on the Highway," "The Promised Land," "Cover Me," "I'm On Fire," "Bobby Jean," "My Hometown," "Born to Run," "No Surrender," "Tenth Avenue Freeze-Out," "Jersey Girl"

IN CONCERT/MTV PLUGGED

Released: Columbia, April 12, 1993, in the UK; August 1993 in the US
Producers: Bruce Springsteen and Jon Landau
Musicians: Bruce Springsteen, Zachary Alford, Roy Bittan, Gia Ciambotti, Carol Dennis, Shane Fontayne, Cleopatra Kennedy, Bobby King, Angel Rogers, Patti Scialfa, Tommy Sims, and Crystal Taliefero
All songs written by Bruce Springsteen
Tracks: "Red Headed Woman," "Better Days," "Atlantic City," "Darkness on the Edge of Town," "Man's Job," "Human Touch," "Lucky Town," "I Wish I Were Blind," "Thunder Road," "Light of Day," "If I Should Fall Behind," "Living Proof," "My Beautiful Reward"

LIVE IN NEW YORK CITY

Released: Columbia, March 27, 2001
Producers: Bruce Springsteen and Chuck Plotkin
Musicians: Bruce Springsteen, Roy Bittan, Clarence Clemons, Danny Federici, Nils Lofgren, Patti Scialfa, Garry Tallent, Steve Van Zandt, and Max Weinberg
All songs written by Bruce Springsteen
Tracks: "My Love Will Not Let You Down," "Prove It All Night," "Two Hearts," "Atlantic City," "Mansion on the Hill," "The River," "Youngstown," "Murder Incorporated," "Badlands," "Out in the Street," "Born to Run," "Tenth Avenue Freeze-Out," "Land of Hope and Dreams," "American Skin (41 Shots)," "Lost in the Flood," "Born in the U.S.A.," "Don't Look Back," "Jungleland," "Ramrod," "If I Should Fall Behind"

HAMMERSMITH ODEON LONDON '75

Released: Columbia, February 28, 2006
Producers: Bruce Springsteen and Jon Landau
Musicians: Bruce Springsteen, Roy Bittan, Clarence Clemons, Danny Federici, Garry Tallent, Steve Van Zandt, and Max Weinberg
All songs written by Bruce Springsteen, except "Detroit Medley" by William Stevenson and Frederick "Shorty" Long; "C. C. Rider" by Gertrude "Ma" Rainey and Leana Arant; "Good Golly Miss Molly" by Robert Blackwell and John Marascalco; "Jenny Takes a Ride" by Bob Crewe, Enotris Johnson, and Richard Penniman; and "Quarter to Three" by Gene Barge, Frank J. Gilda, Joseph F. Royster, and Gary Anderson
Tracks: "Thunder Road," "Tenth Avenue Freeze-Out," "Spirit in the Night," "Lost in the Flood," "She's the One," "Born to Run," "The E Street Shuffle," "It's Hard to Be a Saint in the City," "Kitty's Back," "Backstreets," "Jungleland," "Rosalita (Come Out Tonight)," "4th of July, Asbury Park (Sandy)," "Detroit Medley," "For You," "Quarter to Three"

LIVE IN DUBLIN

Released: Columbia, June 5, 2007
Producers: Bruce Springsteen and Jon Landau
Musicians: Bruce Springsteen, Sam Bardfield, Art Baron, Frank Bruno, Jeremy Chatzky, Larry Eagle, Clark Gayton, Charles Giordano, Curtis King Jr., Lisa Lowell, Ed Manion, Cindy Mizelle, Curt Ramm, Marty Rifkin, Patti Scialfa, and Soozie Tyrell
All songs traditional, except "Atlantic City," "Further On (Down the Road)," "If I Should Fall Behind," "How Can a Poor Man Stand Such Times and Live," "Long Time Comin'," "Open All Night," "Growin' Up," "American Land," and "Blinded by the Light" by Bruce Springsteen; "Jesse James" by Billy Gashade; "Erie Canal" by Thomas S. Allen; "My Oklahoma Home" by Bill and Agnes "Sis" Cunningham; "We Shall Overcome," adapted by Guy Carawan, Frank Hamilton, Zilphia Horton, and Pete Seeger; and "Love of the Common People" by John Hurley and Ronnie Wilkins
Tracks: "Atlantic City," "Old Dan Tucker," "Eyes on the Prize," "Jesse James," "Further On Down the Road," "O Mary Don't You Weep," "Erie Canal," "If I Should Fall Behind," "My Oklahoma Home," "Highway Patrolman," "Mrs. McGrath," "How Can a Poor Man Stand Such Times and Live," "Jacob's Ladder," "Long Time Comin'," "Open All Night," "Pay Me My Money Down," "Growin' Up," "When the Saints Go Marchin' In," "This Little Light of Mine," "American Land," "Blinded by the Light," "Love of the Common People," "We Shall Overcome"

COMPILATION ALBUMS ★★★

GREATEST HITS

Released: Columbia, February 27, 1995
Tracks: "Born to Run," "Thunder Road," "Badlands," "The River," "Hungry Heart," "Atlantic City," "Dancing in the Dark," "Born in the U.S.A.," "My Hometown," "Glory Days," "Brilliant Disguise," "Human Touch," "Better Days," "Streets of Philadelphia," "Secret Garden," "Murder Incorporated," "Blood Brothers," "This Hard Land"

TRACKS

Released: Columbia, November 10, 1998
Tracks: "Mary Queen of Arkansas," "It's Hard to Be a Saint in the City," "Growin' Up," "Does This Bus Stop at 82nd Street?," "Bishop Danced," "Santa Ana," "Seaside Bar Song," "Zero and Blind Terry," "Linda Let Me Be the One," "Thundercrack," "Rendezvous," "Give the Girl a Kiss," "Iceman," "Bring on the Night," "So Young and In Love," "Hearts of Stone," "Don't Look Back," "Restless Nights," "A Good Man Is Hard to Find (Pittsburgh)," "Roulette," "Dollhouse," "Where the Bands Are," "Loose Ends," "Living on the Edge of the World," "Wages of Sin," "Take 'Em as They Come," "Be True," "Ricky Wants a Man of Her Own," "I Wanna Be with You," "Mary Lou," "Stolen Car," "Born in the U.S.A.," "Johnny Bye Bye," "Shut Out the Light," "Cynthia," "My Love Will Not Let You Down," "This Hard Land," "Frankie," "TV Movie," "Stand On It," "Lion's Den," "Car Wash," "Rockaway the Days," "Brothers Under the Bridge ('83)," "Man at the Top," "Pink Cadillac," "Two for the Road," "Janey, Don't You Lose Heart," "When You Need Me," "The Wish," "The Honeymooners," "Lucky Man," "Leavin' Train," "Seven Angels," "Gave It a Name," "Sad Eyes," "My Lover Man," "Over the Rise," "When the Lights Go Out," "Loose Change," "Trouble in Paradise," "Happy," "Part Man, Part Monkey," "Goin' Call," "Back in Your Arms," "Brothers Under the Bridge"

18 TRACKS

Released: Columbia, April 13, 1999

Tracks: "Growin' Up," "Seaside Bar Song," "Rendezvous," "Hearts of Stone," "Where the Bands Are," "Loose Ends," "I Wanna Be with You," "Born in the U.S.A.," "My Love Will Not Let You Down," "Lion's Den," "Pink Cadillac," "Janey, Don't You Lose Heart," "Sad Eyes," "Part Man, Part Monkey," "Trouble River," "Brothers Under the Bridge," "The Fever," "The Promise"

THE ESSENTIAL BRUCE SPRINGSTEEN

Released: Columbia, November 11, 2003

Tracks: "Blinded by the Light," "For You," "Spirit in the Night," "4th of July, Asbury Park (Sandy)," "Rosalita (Come Out Tonight)," "Thunder Road," "Born to Run," "Jungleland," "Badlands," "Darkness on the Edge of Town," "The Promised Land," "The River," "Hungry Heart," "Nebraska," "Atlantic City," "Born in the U.S.A.," "Glory Days," "Dancing in the Dark," "Tunnel of Love," "Brilliant Disguise," "Human Touch," "Living Proof," "Lucky Town," "Streets of Philadelphia," "The Ghost of Tom Joad," "The Rising," "Mary's Place," "Lonesome Day," "American Skin (41 Shots) (Live)," "Land of Hope and Dreams (Live)," "From Small Things (Big Things One Day Will Come)," "The Big Payback," "Held Up Without a Gun (Live)," "Trapped (Live)," "None but the Brave," "Missing," "Lift Me Up," "Viva Las Vegas," "County Fair," "Code of Silence (Live)," "Dead Man Walkin'," "Countin' on a Miracle (Acoustic)"

GREATEST HITS (BRUCE SPRINGSTEEN & THE E STREET BAND)

Released: Columbia, January 13, 2009

Tracks: "Blinded by the Light," "Rosalita (Come Out Tonight)," "Born to Run," "Thunder Road," "Badlands," "Darkness on the Edge of Town," "Hungry Heart," "The River," "Born in the U.S.A.," "Glory Days," "Dancing in the Dark," "The Rising," "Lonesome Day," "Radio Nowhere," "Long Walk Home" (Europe only), "Because the Night (Live)" (Europe only), "Radio Nowhere (Live)" (Europe only)

THE PROMISE

Released: Columbia, November 16, 2010

Tracks: "Racing in the Street," "Gotta Get That Feeling," "Outside Looking In," "Someday (We'll Be Together)," "One Way Street," "Because the Night," "Wrong Side of the Street," "The Brokenhearted," "Rendezvous," "Candy's Boy," "Save My Love," "Ain't Good Enough for You," "Fire," "Spanish Eyes," "It's a Shame," "Come On (Let's Go Tonight)," "Talk to Me," "The Little Things (My Baby Days)," "Breakaway," "The Promise," "City of Night"

COLLECTION: 1973–2012 (COLUMBIA)

Released: Columbia, March 8, 2013 (in Australia); April 2013 (in Europe)

Tracks: "Rosalita (Come Out Tonight)," "Thunder Road," "Born to Run," "Badlands," "The Promised Land," "Hungry Heart," "Atlantic City," "Born in the U.S.A.," "Dancing in the Dark," "Brilliant Disguise," "Human Touch," "Streets of Philadelphia," "The Ghost of Tom Joad," "The Rising," "Radio Nowhere," "Working on a Dream," "We Take Care of Our Own," "Wrecking Ball"

BOX SETS ★ ★ ★ ★ ★ ★ ★ ★ ★ ★ ★ ★ ★ ★

THE BORN IN THE U.S.A. TWELVE-INCH SINGLE COLLECTION

Released: CBS Records, January 1, 1985 (UK only)

Notes: Features four twelve-inch vinyl EPs and one seven-inch vinyl 45, plus a color foldout poster of Springsteen

THE COLLECTION

Released: August 30, 2005

Note: Collection of three previously released full-album CDs

THE COLLECTION 1973–1984

Released: Phantasm Imports, August 24, 2010

Note: Collection of Springsteen's first seven studio albums on eight CDs

THE PROMISE: THE DARKNESS ON THE EDGE OF TOWN STORY

Released: Columbia, November 16, 2010

Notes: Six-disc (three CD, three DVD) box set containing the remastered *The Darkness on the Edge of Town* CD and two-CD set *The Promise: The Lost Sessions* from *Darkness on the Edge of Town*, with twenty-one previously unreleased tracks from the *Darkness* recording sessions. Also included is a 1978 bootleg Houston concert DVD, the feature-length documentary *The Promise: The Making of "Darkness" on the Edge of Town*, and a 2009 E Street Band performance of the entire album in Asbury Park, New Jersey.

COLLECTION: 1973–2012 AUSTRALIAN TOUR EDITION 2013

Released: Sony, March 12, 2013

Note: Two-CD collection released at the time of Springsteen's 2013 tour of Australia, featuring eighteen songs spanning his entire career to date

THE ALBUM COLLECTION VOL. 1 1973–1984

Released: Columbia, November 17, 2014

Note: Eight-CD set of remastered versions of the first seven Springsteen albums, plus a small book

THE TIES THAT BIND: THE RIVER COLLECTION

Released: Columbia, December 4, 2015

Note: Four CDs and three DVDs, or four CDs and three Blu-ray discs, including fifty-two tracks and four hours of concert video, plus a coffee-table book

SINGLES AND EPs ★ ★ ★ ★ ★ ★ ★ ★

1973 "Blinded by the Light" (Mono)/"Blinded by the Light" (Stereo)

1973 "Blinded by the Light"/"The Angel"

1973 "Spirit in the Night"/"For You"

1974 "4th of July, Asbury Park (Sandy)"/"The E Street Shuffle" (Germany)

1975 "Born to Run"/"Meeting Across the River"

1975 "Tenth Avenue Freeze-Out"/"She's the One"

1975 "Rosalita (Come Out Tonight)/"Night" (Netherlands)

1977 "Blinded by the Light" (Mono)/"Blinded by the Light" (Stereo) (Spain)

1978 "Prove It All Night"/"Factory"
1978 "Badlands"/"Streets of Fire"
1978 "The Promised Land"/"Streets of Fire" (UK)
1979 "Rosalita (Come Out Tonight)"/"Night" (Europe)
1980 "Hungry Heart"/"Held Up Without a Gun"
1981 "Fade Away"/"Be True"
1981 "I Wanna Marry You"/"Be True" (Japan)
1981 "Sherry Darling"/"Be True" (UK)
1981 "The River"/"Independence Day" (UK)
1981 "Cadillac Ranch"/"Wreck on the Highway" (UK)
1981 "Cadillac Ranch"/"Be True" (France)
1981 "Point Blank"/"Ramrod" (Europe)
1981 "The Ties That Bind"/"I'm a Rocker" (South Africa)
1982 "Atlantic City"/"Mansion on the Hill" (UK and Canada)
1982 "Open All Night"/"The Big Payback" (Europe)
1984 "Dancing in the Dark"/"Pink Cadillac"
1984 "Cover Me"/"Jersey Girl (Live)"
1984 "Born in the U.S.A."/"Shut Out the Light" (US)
1985 "I'm on Fire"/"Johnny Bye Bye" (US)
1985 "I'm on Fire"/"Born in the U.S.A." (double A-side) (UK)
1985 "Glory Days"/"Stand On It"
1985 "I'm Goin' Down"/"Janey, Don't You Lose Heart" (US)
1985 "My Hometown"/"Santa Claus Is Comin' to Town (Live)"
1986 "War (Live)"/"Merry Christmas Baby (Live)"
1987 "Fire (Live)"/"Incident on 57th Street (Live)" (US)
1987 "Fire (Live)"/"For You (Live)" (UK)
1987 "Born to Run (Live)"/"Johnny 99 (Live)" (UK)
1987 "Brilliant Disguise"/"Lucky Man"
1987 "Tunnel of Love"/"Two for the Road"
1988 "One Step Up"/"Roulette" (US)
1988 "Tougher Than the Rest"/"Tougher Than the Rest (Live)"
1988 "Spare Parts"/"Spare Parts (Live)" (UK)
1992 "Human Touch"/"Better Days" (Double A-side) (US)
1992 "Human Touch"/"Souls of the Departed" (UK)
1992 *Chimes of Freedom* EP with "Tougher Than the Rest (Live)"/"Be True (Live)"/"Chimes of Freedom (Live)"/"Born to Run (Live)"
1992 "Better Days" (US; also issued in different formats and varying song selections for Europe, UK, Spain, and Australia)
1992 "Spare Parts"/"Spare Parts (Live)" (UK)
1992 "57 Channels and Nothin' On (The Remixes)" (US; also issued in different formats and varying song selections for Europe, UK, Spain, Austria, Japan, and Australia)
1992 "Leap of Faith" (US; also issued in different formats and varying song selections for Europe, UK, Spain, Austria, Netherlands, and Australia)
1992 "Lucky Town"/"Leap of Faith (Live)"/"30 Days Out" (CD single Europe)
1992 "If I Should Fall Behind"/"If I Should Fall Behind (Live)" (UK)
1993 "Lucky Town (Live)"/"Lucky Town" (UK)
1994 "Streets of Philadelphia"/"If I Should Fall Behind (Live)"
1995 "Murder Incorporated"/ "Because the Night (Live)" (Europe)

1995 "Secret Garden"/ "Thunder Road (Live)"
1995 "Hungry Heart '95"/"Streets of Philadelphia (Live)" (UK)
1995 "The Ghost of Tom Joad" (US; also issued in different formats and varying song selections for Europe and Japan)
1995 *Blood Brothers* EP with "Blood Brothers"/"High Hopes"/"Murder Incorporated (Live)"/"Secret Garden (String Version)"/"Without You"
1996 "Dead Man Walkin'"/"This Hard Life" (Europe)
1996 "Missing"/"Darkness on the Edge of Town (Live)" (Europe)
1996 "The Ghost of Tom Joad"/"Straight Time (Live)" (UK)
1996 *Blood Brothers* EP with "Blood Brothers"/"High Hopes"/"Murder Incorporated (Live)"/"Secret Garden (String Version)"/ "Without You"
1997 "Secret Garden"/ "Missing"/ "High Hopes"/"The Ghost of Tom Joad" (Europe; also issued in different formats and varying song selections for Netherlands, Spain, Australia, and Japan)
1999 "I Wanna Be with You"/"Where the Bands Are"/"Born in the U.S.A"/"Back in Your Arms Again" (Europe and Japan)
1999 "Sad Eyes"/"Missing" (Europe)
2002 "The Rising"/"Land of Hopes and Dreams"
2002 "Lonesome Day"/"Spirit in the Night (Live)"/ "The Rising (Live)"/"Lonesome Day"
2003 "Waitin' on a Sunny Day"/"Born to Run (Live)"/"Darkness on the Edge of Town (Live)"/"Thunder Road" (UK)
2005 "Devils & Dust"
2005 "All the Way Home" (Europe)
2007 "Radio Nowhere"
2008 "Girls in Their Summer Clothes (Winter Mix)"/"Girls in Their Summer Clothes (Album Version)"/"Girls in Their Summer Clothes (Video)"
2008 *Magic Tour Highlights* EP with "Always a Friend"/"The Ghost of Tom Joad"/"Turn! Turn! Turn!"/"4th of July, Asbury Park (Sandy)" (US)
2008 "Dream Baby Dream"/"Suicide"/"Beat the Devil" (UK)
2008 "Working on a Dream"
2008 "My Lucky Day"
2008 "The Wrestler"
2009 "What Love Can Do"/"A Night with the Jersey Devil" (US limited-edition single for Record Store Day)
2009 "Wrecking Ball (Live)"/"The Ghost of Tom Joad (Live)" (US limited-edition single for Record Store Day)
2010 "Save My Love"/"Because the Night" (US limited-edition single for Record Store Day)
2011 *Live from the Carousel* with "Gotta Get That Feeling"/"Racing in the Street ('78)" (US limited-edition single for Record Store Day)
2012 "We Take Care of Our Own"
2012 "Death to My Hometown"
2012 "Rocky Ground"/"The Promise (Live)" (US limited-edition single for Record Store Day)
2013 "High Hopes"
2014 "Just Like Fire Would"
2014 *American Beauty* EP with "American Beauty"/"Mary Mary"/"Hurry Up Sundown"/"Hey Blue Eyes" (US limited-edition EP for Record Store Day)

BIBLIOGRAPHY

BOOKS

Burger, Jeff. *Springsteen on Springsteen: Interviews, Speeches, and Encounters.* Chicago: Chicago Review Press, 2013.

Carlin, Peter Ames. *Bruce.* New York: Touchstone, 2012.

Clemons, Clarence, and Don Reo. *Big Man: Real Life & Tall Tales.* New York: Grand Central Publishing, 2009.

Davis, Clive, with Anthony DeCurtis. *The Soundtrack of My Life.* New York: Simon & Schuster, 2012.

Dolan, Marc. *Bruce Springsteen and the Promise of Rock 'n' Roll.* New York: W. W. Norton & Company, 2013.

Eliot, Marc, with Mike Appel. *Down Thunder Road: The Making of Bruce Springsteen.* New York: Simon & Schuster, 1992.

Goodman, Fred. *The Mansion on the Hill.* New York: Times Books, 1997.

Heylin, Clinton. *E Street Shuffle: The Glory Days of Bruce Springsteen & the E Street Band.* New York: Viking Penguin, 2013.

Luerssen, John D. *Bruce Springsteen FAQ.* New York: Backbeat Books, 2012.

Marsh, Dave. *Bruce Springsteen: On Tour 1968–2005.* New York: Bloomsbury USA, 2006.

Phillips, Christopher, and Louis P. Masur, eds. *Talk About a Dream: The Essential Interviews of Bruce Springsteen.* New York: Bloomsbury Press, 2013.

Wenner, Jann S., and Joe Levy, eds. *The Rolling Stone Interviews.* New York: Back Bay Books, 2007.

White, Ryan. *Springsteen: Album by Album.* New York: Sterling, 2014.

MAGAZINES

Springsteen: The Ultimate Collector's Edition. Uncut magazine special edition, 2015.

WEBSITES

Absecon-Island-NJ. www.acsurfhistory.wordpress.com/people /9-challenger-eastern-surfboards.

Bruce Springsteen lyrics. www.azlyrics.com/s/springsteen.html.

Bruce Springsteen.net. www.brucespringsteen.net.

Brucebase. www.brucebase.wikispaces.com.

Castiles.net. www.castiles.net.

ARTICLES

Andrews, John Garrett. "Born to (Almost Not) Run." *TheHuffingtonPost.com,* September 4, 2013. www.huffingtonpost.com/john-garrett-andrews /born-to-almost-not-run-ho_b_3863473.html.

Associated Press. "Like Father, Like Son—Douglas and Bruce Springsteen." May 2, 1998.

Bangs, Lester. "Greetings from Asbury Park, NJ," *Rolling Stone,* July 5, 1973.

Barnes, Julian. "Springsteen Song about Diallo Prompts Anger from Police." *New York Times,* June 13, 2000.

Cahillan, Kevin. "Two Guys Left Behind In the E Street Shuffle." *New York Times,* May 1, 2005.

Cashill, Jack. "Bruce, You Ain't da Boss Is dis Garden State." *Cashill.com.* www.cashill.com/natl_general/bruce_you_aint_da_boss.htm.

CBS News. "Kennedy Center Honors Springsteen, DeNiro." *CBSNews.com,* December 6, 2009. www.cbsnews.com/news/kennedy-center-honors-springsteen-de-niro/.

Comaratte, Len. "Dusting 'Em Off: Bruce Springsteen with Steel Mill — Live at the Matrix, San Francisco 1/13/70." *Consequence of Sound.* March 03, 2012. www.consequenceofsound.net/2012/03/dusting-em-off-bruce-springsteen-with-steel-mill-live-at-the-matrix-san-francisco-11370/.

Dolan, Marc. "How Ronald Reagan Changed Bruce Springsteen's Politics." *Politico.com.* June 4, 2014. www.politico.com/magazine/story/2014/06 /bruce-springsteen-ronald-reagan-107448#.Vdyncs61--Y.

Doyle, Jack. "Barack & Bruce, 2008-2012." *PopHistoryDig.com.* December 14, 2012. www.pophistorydig.com/topics/obama-springsteen -2008-2012/.

Dunn, Jancee. "Patti Scialfa's the Boss." *RollingStone.com.* June 16, 2004. www.rollingstone.com/music/news/patt-scialfas-the-boss-20040616.

Elvis Australia. "The Night Bruce Springsteen Jumped the Fence at Graceland." *Elvis Australia.* September 1, 2003. www.elvis.com.au /presley/article_thenightspringsteenjumpedthefence.shtml.

Get NJ. "Asbury Park Guide: Was *Born to Run* Almost the Official New Jersey State Song?" *WelcomeToAsburyPark.com.* 2005. www.welcometoasburypark.com/borntorun121.shtml.

Greene, Andy. "Exclusive: Clarence Clemons Opens Up about Health Problems, Future of E Street Band." *RollingStone.com*. February 24, 2011. www.rollingstone.com/music/news/exclusive-clarence-clemons-opens-up-about-health-problems-future-of-e-street-band-20110224.

Greene, Andy. "E Street Band's Clarence Clemons Dies at 69." *RollingStone.com*. June 18, 2011. www.rollingstone.com/music/news/e-street-bands-clarence-clemons-dies-at-69-20110618?page=2.

Greene, Andy. "Bruce Springsteen Details Massive 'The River' Box Set." *RollingStone.com*. October 15, 2015. www.rollingstone.com/music/news/bruce-springsteen-details-massive-the-river-box-set-20151015.

Hiatt, Brian. "New York Mayor, Police Chief Criticize Springsteen Song." *MTVNews.com*. June 12, 2000. www.mtv.com/news/971923/new-york-mayor-police-chief-criticize-springsteen-song/.

Keller, Daniel. "Bruce Springsteen's 'Nebraska'—a PortaStudio, two SM57's and Inspiration." *TASCAM.com*. July 25, 2007. www.tascam.com/news/display/226/.

Krug, Nora. "Bruce Springsteen on 'Outlaw Pete' and Not Sheltering Kids from the Realities of Life." *Washington Post*. November 3, 2014.

Landau, Jon. "Growing Young with Rock and Roll." *Real Paper*. May 22, 1974.

Lifton, Dave. "'I Saw Rock and Roll Future': The History of Bruce Springsteen and Jon Landau." *UltimateClassicRock.com*. May 9, 2014. www.ultimateclassicrock.com/bruce-springsteen-jon-landau/.

Lifton, Dave. "42 Years Ago: Bruce Springsteen Gets Going with 'Greetings From Asbury Park, N.J.'" *UltimateClassicRock.com*. January 5, 2015. www.ultimateclassicrock.com/bruce-springsteen-greetings-from-asbury-park-n-j-released/.

Lifton, Dave. "Bruce Springsteen's Transformation: The History of 'Born in the U.S.A." *UltimateClassicRock.com*. June 4, 2015. www.ultimateclassicrock.com/bruce-springsteen-born-in-the-u-s-a/.

Lifton, Dave. "35 Years Ago: Bruce Springsteen's 'Born to Run' proposed as 'Unofficial Theme' of New Jersey's Youth." *UltimateClassicRock.com*. April 17, 2015. www.ultimateclassicrock.com/born-to-run-new-jersey-state-song/.

Marcus, Greil. "Record Review: Born to Run." *Rolling Stone*. October 9, 1975.

McGee, David. "Bruce Springsteen Reclaims the Future." *Rolling Stone*. August 11, 1977.

Moser, John J. "How Bruce Springsteen's 'Born to Run' Almost Died in Kutztown." *The Morning Call*. April 6, 2013. www.articles.mcall.com/2013-04-06/news/mc-bruce-springsteen-born-to-run-kutztown-20130406_1_bruce-springsteen-springsteen-saxophonist-clarence-clemons-kutztown.

Nichols, John. "Today Comes the Referendum: Will We 'Take Care of Our Own'?" *TheNation.com*. November 6, 2012. www.thenation.com/article/today-comes-referendum-will-we-take-care-our-own/.

Orth, Maureen, Janet Huck, and Peter S. Greenberg. "The Making of a Rock Star." *Newsweek*. October 27, 1975.

Pilkington, Ed. "Twice in a Lifetime." *Guardian*. February 16, 2009.

Rolling Stone. "Bruce Springsteen Honored at Kennedy Center by Mellencamp, Vedder, Sting." *Rolling Stone.com*. December 30, 2009. www.rollingstone.com/music/news/bruce-springsteen-honored-at-kennedy-center-by-mellencamp-vedder-sting-20091230.

Rolling Stone. "100 Greatest Bruce Springsteen Songs of All Time." *Rolling Stone.com*. January 16, 2014. www.rollingstone.com/music/lists/100-greatest-bruce-springsteen-songs-of-all-time-20140116.

Rose, Caryn. "Bruce Springsteen, 'High Hopes': Track-by-Track Review." *Billboard.com*. January 5, 2014. www.billboard.com/articles/review/5862265/bruce-springsteen-high-hopes-track-by-track-album-review.

Rose, Caryn. "Bruce Springsteen's Most Memorable NYC Concerts." *VillageVoice.com*. December 4, 2015. www.villagevoice.com/music/bruce-springsteens-most-memorable-nyc-concerts-7990874.

Schindehette, Susan, and Victoria Balfour. "Romancing the Boss." *People*. October 10, 1988.

Shea, Courtney. "Springsteen Guitarist Van Zandt Shares His Secrets to Being the Boss." *The Globe and Mail.com*. November 23, 2014. www.theglobeandmail.com/arts/music/springsteens-guitarist-shares-his-secrets-to-being-the-boss/article21703418/.

Solomon, Dan. "Steven Van Zandt Tells the Story of 'Sun City' and Fighting Apartheid in South Africa." *FastCocreate.com*. December 13, 2013. www.fastcocreate.com/3023454/steven-van-zandt-tells-the-story-of-sun-city-and-fighting-apartheid-in-south-africa.

Strauss, Valerie. "The Education of Jon Landau, Bruce Springsteen's Legendary Manager." *Washington Post*. November 11, 2014.

Warner, Ross. "The Week That Made Bruce Springsteen." *JusticeIsComing.com*. July 12, 2012. www.justiceiscoming.com/entertainment/articles-entertainment/the-week-that-made-bruce-springsteen.html.

Varga, George. "'Frank Stefanko' an Exhibit that the Boss Is Sure to Like." *Union-Tribune*. June 12, 2005. www.legacy.utsandiego.com/news/features/20050612-9999-1a12photog.html.

Zeitz, Joshua. "*Born to Run* and the Decline of the American Dream." *TheAtlantic.com*. August 24, 2015. www.theatlantic.com/entertainment/archive/2015/08/born-to-run-at-40/402137/.

INDEX

ABOUT THE AUTHOR

Gillian G. Gaar has written for numerous publications, including *Mojo*, *Rolling Stone*, and *Goldmine*. Her previous books include *She's a Rebel: The History of Women in Rock & Roll*, *Entertain Us: The Rise of Nirvana*, *Return of the King: Elvis Presley's Great Comeback*, and *The Doors: The Illustrated History*. She was also a contributor to Voyageur Press's *Nirvana: The Complete Illustrated History*. She lives in Seattle.